POLICY, LEADERSHIP AND PROFESSIONAL KNOWLEDGE IN EDUCATION

WITHDRAWN

7

Policy, Leadership and Professional Knowledge in Education

edited by

Michael Strain, Bill Dennison, Janet Ouston
and Valerie Hall

P·C·P
Paul Chapman
Publishing Ltd

Paul Chapman Publishing Ltd
A SAGE Publications Company
6 Bonhill Street
London EC2A 4PU

SAGE Publications Inc
2455 Teller Road
Thousand Oaks, California 91320

SAGE Publications India Pvt Ltd
32, M-Block Market
Greater Kailash-I
New Delhi 110 048

British Cataloguing in Publication Data

ISBN 1 85496 444 1
       1 85396 445 X (pbk)

Library of Congress catalog card number

Typeset by PDQ Typesetting, Staffordshire
Printed and bound in Great Britain.

Contents

List of Selected Papers

Full citations of the papers included in the volume are given below. Sincere appreciation is expressed here to these authors, whose only reward can be that some part of their critical writing, over at least a quarter of a century, might now be made known to and benefit many more, through the production and sale of this volume.

1 Strain, M. (1997) Records of Achievement: A Critical Review of Educational Management and Administration. *EMA*, 25.3, pp. 213–42.
2 Smyth, J. (1995) Devolution and Teachers' Work: The Underside of a Complex Phenomenon. *EMA*, 23.3, pp. 168–75.
3 Hoyle, E. (1982) Micropolitics of Educational Organisations. *EMA*, 10.2, pp. 87–98.
4 Bhindi, N. and Duignan, P. (1997) Leadership for a New Century: Authenticity, Intentionality, Spirituality and Sensibility. *EMA*, 25.2, pp. 117–32.
5 Eraut, M. (1993) The Characterisation and Development of Professional Expertise in Education Management and in Teaching. *EMA*, 21.4, pp. 223–32.
6 Baron, G. (1980) Research in Educational Administration in Britain. *Educational Administration*, Vol. 8, No. 1, pp. 1–33.
7 Greenfield, T. B. (1991) Re-forming and Re-valuing Educational Administration: Whence and When Cometh the Phoenix? *EMA*, 19.4, pp. 200–17.
8 Evers, C. and Lakomski, G. (1993) Justifying Educational Administration, *EMA*, 21.3, pp. 140–60.
9 Gronn, P. and Ribbins, P. (1993) The Salvation of Educational Administration: Better Science or Alternatives to Science? *EMA*, 21.3, pp. 161–70.
10 Ranson, S. (1992) Towards the Learning Society. *EMA*, 20.2, pp. 68–79.
11 Barnes, A. and Humble, S. (1978) Governing Schools: Has the Taylor Report got the Balance Right? *Educational Administration*, 6.1, pp. 1–19.
12 Fiske, D. (1981) Education – Going National? *Educational Administration*, 9.3, pp. 1–16.
13 Pring, R. (1988) Privatisation. *EMA*, 16.2, pp. 85–96.
14 Davies, B. and Hentschke, G. (1994) School Autonomy: Myth or Reality – Developing an Analytical Taxonomy. *EMA*, 22.2, pp. 96–103.
15 Simkins, T. (1995) The Equity Consequences of Educational Reform. *EMA*, 23.4, pp. 221–32.
16 Hughes, M. G. (1973) Research Report: The Professional-as-Administrator: The Case of the Secondary School Head. *Educational Administration Bulletin*, 2.1, pp. 11–23.
17 Ribbins, P. and Sherratt, B. (1992) Managing the Secondary School in the 1990s: A New View of Headship. *EMA*, 20.3, pp. 151–60.
18 Gronn, P. (1996) From Transactions to Transformations: A New World Order in the Study of Leadership? *EMA*, 24.1, pp. 7–30.
19 Glatter, R. (1997) Context and Capability in Educational Management. *EMA*, 25.2, pp. 181–92.

Contributors

The Editors

Bill Dennison is currently Head of the Department of Education, Newcastle University. He lectures in Educational Management to a wide range of courses up to, and including, EdD level, as well as being associated with work for departments, schools and LEAs. Most recently, he has become a NPQH trainer. In addition to six books, he has written extensively on education management and related issues, with specific reference to the effective and efficient use of resources.

Valerie Hall is a Reader in Education in the Graduate School of Education at the University of Bristol. She has been a teacher and researcher in schools, further, higher and adult education for over thirty years. Throughout her career she has had a particular interest in the relationship between experience of work and personal biography, social context and adult learning processes. Her research on teaching, managing and leading in education has resulted in a number of publications, including her latest book *Dancing on the Ceiling*, which is a study of women headteachers.

Janet Ouston is a senior lecturer in education management at the Institute of Education. She was head of the Management Development Centre until September 1998. Much of her recent research and writing has been on the impact of OfSTED inspection on secondary schools. She has also written on the use of rational and non-rational models in the management of educational organisations. She is vice-chair of the governing body of an inner-London secondary school.

Michael Strain is Senior Lecturer in Education Management at the University of Ulster, Northern Ireland, where he is also research coordinator in the School of Education. He has taught Classics in secondary schools and worked as an education officer in local government in England. He teaches Education Management on Masters and EdD courses with special interests in education policy and organisation and the concept of a learning society.

The Authors

George Baron is Emeritus Professor of Educational Administration, University of London Institute of Education and former President of the British Educational Administration Society.

Alan Barnes was formerly Headmaster of Ruffwood School, Kirkby, Liverpool.

Narottam Bhindi is Senior Lecturer and Head of the Department of Administration and Training at the University of New England, Australia.

Brent Davies is Professor and Director of the International Education Leadership and Management Centre at the University of Lincoln and Humberside at Lincoln, England.

Patrick Duignan is Foundation Professor in Educational Leadership at the Australian Catholic University.

Michael Eraut is a Professor of Education at the University of Sussex, England.

Colin Evers is Associate Professor in the School of Graduate Studies of the Faculty of Education at Monash University in Australia.

Dudley Fiske was formerly Chief Education officer in the City of Manchester, England.

Ron Glatter is Professor and Director of the Centre for Educational Policy and Management at the Open University, England.

Thomas Greenfield was at the University of Toronto, Ontario, Canada. He died in 1994.

Peter Gronn is Associate Professor in the School of Graduate Studies in Monash University, Clayton, Victoria, Australia.

Guilbert Hentschke is Professor and Dean of the School of Education at the University of Southern California, USA.

Eric Hoyle is Emeritus Professor of Education in the University of Bristol, England.

Mereddyd Hughes is Emeritus Professor of Education in the University of Birmingham, England.

Stephen Humble was formerly Research Fellow at the Institute of Local Government Studies, University of Birmingham, England.

Gabriele Lakomski is Head of the Department of Policy, Context and Evaluation Studies at the University of Melbourne, Victoria, Australia.

Richard Pring is Professor of Education at the Department of Educational Studies, University of Oxford, England.

Stewart Ranson is Professor of Education in the University of Birmingham, England.

Peter Ribbins is Professor of Education and Dean of the Faculty of Education of the University of Birmingham, England. He is also Editor of *Educational Management and Administration*.

Brian Sherratt is Head of Great Barr Comprehensive School in Birmingham, England.

Tim Simkins is Principal Lecturer in the Centre for Education Management and Administration at Sheffield Hallam University, Sheffield, England.

John Smyth is Professor of Teacher Education and Director of the Flinders Institute for the Study of Teaching of South Australia.

Preface

This book is a celebration of 25 years of the British Educational Management and Administration Society and of its journal *Educational Management and Administration*. Throughout this period the Society has sought to facilitate the critical discussion of policy and practice in the management of education and, in particular, to encourage professional exchange among those who teach and research the subject and those who practise it, whether this be at the chalk face of the 1970s or the computer screen of the 1990s. During that period *EMA* has evolved until today it is one of the leading international journals in its field.

Over the period, the pages of the journal have reflected the changing pressures on schools, colleges and other parts of the education system which have arisen from an increasingly turbulent environment and increasingly proactive governments. At the beginning of the period it was almost inconceivable that education could dominate the political agenda; today, in contrast, the politician's cry of 'education, education, education' surprises nobody. Agendas and priorities have changed; yet underlying these changes many issues have retained their pertinence. How should competing demands for accountability and for institutional autonomy be balanced within an increasingly turbulent world? What is quality in education and how might it be assessed? How can demands for an increasingly effective educational system be met within increasingly tight public expenditure constraints? How can equity be assured? What forms of leadership and management are appropriate to different types of institutions and contexts? How can educational leaders of the future best be developed? What can managers in education learn from other parts of the public sector and beyond? What does the experience of education have to offer to others? Underlying all of these questions are more fundamental ones. What is the nature of management and administration in education; how can it be best studied and understood; and how can such understanding contribute to the improvement of practice?

All these issues and many more have been discussed and recontextualised in the pages of *EMA* as the world has changed. They have been explored through case studies of practice and through theoretical discussion; through papers which considered one institutional or national context and those which ranged more widely. Every year papers have appeared whose seminal nature has lent them an authority and relevance well beyond their own time. This book brings together 19 such papers. The editors were not to be envied in their task, but their achievement has been considerable. They have succeeded in putting together a volume which captures the 'leading edge' of writing in education management and which speaks directly to all who wish to understand how we came to be where we are and what can be learnt from the journey of the past 25 years. This should include everybody who works in, thinks and cares about the future of the education service. We owe the editors and authors our thanks.

Tim Simkins
Chair
BEMAS

Acknowledgements

A particular note of appreciation is owed to the authors of these collected papers. This Jubilee publication is essentially their book. As editors we regret the extent to which their finely wrought work has been unavoidably reduced to make possible a wider selection of what we hope are coherent and worthwhile abridgements. We hope too that they agree that the benefits of re-issuing their work on this occasion outweigh any loss of meaning or refinement of argument.

Thanks are due also to our technical and secretarial assistants; they have maintained an essential flow of electronic communications and transfers which made the compilation of material possible in the time available. A special note of thanks is due to Gary Adamson, Research Officer in the University of Ulster, who has made a particular contribution in that way and has worked assiduously to harmonise references among separately edited sections of the book.

Finally, I should like to express appreciation for the work of my co-editors who have struggled to meet deadlines and limitations of length, and have responded so promptly to requests, as well as contributing to our critical discussions as the book took shape. I am grateful too for Jo Donnelly's patience and practical help; she has endured many unsocial hours to make completion of the task possible. The editors hope that a wide readership of teachers and academics in every sort of learning context will find the result useful.

Michael Strain
June 1998

Records of Achievement:
A Critical and Historical Review

MICHAEL STRAIN

ANNIVERSARY REFLECTIONS

Recent education reforms have produced some unintended effects. Measures taken to subject a vast area of public spending to greater predictability and control, to by-pass bureaucracy and give back initiative to teachers and parents, seem to have encouraged quite different and unforeseeable developments.

One of these is that education, as an institution, has become more *reflective* upon itself. From its beginnings in the nineteenth century, public education was dynamic with a sense of missionary social purpose. Dissemination of knowledge, cultivation of enlightenment and provision of opportunity for all were goals which positioned teachers and schools centrally within the nation state's modernising, civilising, project.

Today, we are not so sure of ourselves. Politicians focus on mini-max strategies, re-casting policies which generate least opposition in order to yield as much recordable improvement as can be squeezed from inelastic resource levels. But parents and teachers are more sceptical and unsure; emerging 'partnerships' between them are understood as collaborative, discursive encounters in learning, for their own and their children's personal benefit. Missions are for marketeers, whilst there is 'no mission' for traditionalists clinging to earlier beliefs in 'social progress'. Local 'communities' are now atomised, fragmented, disempowered. Increasingly, individuals search for alternative networks in search of companionship or a livelihood, grasping electronic access to virtual communities for meeting and for learning opportunities which their particular locality is now unable to provide. Access, rather than provision, is the most that can be offered close to home. Education has slipped, somewhat unwittingly, it seems, over the precipice of post-modernity.

Another approach to the past, at a moment of anniversary, is to re-examine the recorded events themselves over the period of 25 years. It was a most turbulent period in the history of British education; Labour's incomplete efforts to introduce comprehensive education were followed by more than fifteen years of Tory reforms, still being implemented and extended, even, most recently, under a New Labour government. LEAs once 'owned' their schools, and, in the 1970s, were urged to adopt corporate management techniques to replace their historic tradition of local or municipal stewardship. The Houghton pay awards acknowledged the increased complexity of schools and encouraged teachers to think that at last they were not only socially valued but would be financially and commensurately rewarded. Implementing ROSLA was on the horizon; then came the 'oil crisis'. Interesting and progressive new curricula were being developed such as MACOS, Nuffield science and the School Council's history project. The main anxieties were about a shortage of student places and teachers, and providing physically and educationally for ROSLA pupils.

Now, 25 years later, we have been 'reformed', yet everyone is searching for a 'role'. The LEA's is diminished and unclear. Parents want to be more actively involved in their children's learning but too few know how, with any confidence. Some schools are still short of teachers, but there is no physical shortage of student places. Most young people stay in education until they are 18 but then enter an adult world undermined by a bewildering array of 'risks' and unequal opportunities (see pp. 30–31) Instead of 'mission', the contemporary climate is one of 'panic', confusion and the search for 'security'. Preoccupations of this generation of parents are about standards, testing, drugs and unemployment. Neither rationality nor its applications in the natural and calculative sciences seem to secure the requisite freedom from life's anxieties.

This book is offered as a celebration of work published in the BEMAS journal between 1972 and 1997, a resource to assist critical review and reflection and, in the limited space available, provides challenging and at times provocative comment by four editors who have collaborated in the selection and editing of the material. The first issue of the journal appeared in the Summer of 1972 as *The Educational Administration Bulletin*, under the editorship of Meredydd Hughes. It was renamed *Educational Administration* in 1975 (Hughes, 1997) and after 1979 was edited by Ray Bolam (1979–1983), under whom it became *Educational Management and Administration*, published by Longmans. Michael Locke was editor between 1984 and 1991 and Peter Ribbins from 1991 to the present.

This review considers a sample of all the papers published over those 25 years. They vary widely in quality, content and approach. Some of them expose earlier research agendas, others illustrate and explore the flux of professional concerns and uncertainties. All the papers identified for discussion will, it is hoped, repay re-reading. One of their most striking features is the extent to which action and outcome have become more important than knowing for its own sake. Theoretical questions, once examined for their intrinsic *epistemic* significance, are now considered primarily for their methodological or positional implications. Performativity, consideration of, for example, what will strengthen the position of educational research in a wider and more open marketplace for research funds, dominates institutional and individual incentive structures. Public policy issues in education are discussed in *EMA* in the early

1980s, but become gradually less prominent as professional and organisational controversies assume increasing importance. Many of these issues form the subject matter of four short editorial commentaries which introduce the four sections of selected papers.

We think some of those papers are outstanding and regret the extent to which they have been abridged. They are felt to be *representative* of the experience of those engaged in education during that time, as well as *indicative* of the journal's significant achievements over the period. In contrast, this essay attempts to anthologise, illustrate and critically review the whole of the journal's output from 1972 to 1997, in its ever-changing historical and educational context. An impossible, perhaps, but not unrewarding task.

I SAYING AND DOING

Meredydd Hughes' first editorial stated the aims of the new Society and its journal as: 'to facilitate the dissemination of knowledge about research, training and practice in educational administration, and also to provide a forum for the discussion of new approaches to the preparation and development of administrators and new developments in research' (Hughes, 1972c). He expressed the hope that *EAB* 'will help to forge the links of the dynastic alliance which will surely follow the obsequies of the old order' (Hughes, 1972b). The 'old order' referred, in William Taylor's phrase, to 'the tired old dichotomy between theory and practice in education which ought to have been dead long ago' (Taylor, 1973, Chapter 8). But was the dichotomy really dead? Recent experience supports scepticism; reforms are increasingly devised and formulated with scant attention to professional or academic advice. Under Sir Ron Dearing the National Curriculum had to be *rescued* by teachers and academics and the government's recent Green Paper on the Learning Society (DfEE, 1997a) seems to have incorporated few of the insights offered, for example, in the Fryer Report (DfEE, 1997b).

Theory and practice: views of practitioners

Yet questions concerning relations between theory and practice in education are enduring and deep-lying. In an early article by H. L. Gray (1972, p.1), the training which senior teachers received was said to be based on 'the learning of practical skills and self-knowledge'; theory was 'a support to an understanding of...skills and self-knowledge' and, through its capacity to explain, can 'provide useful models for analysis and prediction.' The imputed 'power of prediction' itself generated suspicion regarding the value of research. This is evident in the comment of another headteacher (Morrison, 1973) on contributions by academics (McKenzie, 1973; Cumming, 1973). Behind an otherwise restrained endorsement by teachers for the work of academic colleagues, there seems to have lurked a fear that academic research might lead to a loss of professional autonomy for teachers and the replacement of schools as 'communities possessing a kind of organic solidarity' with 'mechanical contrivances powered by direct command.' Another ground for practitioner suspicion emerges from the reference by Cumming (1971) to his classic (and in many ways still isolated) study of educational costs. His article illustrates the inherent futility of conceptualising educational research in manipulative or instrumental terms, an error into which researchers themselves sometimes fall. 'Persons at all points in the education business, including researchers themselves, often unconsciously expect the system to be changed by research as it is currently conceived.' This, for Cumming, is not only a 'crass naivety' but endangers the positive functions of research in fields of social and institutional life. He agrees with Gass (1971) in his OECD review of *Educational Policies for the 1970s* that there is 'an argument against the support of basic research with the objective of obtaining "results" which may be "applied"'. Short-termism and instrumentality are exemplified in the reported response of Scottish Education Department officials to his work. They were 'surprised' to be asked how and when the research data on school and college costs could be used, though it had been gathered in institutions they administered. For 'they, like other administrators, desire, albeit unconsciously, to keep the mystique of their work to themselves and see researchers as the providers of facts which others (themselves) can interpret'. There is more than a suggestion here that identifying clearly what educational research is to be used for will assist definition of what it should be.

Greenfield and the positivists

Greenfield (1976) made his first appearance among contributions to a symposium which he led at the IIP Conference in 1974. None of the reviewers is outrightly opposed to Greenfield's position; Michael Harrison is warmly appreciative of Greenfield's 'connectivity', and its recognition of the human constructedness of organisational life (*ibid.*, p. 3). Pat and John White (*ibid.*, pp. 6–10) are severe on Greenfield's subjectivism and an inconsistency they detect in his rejection of both 'realism' and 'idealism'. They suggest his insights might have been more cogently developed if they 'were not entangled with the trendy nonsense of "phenomenology"'! Hoyle's commentary (*ibid.*, pp. 4–6), though short, is both thoughtful and synoptic in its range of suggestion. He reminds us that phenomenology reveals how individuals *make* their roles rather than *take* them. Today, we might say that they *both* make and take them, from the patterned, differentiated historical circumstances of their lives (Giddens, 1995). But this is an excellent and instructive short essay in criticism; constructive and balanced. It opens windows and invites the reader to explore *theoretically* what is meant by the organisational dimension of the teacher's role in the management of learning.

Greenfield himself, in his rejoinder (Greenfield, 1978a), takes Hoyle's comments very seriously, though the tone of much of his piece is one of quiet resignation in the aftermath of an unholy row at the 1974 IIP in Bristol. He clings tenaciously to what are still today important questions: 'What is real about organisations?' and 'What can theory about them mean, if we do not agree on that reality?' (p. 86). That 'reality' is frequently, for many individuals, a prison, formed of ignorance, poverty, and the unequal distribution of human power to effect change in the disposition of institutional possibilities in the social world. To Griffiths (1977), Greenfield was contesting the self-evident:

> I also wonder about Greenfield's basic contention that organisations are not 'real'. To me, New York University is 'real', the Salvation Army is 'real', IBM is 'real' and the Catholic Church is 'real'.

Greenfield, for his part, wanted to change the way in which such organisations served human ends. Some of those institutions had not always acted in ways beneficial to human development. They tended to pursue their own organisational aims by dedication to internally coherent and 'rational' rules. Yet, as Bauman, Chomsky and countless millions of twentieth century victims of injustice and barbarism have shown us:

> The greatest crimes *against* humanity (and *by* humanity) have been perpetrated in the name of the rule of reason. (Bauman, 1993, p. 238)

Greenfield's integrity of social purpose and justification as a theorist shine through in this paper: 'Social and organisational theories are thus perhaps seen as visions of the world which people act out. In this view, "verification" of theory becomes as much a moral judgement as an empirical process' (1978a, p. 88).

Wisdom and knowledge

Kendell and Byrne (1978), two less well-known American academics, continue the debate, observing that so far it had been concerned with 'victory' rather than 'demonstration' and was therefore essentially a political controversy (pp. 107–8). But there is little evidence in this debate of awareness of the insights of Kuhn (1974), of the work of Bernstein and the sociologists of knowledge, or of the emerging assaults (Feyerabend, Lyotard, Derrida) upon the very concept of knowledge as truth authorised by application of heuristic method. Methods are tools not forms of underwriting truth; their selection is value laden. Similarly, the Vatican's treatment of Galileo turned on issues of core belief and values; an allusion taken up by Greenfield in response to Hoyle:

> The image of the telescope is fortunate, since it evokes the history of another ideological battle about nature and how we should perceive it....Only faith in a new order of things, in a new method of enquiry, and in a new cosmology could bring one to see the rightness of the heliocentric view. (Greenfield, 1978a, p. 91)

Here perhaps is the root of Greenfield's vulnerability. Since the Reformation, a single, authorising 'faith' (in Scripture) had been 'defeated', at least in principle, by the claims of empirical rationality. Greenfield hoped that phenomenology's superior capability to 'account' richly for the experiences and exigencies of lived reality might redeem the failure of positivistic educational theory to show how teachers could enhance what they provided for learners, in particular learning settings. The utter poverty of positivism's contribution to educational practices is revealed starkly in the use made by Kendell and Byrne of Patrick Suppes (1974):

> It is often thought and said that what we most need in education is wisdom and broad understanding of the issues that confront us. Not at all, I say. What we need are deeply structured theories in education that drastically reduce, if not eliminate, the need for wisdom. I do not want wise men (*sic*) to design or build the airplane I fly in, but rather technical men who understand the theory of aerodynamics and the structural properties of metal. And so it is with education. Wisdom we need, but good theories we need even more.

Greenfield saw that this was wrong; that in education we need wisdom more than anything else. Ask any child what is most desirable in a parent – wisdom and goodness or knowledge and power? What Greenfield could not perhaps realise in 1975 was the impossibility of any single theoretical or political perspective providing the necessary ground from which to remove the baneful influence of 'theory' and its instrumentalities. Only now can we dimly perceive that wisdom and its ethical postulates must in future be *plurally* articulated, contested and found room for in a *dis*harmonious social world, replete with *dis*junction, *in*determinacy and radical *un*certainty. Different ethnicities, genders (including their transformations) and value systems must be given freedom to cohabit with their *differences* intact.

Contested control

It would be mistaken to see Hughes' editorship (1972–1979) as dominated by theoretical confrontations. Management training (Vols. 1.1; 3.2; 4.1), the relation between the professional and educational roles inherent in Headship (Vol. 2.1), current innovations in management within local government (Vols. 1.1; 3.1; 7.2), in-school evaluation (Stanton, 1978, 42–53) and the implications for professional as distinct from lay participation and responsibility in the curriculum and, more particularly, in the management of schools, received increasing attention. The publication of the Taylor Report (DES, 1977) was highly influential and perhaps stimulated interest in 'innovation' and 'change' (Vols. 4.1; 4.2; 6.1). A response to Taylor in early 1978 (Barnes, Humble, Davies and Lyons, 1978) concludes with some prescient reservations:

- it is important not to expect too much from structural reform – people and processes will begin to change things but structure by itself will not do. Further attention to decision-making processes and the style of leadership of heads is thus needed.
- there may be no discernible relationships between 'better education' (whatever that may be) and this type of structural change.
- there are other pressures leading to centralisation of decision-making which will effectively counter the decentralisation movement – control of the curriculum, the

economic circumstances, declining school populations, etc.

• we are still left with the fundamental dilemma that, within these proposals there may be little congruence between public and social accountability (embracing the wider community) and financial accountability (still through the LEA).

Indeed, though Taylor turned out to be formative in altering the public and professional 'terms of reference' within which these questions came to be examined, and its core proposal that the curriculum could no longer be a matter solely for teachers (DES, 1977, p.49) was implemented with increasing specificity in the Acts of 1980, 1986 and 1988, some crucial qualitative improvements (participative school leadership, understanding of the relation between forms of school organisation and their educational effects, closer 'fit' between pupils' school experience and the requirements of the social and economic conditions for which they are being prepared), remain as elusive as ever. And the apparently unresolvable conflict between the interests of individuals, localities and central government in matters of social policy are still as much a source of parental discontent as the conflicts between teachers and parents which led to the William Tyndale débâcle (ILEA, 1976) and the establishment of the Taylor Committee itself.

II EDUCATIONAL AGENDA IN A MORE POLITICISED ENVIRONMENT

The Society's first Research Seminar[1] in Birmingham in March 1979 produced a volume rich in historical knowledge and illumination. Current British research is reviewed and there is a comprehensive post-mortem on transatlantic bickerings about 'Theory'. Greenfield's reflections (Greenfield, 1979a) and Hughes and Ribbins' (1979) astute and pragmatic commentary are most valuable.

George Baron (1979a) surveys a decade of 'Research in Educational Administration in Britain' and touches on most of the issues and questions considered in this review. Concerns underlying the academic/practitioner debate are clearly exposed:

The conflict between academic and practitioner arises from each party necessarily inhabiting a different universe. As the researcher develops his approach to his problem, no matter how 'practical' its orientation, he draws on material and ideas from outside the immediate situation to help him in his analysis and explanations. By so doing he distances himself from the administrator who, when subsequently reading the research report, is alienated by what appears to be irrelevant and extraneous material: furthermore, from his experience the administrator brings to his reading a multitude of questions stimulated by the research but not answered by it. (pp. 13–15)

---

1 Educational Administration, Vol. 8, No. 1 (1978/79); subsequent Seminars were held in Birmingham (1981), Birmingham (1986), Sheffield (1987), Nottingham (1993) and Cambridge (1996).

Different mental worlds are revealed here, arising from the multiplicity of interests, knowledge, goals and motives of research users and makers of educational knowledge. There is also a particular kind of knowledge possessed by those professing *education*, as distinct from the knowledge claimed by colleagues in the social sciences and other disciplines (Taylor, 1973, p. 194): '...knowledge about education is to a large and increasing extent *role specific knowledge.*'

Dissatisfaction among users of research is summed up by Shipman (1976): 'From within local government the research enterprise in academia seems to deliver the wrong goods, at the wrong time, without an invoice.'

Lord Rothschild (CPRS, 1971) exemplified for Baron the central government interest being articulated with increasing force in the 1970s, foreshadowing those orthodoxies later enunciated by the Office of Science and Technology (OST, 1993) in *Realising Our Potential*: 'the funding agency says what it wants and the researcher works within a defined brief.'

Believing that the DES, aided by the SSRC, would protect the research community from these onslaughts, Baron separates out 'Policy Related Research', the particular interest of government, from other areas in which the majority of academics can work relatively free from outside interference. He suggests the following four categories:

- Research for Understanding
- Research for Policy Development
- Research into Administrative Structure and Process
- Evaluative Research.

The purpose of Baron's distinction was to protect academic freedom. But today, a different division seems to be emerging; one in which educational research is parcelled into 'soft' areas (action research, school effectiveness studies, curriculum evaluation and monitoring), safely entrustable to the weaker, less well-resourced institutions (obtaining Grade 4 or less in the Research Assessment Exercise), and 'hard' research, large-scale critical investigations of educational structures and goals, which can be cross-fertilised and strengthened by links with contributory social science disciplines, of the kind envisaged by the ESRC thematic programme areas (ESRC, 1997).

Interests and approaches

The phenomenological 'shift' and its applicability to 'case study work' is exemplified by Best, Jarvis and Ribbins (1979) on pastoral care in the comprehensive school. The gap between the (functional) realities of practice and the (heavily prescriptive) rhetoric of practitioner accounts is neither ignored nor allowed to inhibit discovery and innovation. Attempting 'to marry the logic of Falsificationism with the Phenomenological premium on *meanings*', hypothesis testing is undertaken through questionnaires and a 'Rhetoric

Detector' designed to untangle and expose intricacies and substitutions in the language of justification used by practitioners (pp. 64–6). The language in which teachers account for their actions and their pupils' unrealised attainments is as thoroughly permeated by the child-centred philosophy of the Plowden Report as the explanations of their successors today are imbued with terms drawn from accountancy and management. For example, the learner's 'busy-ness', an indication then of fruitful learning in process, is now expressed as an aspect of *efficiency*; the learner's 'readiness' to move forward at an appropriate stage, significant then diagnostically, is taken now as evidence of attainment and becomes an index of the school's *effectiveness*.

At around the turn of the decade, a new and more urgent preoccupation with the relationship between educational research, public policy and the needs of pupils and practitioners is discernible. Policy 'directions' were becoming more prominent in researchers' agenda, at the expense of methodological concerns. Interestingly, Lakomski (1989, p. 43) notes a similar shift in her consideration of Australian work at about the same time:

> This move makes possible the focus on political values, and power, and thus helps address normative issues in educational administration hitherto neglected.

In a brief Conference introduction, Glatter (1981) observes that:

> Whatever the precise meaning of 'research into educational policy-making', it seemed to be agreed that not much of it had actually been done. (p. 5)

This would soon change, along with a developing awareness in the DES of an urgent need for harder-edged, policy-related information and research. Following the publication of the Yellow Book, the Ruskin College Prime Ministerial speech of 1976, and LEA responses to Circular 14/77, in which the disparate and passive role of many local authorities in curriculum matters was exposed, the new Conservative government brought a fresh impetus to the need adumbrated in the Taylor Report to remove control of the curriculum and organisation of schools from its long-standing niche within the traditional 'partnership' shared by teachers, LEA officers and DES officials. Central government (at least, certain political groupings within it) soon began to dismantle fences and poke more intrusively and purposefully among the intricacies of what had been cultivated as a 'secret garden'.

Externalities

Education was being compelled to answer more specifically to its natural aspiration to contribute to the welfare of society at large. Educational research was being required to answer empirical questions, illuminate the relationship between normative changes and their implications for educational organisation and practice, and specify appropriate action which could win public support.

In the terms of Drake's (1981) paper, attending to externalities required a more forceful determination by educational researchers to assist with the discovery of modes of educational and training delivery which were consonant with internal and external efficiency.

> By internal efficiency is meant that combination of resources which yields the maximum achievement of [educational] objectives for a given commitment of resources. By external efficiency is meant the gearing of [education] to objectives external to the [education] system, e.g. production of a desired flow of skilled manpower or meeting certain equity objectives for employment. (p.15)

The introduction of GNVQ and, more recently, Ofsted's campaign to eliminate 'progressive teaching methods' (TES, 1996) may be considered thinly nourished legatees of that rationality. Yet, sadly, too little of the rigorous method of enquiry outlined in Drake's paper has contributed to either educational policy or its implementation in succeeding years. For example, greater attention to 'the effect of financial arrangements on the parties to the [educational process]' has for almost ten years now been used to justify delegation of local financial powers. Schools and colleges will, it may reasonably be claimed, make more efficient and effective decisions if the power to allocate resources is more generally available to them. Yet the equity consequences of assessment-led teaching and the 'marketised' environment in which schools compete on the basis of accredited results have been ignored by central government (Simkins, 1995). Even now, more than twenty years after OECD articulated the need for a shift of resources within education systems from the front-end of statutory provision (5–16) to a more 'end-loaded' investment in 'lifelong' education, with all the implications of such a shift for more equitable and socially relevant patterns of both distribution and learning outcomes, only fragmentary indications of such a redirection, chiefly bearing upon HE funding and in response to fiscal pressures, are apparent.

A noteworthy attempt (Pascal, 1987) to remedy the 'scarcity of empirically grounded studies' is evident in a subsequent study undertaken from 1981 to 1985 in the University of Birmingham. The work of governing bodies and their working relationships with parents, teachers, other politicians and administrators is examined and discussed by reference to four different dichotomies which were identified. The effectiveness and appropriateness of recent reforms of the composition and functions of school governing bodies were studied from four conceptually different but related perspectives: elitist and pluralist models of the distribution of power in the practice of decision-making, assessment of the relative claims of centralised and devolved approaches to the distribution of powers and duties, the extent and consequences of role ambiguities experienced among professional and lay representatives, and the incidence and implications of functional conflict arising from contradictory expectations of support and accountability on the part of parents and the general public. The report concludes that the distribution of powers 'embodied, but not clearly defined, in the 1944 Act, is inadequate and out of date' and that 'major redefinition' is required, beyond that provided in the 1986 Act. Unfortunately, the grant of extensive additional powers to governing bodies in the 1988 Act, as well as in the Teachers'

Pay and Conditions of Service Act of 1991 (DES, 1991b) clarified matters only by adopting a thoroughly managerialised concept of the governing body, without resolving the ambiguities and conflicts inherent in the continuing and extended exposure to the twin claims of accountability and a delegated managerial function. Governors retained responsibilities to represent the community, fulfil the requirements of central policy and regulation, and account to both parents and legally constituted authorities (LEA, employment tribunals, admissions appeal boards, residual powers of the Secretary of State) for what schools managed to achieve within their own exigencies of devolved budgets, subject both to centrally approved formulae and centrally imposed rate capping.

Quality and satisfaction

More generally recognisable than the somewhat forbidding abstraction implied by 'externalities', the term Quality Control in Education was the focus of discussion at the Society's Ninth Annual Conference in 1980 and was accorded a special issue of the journal (Vol. 9, No. 2, 1981). Taylor (1981) points out that quality is a relational, not an absolute property. Indeed, it has no meaning except in relation to some generally understood *function* (*ibid.*, pp. 2–3) and, as such, bears a cost derived from society's agreed allocation of available resources, earmarked to secure desired social outcomes. Quality control, far from being a technically discrete operation, lies at the heart of the political process, in which rival claims on social resources are contested and resolved. Quality always carries a price tag. Achieving it requires intricate estimations of needs and satisfactions which must be explored at the level of both individual and collective consequences (Drake's externalities once again). It is the 'public good' component and its relation to individual consumption and investment considerations which make simplified 'objective' measures so dangerous and lead to Taylor's forthright reminder that 'customer satisfaction is not the sole criterion of satisfaction in educational provision' (p.6). The ambiguous and underdeveloped role and contribution of the Inspectorate in relation to these issues is brought out in the succinct conclusion of Young (1980) to her review of HMI's *Aspects of Secondary Education in England*.

> What was difficult to discern, however, were the underlying models or theories of the nature of teaching and how schools function that were used to make the professional judgements contained in the survey; no framework of theoretical and methodological assumptions was apparent with which to assess the quality of the evidence. I find this a serious omission.

III   CHANGE AND CONTINUITIES

Professional development for senior teachers

Fittingly, Hughes (1982) contributed the opening paper of Volume 10.1 to report on a two-year research project, funded by the DES, to study the extent and nature of courses of professional development. The 1978 Conference had chosen a similar theme and two papers from that earlier conference are also examined here (Glatter, 1979; Baron, 1979b). Under review at the conference had been an issue which, in the words of Royston McHugh, 'was of direct professional relevance and of major importance to *all* members of the Society', as well as that of the future development of the Society itself.

Hughes' report argued for the establishment of a School Management Unit under the general oversight of the Schools Council, itself at that time the subject of review by Mrs Nancy Trenaman. However, the Trenaman recommendation 'that the Schools Council should continue and with its present functions' was not accepted by the government. Her recommendation 'for a representative Schools Council' and a 'new initiative in management development and training for headteachers and senior staff... associated with a widely representative educational body such as the Schools Council' (Hughes, 1982, pp.13–14) was ignored. The aftermath is well known. Extended powers for governing bodies were introduced in 1986 and 1988; locally delegated schemes of financial management and school admissions and a prescribed pattern of curriculum and assessment have followed from the 1988 Act. But little was done to prepare senior staff in relation to their new management duties until the recent initiatives by the Teacher Training Agency. Hughes' recommendation had been for:

- a structured programme of award bearing courses... to meet the long term career needs of those involved in, or aspiring to, management responsibilities in education;
- a flexible programme of short courses of more immediate relevance, focused on particular topics or skill requirements and possibly aimed at specific levels of responsibility. (p. 9)

Teacher unions and the Society of Education Officers were to have had a major role in the provision to be organised by the School Management Unit. BEMAS too was to have lent at least some form of regional support. A question uneasily forming itself on reading these deliberations of more than ten years ago is: could our educational establishment have done more to provide a more secure and well-founded future, at least in relation to a structure of provision for professional development which ensured a constructive and innovative role for members of the profession itself?

Dualism in practice?

The 1978 conference had produced two papers, by Baron (1979a) and Glatter (1979), setting out contrasting approaches to professional development, two quite different conceptions of how the Society and the activity and aspirations of its members should interact to enhance 'effective practice'. In Baron's paper, a pervading dualism, of theory and practice and of thought and action, is evident from the first page:

educational administration... a field of study which contributes to effective practice. (p. 1)

Starting from two key propositions, that educational administration is a field of study, practice and training distinct from other forms of administration and that it should be studied systematically, alongside planned periods of practice, by those holding administrative positions, firm conclusions follow: more resources, more academic departments, more recognised courses and a national accrediting body responsible, among other things, for 'preparing the ground for' a national policy for recruitment and professional development. The paradigm position adopted here appears to be one in which the University/Academy/Professional Body is the significant creator, codifier and repository of knowledge, prerequisite for the shared 'understanding' which it disseminates among professional practitioners. The Public pays the bill for what the Academy (and the Profession?) has prescribed.

Glatter's approach and perspective is very different. While Baron sets himself explicitly to review 'what we have achieved, as measured against the aims...', Glatter entitles his paper 'Future Directions...' and begins by setting out biographically his entry position as 'humble administrator', a practitioner who became an academic in order to 'understand something of the processes in which I was engaged' (p. 19). Dichotomies for Glatter are to be sought out as potential fault lines in a network of social and professional relations, the originating source of practice, not as orienting contours in a process of conceptual clarification and systematisation. The potentially restrictive implications of the term 'professional development' should not be allowed to create an enclave within which professional insiders can more readily arm themselves with jargon, 'psychobabble' and other protective devices. Provision, he argues, should be extended to lay participants, politicians and governors.

On a conceptual level, an emerging dichotomy between policy and management is deplored both because it conflicts with the reality of how educational and governmental institutions actually work and, even more importantly, because 'the separation of values from techniques always seems to me potentially dangerous'. Surveying briefly some current developments in North America and Northern Europe, Glatter argues unequivocally for educational administration, not as a discipline or field of study in its own right but as an applied professional field requiring a theory *of* practice (italics added) 'based much more than in the past on the special features of leadership, management and change in *educational* institutions', rather than relying on 'general theories drawn largely from the social sciences and the broad literature of administration' (p. 25). Much more clearly in Glatter, theory is drawn *from* practice rather than developed in enclaves in order to contribute *to* practice.

What Glatter does most valuably here is to provide colleagues with a contextualized agenda and orientation on the basis of a clearer and more purposeful specification of role and action for those engaged in professional development. Many of the features put forward for emulation in his 1978 paper are now routine currency. In the meantime, however, the 'social sciences and the broad literature of administration' have themselves undergone a sea-change, emancipating themselves and voyaging far from the well-defined territory and positivistic rubrics of functionalist theory and associated research designs, diversifying in terms of their relationships with other disciplines and modes of thought and inquiry. Can education, and the study of education management and administration in particular, attentively serve the interests of learners and absent itself from this plural and formative process, excluding itself from the role which social science now fulfils within a much larger context of radical social change?

> The social and natural worlds today are thoroughly infused with reflexive human knowledge; but this does not lead to a situation in which collectively we are masters of our own destiny. Rather to the contrary: the future looks less like the past than ever before and has in some basic ways become very threatening... In most aspects of our lives, individual and collective, we have regularly to construct potential futures, knowing that such very construction may in fact prevent them coming about. New areas of unpredictability are created quite often by the very attempts that seek to control them. (Beck *et al.*, 1994, p. vii)

Thus defined, the role of social science, within which education is surely a key location, is becoming coterminous with that very process of social re-definition and reconstruction. Is not the paradox of having 'regularly to construct potential futures, knowing that such very construction may in fact prevent them coming about', precisely what teachers experience when they implement a 'whole school' approach to Special Needs and find that the school's curriculum policy has also to be redefined in consequence, or when they establish planned provision for the less able, only to find that it impacts unexpectedly on pedagogy and assessment practice across the school? Glatter's reflective and speculative thoughts in this paper capture, I believe, something of these 'reflexive' uncertainties which are inherent in the task of management in educational settings.

Micropolitics

The conditions of endemic and constitutive uncertainty (Preston, 1996) in which British education is now conducted were the focus of the Society's Tenth Conference, held at Bristol in 1982. The highlights of that collection are three papers by Glatter (1982), Hoyle (1982) and Bailey (1982), which contribute significantly to an understanding of educationalists' managerial tasks. Bailey's rejoinder to Hoyle tries to integrate 'the study of micropolitics into the broader framework of organisational theories'. This is a balanced and pragmatic, more philosophically detached contribution which relates the topic to more enduring and important implications, especially in relation to our obligations to children, as well as to all learners.

> School is for most children their first experience of organisational life and of the wider society beyond the family. The quality of its micropolitics is in itself a powerful educational force maintaining or denying the quality of life in our society. (Bailey, 1982, p. 105)

Pratt (1982) notes changing perspectives within these contrasting approaches. In the decade 1972–82, the preoccupation, associated with the process of local government reform (DoE, 1972) had been 'one of designing structures for the achievement of specified purposes'. This approach came increasingly to be challenged by an opposing camp of 'realists' who resisted imposition of a ' "managerial" view of reality', phenomenologists by method, who looked for theory to be 'grounded' in reflection drawn from practice. What was being questioned by some and rejected by others is the domination in organisational and management studies of a narrowly rational view of human action. Glatter (1982) supports these endeavours to reveal the micropolitics of schools in their conduct of the daily work of teaching. Yet, he points out, the attempt to form and implement policy on a rational basis is also a human propensity which can be and sometimes is attempted with success (p. 161). More significantly, Glatter warns of the danger implicit in expecting too much from a single model. Just as the dominant 'rational' models of the 1960s and 1970s 'were based on an underlying set of values, connected with optimism and a belief in the possibility of progress largely through "technical" means, so the micropolitical approach, which at times comes close to nihilism, is in tune with the cynicism and demoralisation of our age.'

Hoyle exposes a somewhat gloomy picture of school organisations; as Machiavellian, darkly imbricated within mafia-like intrigues and 'hidden agendas'. But he is concerned also to find realistic and illuminative strategies, with a 'theory-for-understanding' which might help schools examine and extricate themselves from obstructive growth, lurking in their routine dynamics of interaction and control, hitherto neither fully understood nor confronted. The paper is a lucidly and economically written introduction to a carefully selected range of writers and ideas drawn from organisational theory.

The politics of management

Pratt (1982) seems to have marked a turning point when he summarised the concerns of members as moving away from the 'management of politics towards... "the politics of management"'. Acknowledging the importance of Greenfield's contributions he notes evidence in the educational literature of a growing recognition 'that structure, function *and process* [are] interactive.' The shift of focus (from macro to micro) and of method (from technical/ instrumental to discursive/interactive) may have been symptomatic of an increasingly general readiness to acknowledge that educationalists were less sure of the direction in which they should go and of the purposes for which their skills should be employed. This sense of a 'turning point' and a felt need of directions amidst the encircling gloom may have prompted the title of the next Conference: *Education Today and Tomorrow: Challenge and Response* (Vol. 11, No. 2). At any rate, out of the turbulence surrounding the discussions and emerging research agenda of the period up to 1982, a new, more exploratory focus on practical problems and the feasibility of their solution is discernible in the period 1983–1995.

Volume 11 also exemplifies the journal's continuing double achievement in identifying new professional perspectives and disseminating studies of organisational practice. 11.1 considers 'the Role of the Deputy Head in Secondary Schools' (Owen, Davies and Wayment, 1983), 'Institutional Factors and School Absenteeism' (Reid, 1983) and 'Microcomputers in Secondary Schools' (Pratt, 1983). This last paper contains an interesting nugget on the role now termed IT co-ordinator. Pratt, drawing upon an NFER study of LEA Advisers and Innovation (Bolam *et al.*, 1979) and an unpublished Bristol MEd dissertation (Reilly, 1982) advocates reversal of received wisdom regarding dissemination of IT expertise: instead of appointing substantive experts as consultants and advisers, 'experienced process experts [should be] required...to acquire the substantive expertise' (p.61). This approach now characterises professional good practice (North, 1991).

In the next volume, a new political focus is followed up by a fresh and more rigorous economic approach to organisational and policy questions (Thomas, 1984; Hough and Warburton, 1984; Crispin and Marslen-Wilson, 1984). New structures and mechanisms which would have significant implications for education at all levels were also being examined in the journal. A small-scale study of the impact of the National Advisory Body on the management of a large college appeared (Bush and Goulding, 1984). The NAB was precursor of the national funding councils (FEFC, HEFC, Funding Agency for Schools), and the Cambridgeshire (Hinds, 1984) and Solihull (Humphrey and Thomas, 1986) pilot schemes of school delegation paved the way for the national introduction of LMS. Two of these authors (Hough and Thomas) were subsequently appointed to Chairs in the Economics of Education and their Inaugural Lectures have now been published in *EMA* (Hough, 1991; Thomas, 1996). In the next section, a number of these papers on financial and economic issues will be discussed as indicative of the journal's contribution to the promotion of studies in this field.

IV AN ECONOMIC APPROACH

Education, like many public services, only recently came to be subjected to economic analysis. The 'dismal science' connotes aims, values and methods of enquiry unrelated if not alien to the aspirations of teachers, carers and healers. Brian Knight expresses similar observations in his short paper 'Attitudes to Educational Finance' (Knight, 1984).

> Why is it that those who work in maintained schools and colleges believe that outside certain limited areas financial information is not important; that they are not concerned with the detailed costs of the work they do; that the financing of a school and college is not a subject for serious study; that interest in such finance is misplaced, even sinister or odd?

A peculiar English sensitivity regarding explicit discussion of money matters may also have inhibited application of economic theory to educational contexts. R. H. Tawney, as Hough (1991, p.219) reminds us, described the economics of education as 'that repulsive hybrid'. The socialist tradition in general, so influential in parts of the English educational tradition, has been especially resistant to application of an 'economic' approach. But those thought worlds, if they ever existed in such a rarefied form, have now disappeared utterly, as schools confront, within a framework of delegated school budgets, the challenges of computer-based Management Information Systems and the opportunities to be made available by the 'Superhighways' Initiative (DfEE, 1995).

The recent origin of the subject is usually dated to the address by Thomas Schultz to the American Economic Association in 1960 and his enthusiastic advocacy of a human capital approach to investment in education (Schultz, 1963). Attention to the subject in this journal may be traced to the pressure of more pragmatic concerns, in particular to the modifications made to local government finance after 1972, which eroded the independence of LEA financial decision-making, to the cumulative effects of associated overall expenditure reductions on education, and to the pressure on schools in particular, following a chronic fall in birth-rate after 1964. Volume 12 is notable for its preoccupation with the consequences of these structural and seemingly irreversible changes, by attention to issues such as: managing effectively in 'small' schools (Mountford, 1984), LEA responses to the effect of the 1981 Block Grant (Crispin and Marslen-Wilson, 1984), and the quality consequences for teachers *and pupils* of the ways in which contraction of the teaching force was being effected (Thomas, 1984). Only Hough and Warburton (1984), in this volume, examine specific questions of individual school costs, in a short paper whose citations reveal both the dominance of American work in this field and the relative lack of attention hitherto accorded to such questions in the journal. This has been remedied to some extent in subsequent issues, notably by the contributions of Simkins (1986, 1995), Boulton (1986), Levačić (1989, 1992), Dennison (1988), Hough (1991) Thomas and Bullock (1992) and Thomas (1996). Noteworthy too is Bondi's Manchester-based study (Bondi, 1988) of the relation of school costs to policy and community variables. In what may be an undeservedly overlooked contribution in this area, her conclusion, that falling school rolls have less influence than had generally been supposed on variations in costs, and *especially* on premises-related costs, is surprising, and, in view of what is now known about some of the effects of formula funding, worrying.

'Patronage, Markets and Collegiality' (Simkins, 1986) exemplifies what few individual papers fully achieve, namely illumination of a general institutional problem through analysis which maintains positive interaction between school-based research data and a simple, but robust, conceptual model. The literature cited is apposite, selective and suitable for the widest possible readership. Simkins (1986, p. 17) argues, perhaps presciently, that 'something of a movement to broaden the scope of schools' financial responsibilities' is afoot.

What strategies are available to schools for ensuring that often crucial marginal choices within tightly constrained limits of discretionary decision are made most effectively in terms of both the school's internal efficiency and its broader, underlying effectiveness as a learning institution in the care of a committed and motivated staff? The paper deserves to be read for its intrinsic qualities, and is a most valuable teaching resource. After almost ten years now during which schools have been working with greater freedom to make independent resource decisions, perhaps it would be timely and profitable to reassess some of the paper's conclusions (pp. 28–9). To what extent have participative decision processes survived? How closely related are current school resource allocation procedures to processes of curriculum decision-making? How widespread and effectively are formulae in use in schools (Boulton, 1986)? Some recent findings (Webb and Vulliamy, 1996) point to the emergence of a damaging divide between the needs of the curriculum and seemingly inescapable organisational pressures within schools. The impact of these has been 'to create "a new headteacher", with more hierarchical forms of management style creating a gulf between headteachers and the staff' (p. 313). In the case of primary schools, Webb and Vulliamy conclude:

> Thus, not only is there currently a tension between the administrative and curriculum leadership demands of primary school headship, there is also a growing tension between collegial and top-down management strategies at the whole school level...The current climate thus encourages headteachers to be powerful and, if necessary manipulative leaders in order to ensure that the policies and practices agreed upon are ones that they can wholeheartedly support and defend. (p. 313)

Structural and qualitative change

A new employment structure embracing both pay and conditions for teachers was established between 1986 and 1992. The professional implications of these impending changes were considered by Henson (1987) in a brief but usefully synoptic review of the literature and the implications of a more hierarchical set of relationships implicit in the Baker proposals. A fundamental question, which has been obscured if not suppressed by the *dirigisme* employed by recent governments in relation to education and by the historically diminished influence of the teacher unions on both government and public opinion, is whether learning can and should be *controlled* by teachers and whether the schools are to be institutions in which learning will be 'delivered' as product, or 'nurtured' as a process in which all are expected to participate. If teachers cannot or should not control the conditions and processes of learning, how can they be 'managerially' responsible for attainment of stipulated learning outcomes? If schools are to belong meaningfully to the communities they are there to serve, can and should they be required to operate with a centrally imposed specification of required learning activities and outcomes?

Perhaps a more inscrutable factor which has inhibited sharply focused consideration of these questions has been the nature and rapidity of changing social and economic conditions. The Callaghan initiative in 1976 to steer schools more pragmatically to meet the needs of the workplace was almost certainly premised upon a conception of work, its nature, value and availability, which is now seriously obsolete. Succeeding governments have moved forward with an ideological, some might say quasi-religious belief in the social and economic virtue of establishing market conditions as prerequisite for the efficient operation of almost every social activity and service. Yet in the globalised economy which every day impinges more directly upon the lives of each individual, it is becoming apparent that the scope for markets is increasingly confined to the *stimulation of the consumption and distribution* of goods; creation and production require the distributive, co-ordinative, informational, and creative qualities and capabilities of a kind which are achieved more effectively within network relations. Levels of mutual trust and qualities of human interaction which suffice in exchange relations are inadequate for an increasing number and variety of human interactions and institutional formations. Might not learning be one of them?

Two contrasting papers (Glatter, 1987; Dennison, 1988) made their contributions to this continually emerging debate by setting an educational agenda for the year 2000. Glatter considers current attitudes and practice with regard to management and policy and identifies five specific issues: staff management; profession/parent relationships; institutional effectiveness; the management/policy interface; and the role of BEMAS. He found it disturbing that the issue of parental involvement seems 'to have been appropriated by one part of the political spectrum.' With hindsight now we are beginning to see some of the consequences of crude attempts to redefine parents and learners as 'consumers' and 'users' and must surely hope that the 'upheaval of reaction' which Glatter refers to will be successful in identifying and winning support for more enlightened community involvement in education. On institutional effectiveness he draws attention to a neglected aspect of the self-concepts of members of organisations, a theme addressed more philosophically by Patricia White (1987). On policy and management Glatter challenged the current ascendancy of the 'accountancy' approach to education policy-making and in particular points to the detrimental effects of an unsustainable separation between policy and management, despite the stubborn refusal of the Audit Commission 'to comment on issues of education policy'. Referring to Maw (1984) and Inglis (1986) he just hints at the threat to professionality inherent in attempts to separate policy and management, which Glatter (1987, p. 9) believed to be 'even more closely intertwined'. If authority over educational values is reserved to 'policy' bodies, the teaching profession may be stripped of the moral basis of its professional role, increasingly technicised, refashioned as chief instrument or conduit for the implementation of policy (Hargreaves, 1994; Webb and Vulliamy, 1996). Implications of these developments were to be explored later in contributions by Ranson (1992) and Strain (1993) and elsewhere, with particular reference to curriculum management, by Hargreaves (1994) and Ball (1993a).

Dennison's paper, 'Education 2000 – Trends, Influences and Constraints to the Turn of the Century' is more avowedly futurological in both aims and approach. Four 'dominant factors' are identified as demanding attention:

- the changing nature and structure of skill requirements in response to technological change;

- the consequences of consumerism on schools and the teaching profession;

- continuing reductions in the volume of public expenditure on education;

- the extended application of IT in learning, school management and staff development.

What we have learnt since then has revealed how little is yet understood which might help us respond practically to these challenges. A further train of thought is suggested; if Dennison's predictive agenda were aptly chosen, have those issues (work-related education, the implications of social change, resources in education and the application of IT) been adequately represented in contributions to this journal? It is hoped that this review might prompt readers to consider such questions.

Financial management in schools and colleges

Notable among papers given at the 17th Conference (Volume 17.2) was Levačić's (1989) discussion of the rules to determine LEA's distribution of formula-based budgets to schools and colleges. She shows how schemes of delegation require a balance to be struck between conflicting sets of preferences regarding anticipated outcomes. Since decision-makers will use formulae to achieve their particular interests and objectives, explicit normative criteria should be stipulated. This enables self-interested or sectional purposes to be disentangled from those based on the values (efficiency, effectiveness, equity, accountability) which the scheme is intended to promote. Schemes are intended to encourage schools to be more efficient by generating savings and using them for chosen purposes; schools are therefore permitted to carry forward budget surpluses. Other elements of the formula, however, seem to allow schools to operate self-interestedly without regard to general principles. In Northern Ireland, for example, the inclusion of a weighting to support provision for children from materially or socially deprived backgrounds encourages schools to *admit* as many children as possible within that category but to *spend* resources differentially in support of learning by those children most likely to succeed in external examinations. In Levačić's words, 'reference to general principles helps in reaching agreed and consistent solutions to specific issues' (p. 89).

Professional understanding of the relations between policy intentions and educational outcomes is indebted to the work of Levačić (1992) and Thomas and Bullock (1992). Both reveal interim indications that some significant improvements in efficiency and accountability may be attributed to the operation of LMS. Cost information is more transparent, inducing more focused accountability, and school autonomy, particularly in respect of virement, is resulting in more efficient resource allocation *within schools* (Levačić, 1992, p. 27). Some more equitable patterns of distribution are also evident, arising from instances where discretionary funding has been replaced by application of general rules. Yet, some disturbing contrary tendencies are also revealed and the interim verdict on the extent to which the reforms have increased equity or contributed to enhanced teaching and learning is sceptical and mixed. Though opportunities for the exercise of parental choice have been increased, resources seem to be shifting away from smaller primary schools in favour of larger ones and away from secondary schools (Thomas and Bullock, 1992). On qualitative learning outcomes, 'important factors found to be associated with school effectiveness – purposive leadership, positive school climate... high expectations, curriculum planning, work-focused activities, recording pupils' progress' are not specifically enhanced by LMS reforms (Levačić, 1992, p. 27).

Competing values

'The Equity Consequences of Educational Reform' are scrutinised a little later in an excellent paper by Simkins (1995) in which he discusses a range of 'input' and 'output' definitions of equity, and points out that a formula and local market circumstances 'only determine the degree of equity *between* schools in the system and hence place constraints on the opportunities which schools can provide for individual pupils' (p. 224). In his conclusion he argues that LMS 'clearly embodies a concept of procedural equity but has consequences for distributional equity too' (p. 230). In this respect, the 'input-based definition of equity with pupils classified primarily on the basis of age' may result in further disadvantage for primary school pupils, especially those in smaller schools, or who have special educational needs or who come from disadvantaged backgrounds. Some of the conceptual difficulties inherent in attempts to resolve these problems are explored further in Thomas (1996, pp. 40–1; on the use of weighting procedures which incorporate non-utility information based upon underlying principles) and Strain (1996, pp. 55–6; on the 'endowment effect' and school strategies to avoid instances of 'local injustice').

How economic concepts illuminate education policy choices and assist practitioners at the institutional level in their efforts to achieve learning aims for pupils is explained by Thomas (1996).

> A 'market'... represents those circumstances where decision-making is decentralised and self-interest is assumed to be the motive force of human action.

The education system in England and Wales is a 'mixed economy' embodying market-like aspects, where agents make decisions on the basis of self-interest, as in circumstances where parents *choose* a particular school or a teacher chooses to take up a professional post, as well as extensive features of a 'command' economy, one in which the resources judged necessary for particular productive processes to take place are *commanded* by a central agency which enjoys authority within a hierarchical set of institutional relations. As Thomas reminds us, even in today's devolved conditions of school management:

> the maintained school system is almost wholly funded by general taxation and, for parents and pupils, is free at the point of consumption. The overall level of spending is determined by government (central and local), and the means of production are largely owned or employed by the government, which also determines the rules for allocating funds to schools. More important still, the curriculum and assessment of pupils is largely determined by the Secretary of State. (p. 32)

Whether the consequences are efficient and equitable is then examined in relation to an earlier study (Thomas and Bullock, 1994). This raises questions such as whether the 'current [irregularly stepped] funding profile' of LEAs in relation to Age-Weighted Pupil Units (AWPU) is consistent with what is inherently required by 'the continuous nature of the education process'. The Isle of Wight is now known to allocate 2.9 times more to provision for 16-year-olds than it does for 8-year-olds, compared with 2.08 times by Sunderland. In the (primary) school size range 122–3 the level of funding per pupil may vary by as much as 25 per cent. With these findings it is indeed possible and necessary to ask more pointed questions about the efficiency and equity effects of current funding practice.

> Is it necessary, for example, for comparable schools to be funded at such different levels in order to provide the same national curriculum? Are the schools with comparatively high levels of funding providing a superior experience and achieving more than the less well-funded schools? (p. 38).

With wry, ironical detachment, Thomas goes on to observe that:

> It is only as a result of the new system of funding schools that there is evidence which enables these questions to be considered – a clear benefit from introducing a greater emphasis on 'command' in the funding of schools.

V NEW WAYS OF EXAMINING OLD QUESTIONS

In this final section, the focus is deliberately restricted to a small number of papers in search of possible new ways of thinking and learning about educational management. Some of these experiments with new methods emphasise continuity with earlier approaches; others attempt radical redefinition of professional and organisational agenda. All assist our understanding of emerging requirements of organisational leadership in schools and colleges and of the role and purpose of 'public' education 'systems', within a 'Learning Society'.

Leaders and followers

Gronn (1996) exposes some significant defects in the 'new' cult of 'leadership', whose rise to prominence he dates from the early 1970s. Recent conventional conceptions of 'leader-followership' posit a cause-effect relationship between leaders and followers, consistent with a range of self-justifying, instrumentalist assumptions associated with 'managerialism' ('the manager's right to manage'; the government's right to govern' etc.).

> Leadership is seen as something performed by superior, better individuals (invariably, ageing white males), rather than by groups, located in *top* positions, and as something done *to* or *for* other inferior, lesser people. Causal significance is achieved when relevant counter-factual conditions are satisfied (e.g. the outcomes for followers otherwise would not have transpired but for the leader's leadership; all rival candidate explanations for the outcomes have been eliminated). (Gronn, 1996, p. 12).

Recalling the 'critical role' accorded to followers by Max Weber, Gronn most persuasively cites 'an emerging consensus that leading is an inherently symbolic activity', an activity imbued with the intrinsically human capacity to frame meaning, 'to make sense of one's own and others' experiences of the world'. If leadership activities are to contribute as we would wish to the construction of a shared social reality, support of the group must be mobilised through exchange of shared symbols and meanings. This is how *identities* are formed (Anderson, 1991). For these processes to be active, a level of consent and participation will be necessary on the part of the group. Transforming organisations is part of a cultural project. Identifying the extent and organisational forms by which this can become operative and fruitful, is a central task in a continuing, interdisciplinary endeavour.

> it is enduring moral values and culture which give organisations their distinctive characters and styles. Any cult of efficiency and effectiveness is of secondary import; these are essentially instrumental and operational values, necessary conditions for the persistence of the co-operative system that constitutes organisation...but not sufficient. For, antecedent to both efficiency and effectiveness is some overall abiding purpose or end, a moral economy, which provides people's willingness to co-operate with its justification from the outset. (Gronn, 1996, p. 24)

Gronn's paper accords well with the aims and methods attempted by Ribbins and Sherratt (1992) in their efforts to supplement a large-scale research project examining 'the changing patterns of governance and management...in response to recent legislation' through the use of ethnographic accounts of what is actually happening in schools. As well as using traditional sources of evidence, such as collections of documents, interviews, diaries, discussion and observation, they try to set the Head's accounts against those of other key actors and to involve Head, teachers and researcher in a process of reflection and interpretation which they term 'a dialectic of biography and autobiography'.

Professional implications and principles

Busher and Saran (1994), after exploring 'the various models which might be used to illuminate the work of headteachers', argue convincingly for 'the need for micropolitical theories of organisational life to be inclusive of both formal and informal aspects of organisations' and to support positively the development of 'consensual interactions' without neglecting conflictual elements. They identify the main features of leadership activities in schools as: constructing an organisational culture which embraces the shared values and beliefs of members, managing the external environment and 'using and diffusing power to handle conflicting values and interests between stakeholders' (p. 8). Their distillation also retains the essential characteristics of a *political* model of organisation, in essence a human social construct whose purpose and processes are defined through uncoerced discourse which responds primarily to moral, rather than technical, claims. These purposes in turn derive from 'a duty to serve the best interests of the pupils':

> heads who acted in this way built their credibility as professional leaders with teachers.
> (pp. 11, 12)

Further exploration of how these qualities of leadership might be developed and practised in a morally defensible organisational framework (Hodgkinson, 1993) can be found in Volume 21, No. 3. The merits of generic as distinct from sector specific standards of competence are reviewed by Earley (1993); Ouston (1993) examines management competence specifically in relation to the findings of school effectiveness studies and teachers' assessment and training needs. Eraut (1993b) delves more analytically into what must be a prerequisite for significant advance on these fronts by arguing the need for a new epistemology to fulfil the aims outlined in Schön's *Reflective Practitioner*. Such a model incorporates the personal and professional knowledge which teachers actually draw upon in their teaching and managing in schools. The paper is both carefully constructed and conceptually rich. Following Argyris and Schön (1976), listening and actively seeking feedback from colleagues is encouraged in order to correct for the tendency 'of people's perceptual frameworks to be determined by what they want or expect to see' (p. 230). These are termed 'meta-processes', which assist continuing critical adjustment of cognitive frameworks and assumptions. They are essentially processes concerned with self-knowledge and self-management. Eraut later adds 'the conception of a meta-evaluation framework' as central to the notion of professionalism. In the case of teachers, he suggests, such a framework should be founded on two moral principles: the twin obligations to practise child-centredness and, for the sake of future generations, continuously to improve one's own professional expertise.

The learning society

The importance of principles, assumptions or values such as these lies not in their embodiment of intrinsic authority or some immanent guarantee to practitioners of being 'right', or of enabling them through practising them more reliably to 'do things right' – their significance is, much more elusively, that they *constitute* the foundation of any education system. One Head's expression of belief in his own school's *constitutive* values was recorded by Ribbins (1992):

it has to do with how we value children; all children and not just some children. We believe that all children have a right ... to achieve. Our first job as teachers is to enable them to achieve. This still applies even if they don't want to achieve. I do not believe that children always know what is best for them ... I think also we have sometimes to say to parents as well that something is good for their child. Within this we have a firm commitment to equal opportunities. We want to help all children to broaden their horizons and visions. We want to help them all to understand there is a world beyond the one they know and that they can all participate in it. The school is just a step to this and teachers are there to help to make it possible. My task is to create the conditions which make this possible for teachers and children to achieve. It is not a task I can achieve alone. (p. 67)

Of course, values espoused are not always or entirely matched by results in practice. In particular, entrenched historical and social patterns of under-achievement are hard to change. Introducing his seminal essay 'Towards the Learning Society', Ranson (1992) notes the 'stubborn statistic', recently acknowledged by HMI (DES, 1990), of one in three children receiving a poor education, underachieving. He attributes this to 'the long cultural tradition of educating a minority'.

Underachievement, Ranson argues, is *institutionalised* in our schools 'because of principles and assumptions which are constitutive of the education system'. Many of these assumptions, by their appearance of being 'only common-sense', conceal the shaping force of underlying values which contribute to the 'distribution' of unequal, unjust or undesirable educational consequences, such as underachievement. Ranson lists some of these influential and readily recognisable 'principles'. Education is an activity for schools and parents, when children are young; training is for colleges and employers. Learning involves instruction by those whose authority to teach derives from their knowledge and skills. The Curriculum should also transmit skills in identified areas of (objective) knowledge. The learning outcomes of education processes should be measured by universal objective tests whose results should be published to reward and enhance the credibility of the successful, encourage the average and penalise the 'failing' institutions. By these latent mechanisms or constitutive principles, failure to 'deliver' what central government specifies to be the appropriate 'outcomes', which may or may not match the kind of organisational values articulated by the Head quoted earlier – to enable children to achieve even when they don't want to achieve – is transmitted and explained publicly as the failure of the school itself, a failure of professional competence or application, or, more unfairly still, the fault of the individual child and its family.

The remedy proposed by Ranson is to alter fundamentally many of these constitutive principles by replacing them with new, socially agreed conceptions of the place of learning in society and of a more 'civil-ized' working relationship between working, civic, learning and caring roles in the lives of individuals. These constructs, institutions which sustain and mediate our social relations and experiences, are the responsibility of all, in common. Learning is an indispensable part of such a polity at all stages of an individual's life. This is the conception of

'The Learning Society' whose advocacy Ranson concludes with:

> A different polity, enabling all people to make a purpose of their lives, will create the conditions for motivation in the classroom. Only a new moral and political order can provide the foundation for sustaining the personal development of all. It will encourage individuals to value their active role as citizens and thus their shared responsibility for the common-wealth. Active learning in the classroom needs, therefore, to be informed by and lead towards active citizenship within a participatory democracy. Teachers and educational managers... can, I believe, play a leading role in *enabling* [original italics] such a vision to unfold not only among young people but also across the public domain. (p. 79)

The end is where we start from[2]...

This review has attempted to sift and encourage a second reading of some of the enquiries and debates which have been published in this journal. It has not attempted to assess their intrinsic merits as publications but from them to recapture and re-present still pertinent ideas, experiences and ways of examining the challenges now facing teachers and learners.

Our practical understanding of the relation between theory and practice in education has changed beyond recognition since the early days of the *Bulletin* and the 1974 IIP Conference. The recognition of the value of action research for teachers as both practitioners and researchers has been crucially influential in this respect. Yet the logical and conceptual foundations underpinning such activities still exercise the concern of theorists. Evers and Lakomski (1993, p. 150) opt for explanations of social behaviour which are reconcilable (coherent) with those of natural science. Others, notably Hodgkinson (1993, p. 184), resist tenaciously all attempts to blur the line between 'fact and value', insisting on the separate, moral, humanistic nature of administration. The domain of the 'social', what is experienced routinely, intersubjectively and in common among human beings, is almost lost sight of in this long-running battle between positivistic 'coherentists' and humanistic 'idealists' (Bates, 1993, p. 174–5). My own preference is to insist, with Bates, on the primacy of the intersubjective and the 'social' (Strain, 1996, pp. 50-51), to continue to search for 'real' possibilities of learning.

This chapter is a substantially revised version of a paper previously published in *EMA* as 'Records of Achievement: a critical review of *Educational Management and Administration*', *EMA*, Vol. 25, No. 3 (1997), pp. 213–242.

---

2 T. S. Eliot, 'Little Gidding', *Four Quartets*. London: Faber, 1959.

PART 1
TEACHERS

Teachers in Organisations

JANET OUSTON

INTRODUCTION

Choosing four papers from *EMA* for this collection has been a great privilege: many others could have been included. My commission was 'teachers and the future'. I have interpreted this as the role of teachers, how they behave towards each other in their professional lives, and how they might in the future. In this commentary I will try to draw out the ways in which the papers might be seen as 'talking to' each other, and clarify why I have chosen them from the wide range of excellent papers available.

All the papers are concerned with people in the management of education: they do not focus directly on systems nor with technical issues such as funding although Smyth's paper on the impact of the introduction of local management on teachers and schools takes this as its starting point. All assume that educational institutions are complex, and cannot be understood as rational organisations (Ouston, 1998). Morgan's (1996) machine metaphor has no place here. All challenge the reader to think about alternative approaches to how we conceptualise organisations and all raise more questions than they answer. As Hoyle says, pointing out that organisations are not entirely rational, and that the lack of rationality should not seen as failure:

> everyone working in organisations is all too aware of their often idiosyncratic, adventitious, unpredictable and intractable nature when every day brings a new organisational 'pathology' to disrupt well laid plans. (p. 42)

Bhindi and Duignan comment that:

> There was a time when leaders could control and manipulate organisations more readily than they can today. (p. 52)

Could they? Was there ever such a time, or is it that our perception has changed? Hoyle argued that micropolitics is an inevitable part of the nature of social organisations and would, I think, question whether leadership was ever as clear-cut as Bhindi and Duignan assert.

THE PAPERS

The papers are discussed in the following order:

- Smyth's paper sets the scene for the present and likely future of school management.

- Hoyle, for the first time, argues that the 'dark side' of the organisations can be approached through an analysis of their micropolitics.

- Bhindi and Duignan offer their analysis of leadership for the next century, but also, and perhaps even more importantly, they advocate quite different criteria for understanding and acting within organisations.

- Eraut offers a conceptual framework for considering how professional expertise is developed.

DEVOLUTION AND TEACHERS' WORKS: THE UNDERSIDE OF A COMPLEX PHENOMENON

Smyth's paper starts with the angry assertion that:

> school-based management...is an area that is rapidly becoming a tangled web of misunderstandings, distortions, half-truths and downright lies. (p. 34)

The first section of his paper offers an excellent, concise, explanation of how the local management of schools can be seen as a response to wider political changes. The middle of the paper discusses the consequences for the education service (what an old-fashioned term that is in the current climate!) and argues that devolution has shifted power to the centre, devolved blame to schools and increased inequity for students and communities. He quotes from Hartley to support this argument, which has been powerfully confirmed by recent research by Whitty, Power and Halpin (1998) and Simkins' paper in this volume.

Smyth's analysis is mainly pessimistic. In the final paragraphs he asks 'What is the alternative?' (p. 40). He rightly urges educationalists to convince themselves that the current direction of education policy 'is not in the interests of teachers, students, or society generally'. While I would not wish to disagree with his position, we as readers need to take on two sets of questions: how can the policy context of schools be changed to ensure good education within an equitable context, and how can our schools be run to compensate for the adverse impact of devolution? But it should be noted that other writers (for example, Levacic, 1995 and Bullock and Thomas, 1997) have commented on the positive aspects. Part of the 'problem' seems to me to be schools' – and some inspectors' – interpretations of the OfSTED criteria which have become so dominant in teachers' thinking. Creativity, flexibility and high quality exciting teaching are not 'forbidden' by OfSTED guidelines. But some teachers (particularly those in the inner cities where equity is disappearing, pressures are increasing and performance may not reach the national average) are understandably anxious about 'failing' and have become more and more compromised in their professionalism.

MICROPOLITICS OF EDUCATIONAL ORGANISATIONS

Moving back thirteen years, Hoyle's paper is a classic. Reading through previous volumes of *Educational Management and Administration*, people are almost invisible. Many of the papers are to do with systems and with 'administration'. Out of the blue this paper challenges the scientific approach to administration, not by saying that there are inevitable and regrettable failures of that model, but that it was a flawed model in the first place. Greenfield's and Ranson's paper in this volume also reject this model. People, and their behaviour in organisations, became high profile for the first time. At this point in my reading of the early – rather dull – volumes of the journal I was excited to find it, and it obviously had a major impact on subsequent writing. Hoyle says that:

> This paper offers no solutions... its purpose has been to put micropolitics on the agenda. (p. 51)

He succeeded.

Hoyle explores the strategies used by interest groups to obtain power, and sees these as an inevitable part of organisational life. Moving to the current context, his micropolitical analysis is often evident not only in the relationships within schools, but between the school and its LEA and community. The modern reader is faced with two questions: is the existence of micropolitics in organisations inevitable, and should steps be taken to minimise its harmful effects? One of the implications of the analyses in the very different papers by Eraut, and Bhindi and Duignan, is that the pervasiveness of micropolitics in some organisations might be damaging and that it might be countered by an explicit focus on increasing transparency and developing common values. Micropolitics, while they might be inevitable, can lead to organisational damage.

LEADERSHIP FOR A NEW CENTURY:
AUTHENTICITY, INTENTIONALITY, SPIRITUALITY AND SENSIBILITY

Bhindi and Duignan's paper is set in an entirely different conceptual mould. Here the small-scale analyses of micropolitics are replaced by the wider view of leadership values. It is argued that educational leaders should have authenticity, intentionality, spirituality and sensibility. They argue that leaders for the future should be driven by ethics, values and principles. This is in striking contrast to the can-do culture of much current thinking about educational management and leadership. The NPQH, for example, has little space for profound and critical thinking about these issues.

This paper separates out leadership from the overall management of the school – an increasingly frequent, and to this commentator unhelpful, approach – which has, however, become so prevalent that it has captured the discourse of education management. We seem to have no choice but to accept it. But it has dangers: in particular that the (by implication lowly) management activities can be undertaken without reference to the values which underpin the leader. Creating a values-driven school culture, which by definition might curb the worst excesses of micropolitical activity, will not be achieved unless the leadership and management activities of all staff are set within broadly similar sets of values and where decision-making is devolved. Stacey (1992) and Fullan (1993) both argue that the rapidly changing future will demand flexibility and devolved decision-making. Thus a values-led leadership as argued for by Bhindi and Duignan will have to incorporate strategies for giving that leadership away.

THE CHARACTERISATION AND DEVELOPMENT OF PROFESSIONAL EXPERTISE IN SCHOOL MANAGEMENT AND IN TEACHING

Eraut's perceptive and articulate paper explores the ways in which teachers with management responsibilities learn. He argues that much personal knowledge is acquired through experience and is tacit. It cannot be fully under critical control and evaluated (p. 64) unless it is made explicit. The four key values of Bhindi and Duignan could be seen as underpinning personal knowledge, which needs to be understood and subjected to evaluation through disciplined professional reflection. The second part of the paper looks at the learning of deliberative processes and these too will be influenced, perhaps unconsciously, by the values held.

What might be the relationship between professional learning and explicit expertise, and micropolitics? Micropolitics can be seen as mainly providing opportunities for manipulative action, making the organisation and people within it do what you want them to do. It is a conscious activity, where individuals are very aware of the strategies they use to further their interests. Eraut's paper raises for us the possibility that these strategies may be founded on learning which has remained tacit, and where professional knowledge, values and attitudes formed earlier in life may guide micropolitical actions (Hirschhorn, 1990). We have, therefore, a double darkness in the organisation: personal values agendas which people are unaware of, leading to micropolitical action which is by definition difficult to locate. While both are inevitable, the combination may significantly contribute to the formation of Smyth's 'tangled web' and provide a profoundly damaging context for school management practice. Eraut's emphasis on examining tacit personal knowledge and expertise, is of critical importance.

ENDNOTE

These papers were chosen because of the pleasure and insights they gave me. For very practical reasons of space they were cut, hopefully with respect for the intentions of the authors. Do read the originals, too. They will challenge your thinking.

Finally, I would like to point out that only one of these papers has a woman author. I hope that during next twenty-five years of *EMA*, writing by women about education management will become more prominent. It is also surprising that gender is not mentioned in any of these papers: many would have been enriched by this additional perspective, particularly in a profession in which women far outnumber men.

Devolution and Teachers' Work: The Underside of a Complex Phenomenon

JOHN SMYTH

Devolution, school-based management, or site-based management is an area that is rapidly becoming a tangled web of misunderstandings, distortions, half-truths, and downright lies. We need to start unravelling some of the complex issues, some of the undisclosed interests, and some of the manipulation that is masquerading under the rubric of devolution.

To make my point at the outset, and in the most direct way possible. Last year I presented the keynote address to a teachers' conference in New South Wales, where devolution was a hot issue. Before my presentation, a teacher (as part of the general business of the meeting) made a statement that captured the essence of what myself and many others were struggling with. It went like this:

> I feel like we have been taken to the cleaners. When you go to the dry cleaners you get a note that says: 'All care but no responsibility'. With this devolution and self-management stuff, 'it's all responsibility and no power'. (Smyth, 1993, p. 1)

This teacher's words serve as a poignant reminder that devolution does not mean the same thing to everyone. If devolution is to mean anything, then we have to be serious about listening to what teachers say, think and feel – a fact that is not all that self-evident in the rash of educational reforms and educational re-structurings currently occurring around the world.

If we are to move beyond much of the humbug that has come to characterise devolution, we also need to be more open and honest about several key questions – questions like:

– whose interests are served (and whose denied) by devolution?

– why is devolution happening with such intensity now? (notwithstanding the arguments from some quarters, that this is merely a natural progression of a process already well underway)

– what does this do to the nature of relationships within/between schools?

34

- what kind of alternatives might be possible?

The starting point for the discussion of these matters has to be: where does devolution fit into the 'broader picture' (the context if you like)? If we go down this route, it may just turn out that *the context* proves to be the most important and revealing of all. The context, as I see it being described, is one of:

- global re-structuring
- international competitiveness
- leaner forms of production
- flexible workforce and multi-skilling
- international best practice
- post-Fordist forms of work organisation
- free-market thinking, and
- severe fiscal austerity.

As I hear the arguments being rehearsed, they go something like this. If we are to extricate ourselves from the economic quagmire, then we need to do certain things:

- dismantle inefficient structures that have surrounded the work of schools and that are too costly – particularly inefficient educational bureaucracies;

- create flatter organisations, in which the lines of communication are truncated;

- make decisions closer to the workface, by people who are in touch with the work, and who know what they are doing;

- be much more flexible and responsive to our 'clients', and provide better service;

- operate in ways in which we are more accountable, through the measurement of 'outcomes', the use of 'report cards', and through the publication of 'league tables';

- work in ways in which 'consumers' are in the driver's seat, not the 'producers'; and above all

- operate according to the entrepreneurial principles of the private sector – 'user pays', 'managing image and impressions', 'watching the bottom line', and 'being rugged and competitive individualists'.

A key factor feeding into all of this is the resurgence of 'human capital theory' – a view that regards individuals as being maximisers of their own advantage, and as pursuing self-interest 'primarily towards the acquisition of wealth, status and power' (Lauder, 1987, p. 5). According to Marginson (1989), human-capital theory encapsulates four principles:

1. people are calculating players who act to maximise their own personal economic utility;
2. the only benefits to education are economic;
3. the benefits of education are primarily individual; and

4. the social benefits of education are no more than the sum of the individual benefits.

In this quick snapshot, I have tried to capture the spirit of the changing context accurately – and if I haven't, then my omission is in the detail, not in the general essence of things. I should hasten to add that some of the practices I have alluded to are worthy and fine ideals (in a limited kind of way). They sound natural and commonsensical; perhaps that's because we have been bombarded with them so intensively by the media. But they also mask a lot of unanswered questions, particularly when applied to education....

The immediate question that needs to be addressed is 'why are we having devolution now?' The explanation is not simple, but it does have quite profound consequences for places like schools and what transpires within them. The reason we are seeing and hearing so much about devolution is that we are experiencing a 'crisis of the state' – that is to say, an increasing inability of the collective institutions and apparatuses of government to actually do their job. Without going deeply into social and political theory, what is occurring at the moment amounts to a shift of the economic epicentre from the USA and Europe, to the Asia and Pacific region – a process brought about by low labour costs, vastly improved information technology, instantaneous communication, and transportation. We are in a context in which capital is footloose and able to take advantage of the 'best' conditions anywhere in the world.

In situations like this, of extremely high fluidity, uncertainty, and unpredictability, the process of governance becomes much more difficult. Tax bases are no longer predictable in the way they used to be; profits are much more volatile with corporations becoming franchised operations headquartered in New York, London or Tokyo; and geopolitical boundaries and national sovereignty are practically meaningless. Little wonder that national governments are finding it extremely difficult to govern.

What happens in circumstances of virtual ungovernability like these is that the state tries to ameliorate the worst effects of the pendulum-like action of the business cycle, through forms of technical/rational planning. The state retreats in a fiscal sense from many areas in which it has traditionally been a 'provider' of infrastructure, like telecommunications, transportation, gas, electricity, banking, and schooling – at the same time that it centralises and hardens its 'regulatory' function. That is to say, in situations of such 'overload' (Nash, 1989) it portrays itself as providing the broad policy directions, guidelines and frameworks, within which private (and quasi-private) providers can do their stuff....

In the remainder of this paper I want to argue that devolution is a part of this complex puzzle, and that it has profound influences on how we think about and operate schools, and that it might not be a notion that is readily transferable from other spheres of activity.

As it applies to schooling and education, devolution does certain things. What it *actually* does may not be what it *purports* to do – but that *could be* part of the process! As long as devolution is an element of the state repositioning itself in a dramatically changing set of circumstances, then certain features become clear:

1. Governments can no longer sustain educational expenditure of the order of magnitude of the past. Neither can they continue to be providers, at least in terms of what we have come to know as large educational bureaucracies that have historically supported the work of teachers and schools. They have tried shifting parts of bureaucracies around, by regionalising, but there are no real cost reductions there.

2. What governments seem to have done strategically is to admit that they got it wrong; bureaucracies really are an inefficient form of provision, and they should be dumped! Given the unsavoury experiences the general population has had at the hands of petty bureaucrats, there are few problems with the overall legitimacy of dismembering so-called inefficient bureaucracies. What is overlooked, of course, is the crucial mediating function bureaucracies perform in terms of seeking to ensure at least a modicum of social justice, equity and participation across vast distances (in the case of countries like Australia), along with the attempt to handle a student clientele with increasingly disparate abilities, cultural and socioeconomic backgrounds.

3. Coupled with this deconstruction of inefficient bureaucratic methods is the argument that we need decisions that are made as close as possible to the workface. Collectively, we are prepared to accept this, at least at face value; it sounds as if it fits within the philosophy of industrial democracy.

4. At the same time as we dismantle the machinery of rules and regulations (the hallmarks of bureaucracy), we posit in their place the claim that what is needed is a dose of free marketeering – that is to say, competition and deregulation. Schools, it is claimed, need to be shifted away from being sheltered workshops so as to get them to compete against one another (even to tender) for resources and students – and this is a good thing!

   In this, we are invited to embrace the logic of the sporting analogy of competition. It must be good, otherwise how can we explain our frenzy of support for football, or even the Olympic Games? We all know that competition produces efficiencies. There are winners, and there are those who had better lift their game, or get out. This is a line of argument that is almost irrefutable. It has obvious appeal to industry because it positions them to be able to more directly shape the output or outcomes of schooling, by having a larger say in what ought to constitute a more literate and numerate workforce – something they argue that has long been holding them back, making them uncompetitive. Schools have been hopeless, so industry argues, at doing things, and what we need is an education system that has a 'corporate and entrepreneurial culture'. And if it doesn't work, schools can still be blamed, as they have in the past, because they didn't listen carefully enough to the captains of industry.

5. These arguments are inextricably linked to the false (but highly plausible)

claim that the reason for our economic woes is that schools have not been doing their job properly – too many illiterates; schools falling apart because of lax discipline; excessive violence; not enough testing and measurement against standards; too much soft and spongy curricula; and so on.

The reason arguments of this kind are wrong-headed is that in respect of 'the economy', the analogy of competition somehow becomes hopelessly confused. It tangles itself up in 'who are winners' and 'who are losers' . . . .

Who the 'consumers' of education are has been dramatically re-defined at a policy level, so that there is a much closer nexus than ever before between industry and education. We can see this in terms of the spokespersons for education who are increasingly Business Roundtables, Industry Education Forums, and Chambers of Industry and Commerce. In a devolved view of education, these groups have a much closer relationship with education, on the grounds that schools 'need to be more responsive' . . . .

There are other questions too, about what is genuinely being devolved – is it real power, or merely the responsibility for implementing a bigger agenda decided elsewhere, far removed from schools? The evidence seems to be that far from shifting power from the centre, the reverse is actually happening. Central policy-making groups are actually acquiring more power to determine policy centrally through guidelines, frameworks and directions documents, with responsibility being shunted down the line to schools.

None of this is to say that devolution, *per se*, is necessarily a bad thing. Basically, what it represents is a marked change of ethos in the way schools are organised – from an educational focus to an entrepreneurial and marketing one – from a system of state regulation that kept an eye on questions of equity and resourcing, to a competitive market-driven approach. At the level of individual schools, devolution becomes something quite different to what it purports to be – it is a budget-cutting exercise masquerading under the banner of schools getting more control of their own affairs. There will be more responsibility to schools for managing their own cuts – but *no more power*. Furthermore, there is a paucity of evidence that in handing budgeting, management, and marketing to schools, teaching and learning improves as a consequence. If anything, the evidence available suggests the reverse (Murphy, 1990). The administrative load of schools increases significantly as schools engage in commercial/entrepreneurial activities just to stay afloat.

The removal of central bureaucracies might seem to make some sense, but the evidence is that other ones just as big and as expensive take their place to check that things are done according to central guidelines and frameworks – curriculum audits, Review Units, and central office personnel who ensure that expenditures conform with requirements. There is no net gain to schools. Overall, this is a recipe for increasing central power, not reducing it. Policy Units and the like become even more powerful than the bureaucracies they replaced. The only role for schools is in the implementation of real educational decisions, made centrally.

Emphasis is increasingly on 'impression management' as schools are driven by the need to rank high on published league ladders of achievement. The basis of what constitutes schooling and education will be narrowed as schools are pushed increasingly to market themselves. Turning schools into businesses is not the way to make them efficient or accountable – schools are infinitely more complex social institutions than that. The claim that in a devolved situation, parents will have choice, in the same way they would in a shopping mall, actually turns out to be completely inaccurate. The reverse actually happens – schools choose the students. The more affluent schools will cream off the students that are to their liking (mostly the ones from affluent and middle-class backgrounds), and the rest will be left behind in 'sink', 'residue' or ghetto schools. This separation of 'haves' and 'have nots' is an extremely divisive social agenda....

If I can summarise my argument so far. The reason we ought to be extremely cautious about notions like devolution is that they are playing loose and fast with language. They are not what they seem to be about, and we can only get a good sense of that when we look at the bigger picture. In short, it is not about handing over control; for that to happen, we need quite a different context, quite a different philosophy, and a radically different set of values. What we have at the moment under the banner of devolution is a set of practices that amount to nothing less than a 'political and managerial solution' (Jackson, 1993) to problems of contemporary government....

The implications for schools are becoming clearer.

First, a discourse about the work of schooling is constructed that becomes unassailable. For example, we naturalise the discourse so that we need more 'skills profiles' and 'task analyses', in order to produce 'needs statements', against which to produce highly structured 'performance objectives', so that 'outcomes' can be measured against 'standards'. Presumably the intent (although it is not put this way) is to produce labour that is more compliant. Opposition to this line is branded as being deviant, old-fashioned, or just out-of-touch.

Second, policy-making in contexts like this becomes a process of 'exhortation' (Crowe, 1993). As long as teachers are exhorted to be 'clear', 'precise' and 'consistent' about their teaching, and to pay proper regard to 'missions', 'goals', 'operational procedures', 'outcomes' and 'measurement' – then it all looks as if teachers are the problem....

Third, what is worrying about this is that the real interests being served are not disclosed. In being told that education is being re-structured 'in the national interest' we are not being told the truth. Forms of education that are about efficiency, effectiveness, excellence and quality are really about responding to the needs of industry....

If we allow schools to follow this market-driven view of education, which is part of the devolution agenda, then we will end up with a scenario of the kind described by David Hartley (1993) when he says:

> Within schools there will be an ever-increasing division between those who control files and finance, on the one hand, and those who educate, on the other. The former

will work to stave off the financial bankruptcy of the school, while the latter will toil to keep it educationally solvent. Freire's 'banking concept' will come to have an entirely new meaning. But these micropolitical divisions will be as nothing compared to the inter-school divisions that will ensue. Caught in the crossfire will be children, especially those unfortunate enough to be born to poorer parents. But above the fray the market makers and their mandarins – honest brokers to a man – will monitor the movement of some kind of Times Educational Index (in our terms, an Educational All Ordinaries Index, and boy will it be ordinary), checking the balance sheets and a accounts, downgrading one school's 'stock market' rating, taking out options on another, and sadly closing their position on others. All this constitutes a financial audit. But what of the moral audit? It is not sufficient merely to invoke the democratic principle of liberty, or the freedom to choose, as a moral justification of these policies. When the pursuit of liberty – individual liberty – proceeds beyond the point when the public good is served, then the whole democratic basis of 'choice' education policy will be cast into doubt. Perhaps the academic standards of some children will be enhanced, but the overall academic standard of all our children is set to fall. The public good will not be served when inner-city children are left to languish in 'sink' schools, schools which are not of their making. For these children, it is chance, not choice, which will determine their educational fate. By the end of the day the government may still claim to be able to exonerate itself, for it will surely suggest that all of these arrangements to do with self-management (at whatever level – pupil, teacher, school) are optional – if they are not taken up, then that is a matter for the pupil, the teacher or the school. Therein lies the choice – therein lies the liberty. (p. 112)

WHAT IS THE ALTERNATIVE?

As it happens, there is an alternative, but it looks dramatically different. It is one in which schools are educationally vibrant places where parents, teachers, students and the community feel they are able to freely engage in discussion and debate about what is going on, why and with what effect. There is also an absence of schools being bludgeoned into submissiveness using crude and narrow economic agenda. There are genuine opportunities for dialogue, chances to understand one another's perspectives outside of coercion, and a greater tolerance, difference and diversity in contrast to conformity and uniformity produced by some centrally determined market model.

This vision has implicit within it a quite different set of social relationships too, about the nature of teaching as an occupation that is primarily concerned with the exercise of professional judgement (Tripp, 1992). There is less measurement against standards of performance, and more concern with ways of enabling teachers to connect with the lives of their students. The emphasis is on better ways of helping teachers to counteract mindless bureaucratic incursions into their classrooms, that have no educational foundation to them. Teachers are able to see in what ways their voices are being progressively silenced in the debates about school reform, and how the media hype about accountability is being used as a way of legitimating managerialism. In the process they are equipped with ways of exposing and transforming authoritarian and hierarchical structures that have come to captivate them and their students, devising better ways of celebrating (Boomer, 1985) what it is they do in teaching, through creating better self images. None of this is to underestimate the magnitude or the difficulties of the job of winning back schools and the work of teaching. The struggle by educationists must be multi-layered – pragmatic, symbolic, philosophical and theoretical. But first, we have to start out by convincing ourselves that the direction in which education is being re-structured is not in the interests of teachers, students, or society generally. To borrow from Michael Fullan and Andy Hargreaves (1991) – we need to be coherent as to 'What's worth fighting for'.

Micropolitics of
Educational Organisations

ERIC HOYLE

Both practitioners and theorists regard administration as an essentially rational process. Although the current emphasis on contingency theory recognises that effective patterns of administration are relative to the contexts in which they are to operate, there remains the fundamental assumption that if plans are well-conceived, clearly set out, and adequately communicated, then systems can be improved. Yet everyone working in organisations is all too well aware of their often idiosyncratic, adventitious, unpredictable and intractable nature when every day brings a new organisational 'pathology' to disrupt well laid plans. This uncertainty occurs at the highest levels of policy-making and implementation. In his much cited work on the Cuban missile crisis, Allison (1971) showed that what had been interpreted as the outcome of carefully considered and rationally enacted policies could be viewed as the result of actors within a highly uncertain situation bargaining within their own camps as well as across national boundaries. In an interview, Zbegniew Brzezinski, President Carter's adviser on national security, stated: 'My overwhelming observation from the experience of the last four years is that history is neither the product of design nor of conspiracy, but is rather the reflection of continuing chaos. Seen from the outside, decisions may often seem clear and consciously formulated . . . but one learns that so much of what happens . . . is the product of chaotic conditions and a great deal of personal struggle and ambiguity' (Urban, 1981). Policy-makers and administrators in the less lethal field of education will recognise the aleatory dimension of the institution – described by Kogan (1975) as 'pluralistic, incremental, unsystematic and reactive' – as they attempt to improve the service in conditions which appear to be perennially turbulent.

Evidence of the quirky and idiosyncratic nature of social institutions could lead one into a consideration of fundamental questions about the nature of the social sciences. However, this path will not be taken in this paper. The question to be considered is whether social scientists have explored sufficiently all dimensions of institutions as a source of explanation of what, within the prevailing paradigms of social science research, appears to be irrational, adventitious and peculiar to a unique setting at one point in time. It is the purpose of this paper to suggest that there is one dimension of organisations which has been largely ignored in administration and organisation theory. We can refer to this as the 'micropolitics of organisations'. It is an organisational underworld which we all recognise and in which we all participate. We acknowledge it when we speak of 'organisational mafias', 'hidden agendas', 'playing politics' and 'Machiavellianism'. It is a dark side of organisational life which provides the source of much staff gossip. Ironically, micropolitical activity is engaged in by the very administrators who profess a rational theory of administration. Yet it is very rarely made the focus of academic study. For enlightenment on micropolitics and for enjoyable confirmation of what we know of this dimension of organisations, we go to television serials, films, plays and novels:

'Wilt' does more than Weber can
To reveal the FE world to man.

There may be good reason for the academic neglect of micropolitics. It is perhaps considered slightly unrespectable, or too self-indulgent ('the cute school of organisation theory', Ouchi, 1981), or a threat to conventional administrative theory which it is, or as having no practical application – which it may not. Or it may be that it simply is not a single dimension of organisations at all but a range of different processes each best handled separately through existing bodies of theory and research.

The purpose of this paper is simply to put the issue of micropolitics on the agenda. The sections which follow deal with the hypothesised domain of micropolitics, reasons for its omission from the major approaches to the study of organisations and their administration, the approaches to organisation and administrative theory which deal to some degree with micropolitics, and implications of micropolitics for the training of administrators.

THE DOMAIN OF MICROPOLITICS

Micropolitics embraces those strategies by which individuals and groups in organisational contexts seek to use their resources of power and influence to further their interests. The cynic might well say that this is simply a definition of administration. It is true that the relationship between administration and micropolitics is symbiotic in that in practice they are inextricably linked, but it can at least be hypothesised that there is some measure of independence. Administrative theory focuses on structures and the associated processes of power, decision-making, communication, etc. But the space between structures is occupied by something other than individuals and their motives. This 'other' consists of micropolitical structures and processes. It is characterised more by coalitions than by departments, by strategies rather than by enacted rules, by influence rather than by power, and by knowledge rather than by status. The micropolitical dimension may be largely shaped by the formal structure – which may well be the dimension which best accounts for organisational activity – but it is nevertheless worthwhile reversing the traditional approach by treating the micropolitical as the 'figure' and the administration as the 'ground' to explore whether this throws a different light on the operation of organisations. Such a procedure would lead to a focus on the major elements of micropolitics: interests, interest sets, power and strategies.

Politics is inevitably concerned with *interests*. Administrative theory often underestimates the plurality of interests in organisations because it tends to be attuned to organisational goals as determined by the leadership. That there are interests other than those of organisational effectiveness has of course long been taken into account by most administrative theories, but they nevertheless tend to be treated as recalcitrant, a suitable case for leadership, or socialisation or coercion. It is beyond the scope of this paper to offer a taxonomy of interests, but any classification would at least include personal, professional and political interests. Personal interests would include autonomy, status, territory and rewards....

It is easily seen that, taking these three areas of interest alone, it is difficult to disentangle the personal, the professional and the political at a substantive level. The tendency is perhaps for personal or political interests to be presented in terms of the professional, since normatively this is the most 'respectable' form of interest in education. Thus a proposed innovation which threatened the territorial interests of a teacher might well be resisted by mobilising 'professional' arguments against it. Similarly, political interests can be presented as professional interests. However, it can be seen that here even the conceptual distinction is very difficult to sustain....

Interests constitute the content of micropolitics but it can be seen that the area is fraught with conceptual and methodological difficulties. It is perhaps for this reason that those who have addressed themselves to micropolitics have tended to focus on strategies rather than content. Interests are pursued by individuals but frequently they are most effectively pursued in collaboration with others who share a common concern. Some of these may have the qualities of a group in that they are relatively enduring and have a degree of cohesion, but others – which are perhaps best referred to as *interest sets* – will be looser associations of individuals who collaborate only infrequently when a common interest comes to the fore. Some interest groups will be coterminous with formal organisational groupings, e.g. departments or teams. These will be particularly strong. Others will transcend formal boundaries and will form when a common interest has to be pursued. The basis of group or set association may be age, sex, professional interests, politics, union activity, etc. Burns (1955) distinguished between cliques which are committed to sustaining the status quo and *cabals* which are committed to organisational change....

Some interest groups will be permanently mobilised; interest sets will mobilise as and when their interest becomes salient. Components of the formal structure will remain the most powerful set of groupings in an organisation, but there is at least a case for viewing an organisation in terms of the alternative structure of shifting interest sets which, in fact, interpenetrate with the formal organisation at many points.

Power is one of those social science concepts which refer to an important social phenomenon but about which there are theoretical and empirical disputes which are likely to remain unresolved. Given the libraries of works on power produced by political scientists, philosophers, sociologists and social psychologists, it would be impossible to review the complex theoretical and methodological issues involved in this short paper. Thus the remarks made will be those of particular relevance to micropolitics.

The distinction between two major aspects of power are important. *Authority* is the legally supported form of power which involves the right to make decisions and is supported by a set of sanctions which is ultimately coercive. *Influence* is the capacity to affect the actions of others without legal sanctions. The distinction is conceptually important but difficult to sustain empirically because, since authority can be latent, it is difficult to establish when control is exercised through influence or through latent power. However, the distinction between authority and influence remains potentially useful since the power deployed in micropolitics frequently takes the form of influence since interest sets will draw on resources other than those of authority to achieve their ends.

Administrative theory tends to focus on authority which has its source in the hierarchical structure of the organisation. Micropolitical theory would give greater prominence to influence. Influence is derived from a number of sources, e.g. personality (charisma), expertise, access (especially to information) and resources (material or symbolic). Influence differs from authority in having a number of sources in the organisation, in being embedded in the actual relationships between groups rather than located in an abstract legal source, and is not 'fixed' but is variable and operates through bargaining, manipulation, exchange and so forth.

The headteacher in Britain has a high degree of authority; but his exercise of this authority is increasingly modified as teachers' sources of influence through expertise, access to symbolic resources, etc., increase and thus involve the head in a greater degree of exchange and bargaining behaviour (Hoyle, 1981). These are the aspects of power which are the appropriate focus of micropolitics.

Micropolitics takes account of the *strategies* used by interest sets to attain their ends and gives these greater attention than formal procedures....

There is so little discussion of micropolitical strategies in educational organisations that it is perhaps appropriate to invent some examples: an FE college may have a 'collegial' structure, but the principal, caught in the dilemma of all who would manage pluralistic organisations, i.e. the reconciliation of legal authority and the expectation of participation, may indulge in micropolitics in order to cope with this dilemma. Thus he may attempt to handle situations by: 'losing' recommendations from working parties by referring them to other groups in the hope that they will disappear or become transformed, 'rigging' agendas, 'massaging' the minutes of meetings, 'nobbling' individuals before meetings ('I'm glad you see it my way. I hope you'll make your views known at the meeting'), 'inventing' consensus ('Well, we all seem to be agreed on that') when consensus has not been tested, 'interpreting' the opinions of outside groups ('The governors would never accept it', 'The LEA wouldn't finance it') and so forth. As Noble and Pym (1970) discovered, 'collegial organisations are characterised by a 'receding locus of power'. The course of power is difficult to identify in a collegial organisation. The principal can draw on his resources of legal power, but other members of staff have their own resources.

Thus micropolitics involves a study of interests, interest sets, power and strategies. These are intimately related to the more formal aspects of an organisation which is the main focus of much administrative theory, but the political dimension of an organisation constitutes an alternative focus for understanding organisational processes. However, from the brief discussions of these four components in this section it can be seen that it is likely to be a conceptually and methodologically complex area of enquiry.

THE NEGLECT OF MICROPOLITICS

Theories of organisations and administration are *relative*, i.e. products of their place and time, *partial*, i.e. in adopting one theoretical perspective others are inevitably excluded since a total perspective is not a possibility, and *normative*, i.e. to a greater or lesser degree they are infused with values.

The dominant paradigm in organisational and administrative theory is one in which political aspects do not easily fit. Although it is a great over-simplification to group all prevailing theories within one paradigm, and although it is impossible to do justice to the diversity of existing theories, some broad points can be made in order to illustrate the reason for the neglect of micropolitics.

Current organisation theory has two origins: Weber's theory of bureaucracy and early theories of management. These two strands converge and diverge at many points in the development of theory. Sociological theory in the Weberian tradition is potentially concerned with understanding organisations; management theory is potentially concerned with improving them. However, theories of management need to be based on understanding if they are not to be merely recipe theories, and organisation theory has not retained a detached purity since its protagonists have also been concerned with improving organisations in various ways: their efficiency, the quality of life of participants, and, hopefully, both. Hence they share a common paradigm which can be termed the *maintenance* paradigm....

The operation of the maintenance paradigm in education can be – again in a gross over-simplification – summarised as follows: educational organisations – schools, colleges, polytechnics and universities – have to cope with changes in their environment: cultural, technological, economic and political changes of various kinds. Political changes are initiated at the macropolitical level and tend to focus on the allocation of resources, legal enactments and overall structure with rather less focus on matters of curriculum and pedagogy. It is assumed that practitioners will interpret these external changes in an attempt to keep in balance the interests of society and the interests of clients. Hence the expectation is that innovation will be professionalised rather than politicised. In order to equip institutions and practitioners to cope with the professional demands of innovation, programmes of professional development, organisational development and the development of interpersonal skills have emerged. The appropriate strategy of change, within the coercive strategies of national and local government, is considered to be a mixture of rational and re-educative approaches.

A major alternative is the *action* paradigm which again has a complex history and embraces a wide range of perspectives so that to bring them together under one heading is to over-simplify. Nevertheless the lineaments of the action paradigm are as follows: its metatheory holds that the social world is nothing other than the construction of minds of men and has no objective reality 'out there'. Social life is sustained because men, through their daily interaction and their language, create intersubjectively shared meaning. These meanings may be relatively persistent and perhaps come to have the appearance of objectivity but, in fact, as men continue to solve the problems of their daily lives, they can voluntarily construct new meanings. It follows then in strict terms there can be no action theory of organisations since organisations are not 'objects' but social constructs, and the meaning attached to them will differ according to one's perspective. The action theorist is interested in activities within what are conventionally termed organisations because he is interested in how participants construe organisations and their processes. He treats as 'problematic' the organisational structure and the administrative processes which organisational theorists take for granted. As there can strictly be no organisational theory, there can likewise be no theory of management since management is only a constructed label for a group of organisational processes dominated by those who have resources of power which tend to become problematic only if treated phenomenologically. It should follow that an action perspective is neutral in relation to change since it is a paradigm more concerned with understanding the world or, more precisely, understanding others' understanding of the world – than with initiating change. Its active contribution to the change process is the assumption that social theorists of this persuasion should work with practitioners at any level of the organisation helping them to clarify their own perspectives, helping them to question what had previously been taken for granted which then becomes potentially amenable to change. Thus it generally encourages an 'active' stance on the part of participants. This sounds rather like the process consultant operating within the maintenance paradigm but whoever the process consultant is, however independent of management he may profess to be, ultimately he is concerned with improving organisational functioning in relation to the goals of management. The action theorist tends to be orientated towards enabling the lower participants to perceive the possibility of reconstructing the organisation in ways alternative to that perceived as 'effective' by management. In short, action theory, like maintenance theory, is relative, partial and normative. Yet there is more potential within the action perspective for focusing on micropolitical activities since these are actions which can be made the strict focus of enquiries and not treated as pathological or deviant activities.

What can be termed the *radical change* paradigm has political activity at its centre. It is concerned with understanding the social world in order to change it in accordance with a set of political beliefs. This perspective is strongly Marxist in orientation. Again, at risk of great over-simplification the following are some of the main characteristics of this approach: the metatheory may, according to the particular view of Marx taken, share the same view of the world as the maintenance theorists, in that it is taken that there is an objective world out there which is amenable to scientific understanding and control via the manipulation of structures and the socialisation of individuals, or as the action theorists. Essentially it is not an organisation theory but a broad socio-political theory in which organisations are seen as arenas in which occur the clashes between the prevailing ideology and the alternative radical ideology. Thus the political transformation of organisations is a necessary step towards transforming society.

APPROACHES TO MICROPOLITICS

The chief elements of micropolitics – power, coalitions, strategies and interests – have been the focus of studies in a number of social science disciplines. In social psychology there has been considerable study of interpersonal power particularly in group settings. However, the socio-psychological study of organisations has been largely concerned with problems of leadership and communication and is clearly located within the maintenance model. Weick (1979) is an exception to this trend in that he has concerned himself with the 'negotiation' of organisational order, but the focus has not been directly upon the micropolitical. The concern of political theorists has been games, choice and coalitions (Brams, 1975; Laver, 1981). They have tended to be concerned with establishing formal theories rather than with understanding political activity *in vivo*.

In decision-making approaches to organisation, Simon's (1964) notion of 'bounded rationality' is concerned with the boundary between rational and non-rational aspects of social behaviour. The 'non-rational' – which we would now, in these post-phenomenological days, refer to as 'alternative rationality' – relates to the activities which we have referred to as micropolitical. However, in the theories of March and Simon (1958) organisational analysis remains well within the maintenance framework in noting these aberrant behaviours as evidence that organisations do not in fact function according to the rational model.

Three organisational theories which are more directly concerned with micropolitics can be noted. The first is the later work of March who now appears to have brought what was earlier considered to be 'non-rational behaviour' in the decision process, i.e. micropolitics, to the centre of the stage. In *Ambiguity and Choice in Organisations* (March and Olsen, 1976) he and his colleagues concentrate less on how decisions ought to be made if they are to conform to canons of rationality, than on how in fact they are made. What is described is how decisions, which are rarely the clear-cut events usually described, emerge out of a complexity of micropolitical activities. They advance what is now their well-known 'garbage can' model of decision-making:

> Although choice opportunities may lead first to the generation of decision alternatives, then to an examination of the consequences of those alternatives, then to an examination of the consequences in terms of objectives, and finally to a decision, such a model is often a poor description of what actually happens. In a garbage can situation, a decision is an outcome or an interpretation of several relatively independent 'streams' within an organisation.

They consider four streams which might go into the 'garbage can':

Problems: These are the personal problems of participants as they relate to such matters as pay, status, promotion, personal relationships, families and even the problems of mankind.

Solutions: They reverse the normal view of solutions and see them as sometimes preceding problems. They cite the installation of a computer in an organisation which may represent a solution to problems not yet conceived. In the educational context one could conceive a new curriculum or a plan for school-focused in-service training generating new problems rather than solving existing ones.

Choice opportunities: These are occasions such as those when a new member of staff is to be appointed or where a responsibility allowance is to be allocated which generate behaviour which can be called a decision.

Participants: Individuals come and go and their different attributes will shape the outcomes which are termed 'decisions'.

The rates, patterns of flow and confluence between these four streams shape certain organisational events which come to be labelled as 'decisions'. March and Olsen write of organisations 'running backwards' in the sense that organisational events are the outcome of bargaining, negotiating and exchange and only after they have occurred is their history 'rewritten' by managers to give them the appearance of having been the outcome of a rational decision-making process.

Michel Crozier (1964) has long been interested in how power and influence operate in organisations and has developed the view that organisational processes are best understood by focusing not on formal organisation and power as on the games which individuals and groups play in order to solve problems and in which power is treated as a bargaining relationship. He argues for a change in paradigm. Thus the research problem is to explore how different systems of games can solve the problems which organisations face. He believes that the way forward is to learn more about current games in all forms of organisation and the forms of regulation inherent in these games. This will be best approached by case and comparative studies at the present time with the prospect of formalisation and measurement left until the future.

In sum, there have been a number of approaches to the study of micropolitics, but at the present time they cannot be said to constitute a coherent body of theory. The question is whether such a coherence is likely to be achieved and, if so, what its contribution to the study of educational administration might be.

Empirical studies of micropolitics are extremely rare. Some exceptions are Thompson (1967) in the USA and in this country Pettigrew (1973) and Mangham (1979) but none of these studies was conducted in educational organisations.

THE PROSPECTS FOR MICROPOLITICAL STUDIES

This paper is based on the assumption that a considerable gap exists between the organisational world which is presented in theory and research and the organisational world which we all experience. This gap is acknowledged by administrators who perhaps gain little help from administrative theory because it is not of their world, or at least it relates to a rather sanitised version of the world in which they function. The gap is also increasingly recognised by theoreticians and researchers who have become somewhat disenchanted with the prevailing paradigm but are not wholly happy with the action and radical change alternatives. Thus the importance of the micropolitical world is existentially acknowledged. The question is: can it be captured by the theories and methods of the social sciences and, if so, will what is learnt be of value to practising administrators?

The answer to the first of these questions must remain tentative. There are two basic levels of answer. One relates to the fundamental problem of the social sciences of whether in principle a knowledge of the social world can be attained by the methods of objective enquiry. This is no place to rehearse the arguments yet again, except to note the three broad positions: that a knowledge of the social world is in principle impossible, that it is possible only through an understanding of the meanings which actors ascribe to situations, and that the social world is in fact knowable by the procedures of the natural sciences. If we make the assumption that it is, in principle, knowable, then we have to ask *how* it might be knowable. It could be argued that the micropolitical world is so ideographic, idiosyncratic, contingent and volatile that in practice it cannot be grasped. It could be further argued that it is indeed of this character but it can be grasped in its particular concrete setting via a detailed case study, but that generalisations are very difficult to achieve in practice. Or it can be argued that the micropolitical world is amenable to study by the methods of the social sciences which permit generalisation.

If one takes the latter position, then two things have to be said. One is that 'the real stuff' of micropolitics is particularly elusive. As we have seen, different approaches focus on different components of micropolitics, so the interactive nature of power, coalitions, interests, and strategies is unclear. However, if studies concentrate on one or other of the aspects in an effort to clear the way towards formal, testable theory, then the configuration disintegrates. Thus we are left, as we often are in the social sciences, with a choice between case studies providing rich data and formal studies providing – hopefully – generalisable findings. And one inevitably comes to the familiar conclusion that both approaches should proceed, if, indeed, it is worthwhile pursuing at all the study of micropolitics in education. It may be that it is not a viable area of study as a whole and that its components are better pursued independently.

If one concludes that it is worthwhile getting to grips with the micropolitics of educational organisations, by whatever method, one has to ask whether the outcome is likely to improve the practice of educational administration. Would it, in fact, provide theory-for-understanding or theory-for-improving? It would appear more likely to provide theory-for-understanding. Studies of micro-politics could well bring the area much more into the arena of open discussion, but it isn't easy to see in what ways this might improve the quality of administration or the quality of life in educational organisations for participants. It is even more difficult to see how the outcome of the study of micropolitics would feature in courses for practising administrators other than as a general mirror-raising component and as theory-for-understanding. In what sense could it contribute to improvement of skills? It could form the basis of various forms of simulation and games, but the degree of transfer from gaming to practical decision-making contexts must be somewhat dubious. And even if it were possible to teach micropolitical skills to practising administrators, this would – to say the least – generate some obvious moral issues.

It is clearly the case that micropolitics is difficult to embrace within the conventional theory, research and training patterns of educational administra-tion since administrative theory is normatively oriented to rationalising order and control and eliminating the alternative world of micropolitics. This paper offers no solutions. As stated at the outset, its purpose has been to put micropolitics on the agenda.

Leadership for a New Century: Authenticity, Intentionality, Spirituality and Sensibility

NAROTTAM BHINDI AND PATRICK DUIGNAN

INTRODUCTION

There was a time when leaders could control and manipulate organizations more readily than they can today because organizations were seen as less complicated, environments were more stable, and power and wisdom were perceived to flow from their 'heroic' figures. The emphasis was on goal achievement rather than on serving the customer; on productivity rather than on market needs and quality; on outcomes rather than on ethical and moral responsibility; on dependency rather than mutuality; on predictability rather than continuous change and improvement; and on gamesmanship rather than on leadership authenticity. However, many complex forces have emerged over the last decade or so to put both organizations and their management under greater scrutiny.

In Australia, there have been convulsions in established organizations such as the churches, police forces, public service, universities, health services and businesses. These organizations are being challenged as never before. Their management and leadership are no longer regarded as 'sacrosanct' and are subject to increasing criticism. Included among the forces which have contributed to the complexity and turbulence of modern organizational environments are: the expanding information society; discontinuous changes; a marked resurgence in probity and social justice issues of gender, access and equity; and the increasing stranglehold of economic rationalism. Environmental complexities and turbulence have brought to the forefront fundamental issues and tensions relating to leadership, organization structures, culture and management practices.

These challenges, which appear to be worldwide phenomena, have placed leadership, its basis and function, under critique. There is, especially, a re-examination of the concepts of power and authority and how they are exercised and legitimized. Leadership and management are being redefined and there are increasing calls for a clear shift away from traditional hierarchical control mechanisms and processes as a basis for influence to notions of leadership as service and stewardship.

... Block (1993) advocates leadership as *stewardship* which emphasizes partnership, empowerment and an end to paternalism. In recent years there has also been a noticeable concentration on leader-follower dynamics. In this view, leadership is *bestowed* on the leader by those who are led and therefore leadership must be *earned* (Cox and Hoover, 1992). Chaleff (1995, p. 49) bemoans the 'awesome shaping powers of school, organised religion, sports teams, the military and large corporations in seeking obedience and conformity' among their followers. She pleads for 'a dynamic model of followership that balances and supports dynamic leadership'. Rosenbluth and Peters (1992) have also demanded that 'our followers, not customers come first'.

These perspectives on leadership are paralleled by shifting views on the nature and function of management in organizations. Very few organizations have escaped the seductive pull of this 'management revolution' following Deming's *Total Quality Management* (Milakovich, 1991; Aguayo, 1992; Schmoker and Wilson, 1993; Romagna, 1995), Senge's *Learning Organization* (1990), Peters and Waterman's call for *excellence* (1982; see also Selvarajah *et al.*, 1995) and Champy and Hammer's advocacy of re-engineering (1993), to mention a few.

A major paradigm shift is occurring in the way we construe our world, work, relationships and leadership (Senge and Kofman, 1993; Gunn, 1995). The current emphasis on corporate managerialism, the excesses of leadership expediency and obsession with self-interest and narcissistic behaviour (Kets de Vries, 1993), personal advantage and lust for power and privilege have contributed to a persistent feeling among the followers of being used, cheated and even demeaned. This disquiet about excessive managerialism has led to the call for the 'transformation' of managers and administrators into leaders (see e.g. Conger, 1992; Murphy, 1995). It has also led to a concern about 'the paralysis of moral patterns' of life (Pirsig, 1992, p. 357) and a great yearning to reclaim the moral-ethical-spiritual domain of leadership (Covey, 1992; Kets de Vries, 1993; Conger, 1994; Messick and Bazerman, 1996).

In this article the authors argue for *authentic leadership* based on: *authenticity*, which entails the discovery of the authentic self through meaningful relationships within organizational structures and processes that support core, significant values; *intentionality*, which implies visionary leadership that takes its energy and direction from the good intentions of current organizational members who put their intellects, hearts and souls into shaping a vision for the future; a renewed commitment to *spirituality*, which calls for the rediscovery of the spirit within each person and a celebration of the shared meaning and purpose of relationship; a *sensibility* to the feelings, aspirations and needs of others, with special reference to the multicultural settings in which many leaders operate and in the light of the increasing globalizing trends in life and work....

AUTHENTICITY

The concept of authenticity in leadership calls for a radical shift away from the traditional, conventional wisdom about leadership. It is based on personal integrity and credibility, trusting relationship (Kouzes and Posner, 1991; Duignan and Bhindi, 1995) and commitment to ethical and moral values (Hodgkinson, 1991; Nair, 1994). Leaders *earn* their allegiance through authentic actions and interactions in trusting relationships, and through the shaping of organizational structures, processes and practices that enshrine authentic values and standards. Such leaders help nurture, inspire and empower others. They encourage sharing and partnership based on the recognition of mutuality and interdependence in relationships....

Authentic leadership is centrally concerned with ethics and morality and with deciding what is significant, what is right and what is worthwhile (Duignan and Macpherson, 1992). It supports a view of leadership as 'moral art' which elevates the actions of the leader above mere pragmatics or expediency (Hodgkinson, 1991, p. 50). Authentic leadership is partly a visionary activity based on 'right action'; it is 'a venture in moral philosophy' comprising the ideals of 'honour, dignity, curiosity, candor, compassion, courage, excellence, service' (Bogue, 1994, p. 13). Bogue argues that these authentic ideals find their highest promise

> in the lives of these leadership artisans who have spiritual scars and calluses on their characters, the evidence of their having struggled with difficult moral issues, weighted contending moral calls that defy neat solution, agonized over the conflict between their own conscience and the judgment of an opposing majority.

...Authentic leadership is a counterbalance to the often cynical and dehumanizing behaviours of managers which can 'debilitate, coerce and frustrate people inside and outside the organisation' (Starratt, 1993, p. 63). The focus is on 'elevating leaders' moral reasoning' (Terry, 1993, p. 46) which is also central to Burns's (1978) distinction between leadership which is transactional and that which is transformational. Burns (1978, p. 20) states that transforming leadership

> occurs when one or more persons *engage* with others in such a way that leaders and followers raise one another to higher levels of motivation and morality [and it] ultimately becomes moral in that it raises the level of human conduct and ethical aspiration of both leader and led, and thus it has a transforming effect on both.

Such leadership is also 'transcending' in its effect and as it works through the dynamism of meaningful relationships is, in essence, 'leadership *engagé*' (p. 20).

This incorporates elements of some other views of leadership (e.g. leadership as service, stewardship, moral art, ethical standards, transformation) within a more comprehensive and inclusive framework that emphasizes leadership action that is

> both *true* and real in *ourselves* and in the *world*. We are authentic when we discern, seek and live into truth, as persons in diverse communities and in a real

world...[authentic] leadership calls for authentic action in the commons. (Terry, 1993, pp. 111–12, original emphasis)

It derives its energy, purpose and direction from the discovery of 'true self', which is partly defined by meaningful and significant values; sensibility in relationships; and from the creation of and maintenance of organizational structures and processes that are built on authentic values and standards. This may appear to be an eclectic view of leadership or overly ambitious, complex or comprehensive. We do not think so. We propose that the four qualities of *authenticity, intentionality, spirituality* and *sensibility* are the threads which can be woven together into the fabric of leadership in organizational settings to make it more authentic. As in nature where complexity seems to be produced from endless iterations of simple formulae, so we believe that constant repetition of the four qualities in the practice of leadership and management, in all relationships at all levels of systems and organizations, will radically change organizational dynamics and encourage and support more authentic processes and practices.

There is a need to develop an awareness in our organizations of the potential for inauthenticity, especially in information and technologically driven societies that can intentionally or otherwise create the illusion of reality – a 'virtual reality characterized by *spin control, plausible deniability, disinformation, double speak and docudramas*' (in the latter, fiction is merged with fact in such a way that only those who intimately know the event or situation can judge its authenticity – Terry, 1993, p. 118, original emphasis)....

But what is meant by the word *authentic*? Can it easily be defined? How does it relate to such concepts as ethical action and sincerity? The authors propose that leadership is authentic to the degree that it *is* ethical action (Terry, 1993; Duignan and Bhindi, 1995). It implies sincerity, genuineness, trustworthiness in action and in interaction and rejects motives and actions that are deceptive, hypocritical, duplicitous. However, if sincerity or genuineness means only 'being true to oneself then it can limit a full explanation of self *and* world, and it, therefore, falls short of authenticity' (Terry, 1993).

...While excluding the Hitlers of this world from the authentic category, our concept of authentic leadership is not about saints or pious, self-righteous leaders. It is about everyday full-blooded creatures who are politically and spiritually aware, credible, earthly, practical and, despite their human frailties, strive to be ethical, caring, and conscience driven. They don't always get it right but they try to live their values to the best of their ability. They make mistakes but they learn from them. As stated elsewhere in this paper, these are often the people with spiritual scars and calluses on their characters from taking that last stride and stepping over the edge. They are usually those people who have plumbed the dark depths of the lake that is within and have released the energy, the fire that smoulders within the self. As Whyte so eloquently phrases it in his poem 'Out on the Ocean':

Always this energy smoulders inside
when it remains unlit
the body fills with dense smoke.

Whyte (1994, pp. 91–2) says that a vitality smoulders inside and when it remains unlit, the 'toxic components of the smoke are resentment, blame, complaint, self justification and martyrdom'.

Of course we can be trapped within our endless preoccupation with self as if the 'self' can be isolated from the world in which we live, work and play. Whyte talks of a 'core delusion' typical of contemporary life 'that narrows our sense of self and ignores the greater world beyond'. Or else we define self in the world simply in terms of ambition and career within an organization and, thereby, 'we allow our dreams and desires to be constricted and replaced by those of the organisation and then wonder why it has such a stranglehold on our lives' (p. 277). Whyte, who makes a plea for the preservation of the 'soul' in corporate America, argues that the first step in preserving the soul in each of our lives is to recognize that the world around us has a soul that is linked to our work and destiny.

... The second element in the authentic leadership framework, the concept of *intentionality* is now discussed.

INTENTIONALITY

Where there is no VISION, the people perish. (Proverbs 29, 18)

Authentic leaders help build and sustain strong organizational visions. Whether negotiated or shared, a strong vision, deriving its sustenance from organization beliefs, values, aspirations and history, is necessary to facilitate clarity of purpose and direction for organizational members. Strong, clear visions can also provide direct psychological comfort in times of crisis and turbulence....

In times of major change, reform or restructuring, a complete reorientation of the existing vision may be necessary, whether the focus is on quality cars, excellent schools, or better, caring hospital services. Much recent research and writing on management and leadership extol the centrality of vision as a necessary ingredient in leadership effectiveness and strategic repositioning of organizations (Kouzes and Posner, 1987; 1991; Conger, 1992; Champy, 1995). For example, in their important research on leadership, Kouzes and Posner (1987, p. 279) identify shared vision as one of the five fundamental practices of exemplary leadership. They say that effective and credible leaders

> passionately believe that they can make a difference. They *envision the future*, creating an ideal and unique image of what the organisation can become. Through their strong appeal and quiet persuasion, leaders *enlist others* in the dream. They breathe life into visions and get us to see the exciting future possibilities.

Weick and Leon (1993) identify *visualizing and vision transformation* as one of the 'five power tools of learning' about client, service, products, competition and repositioning. Klein and Saunders (1993) emphasize *mapping out of a shared vision* as one of their ten steps towards the Learning Organization.

Shared vision helps organizational members focus on the bigger picture while assisting them to understand and appreciate their role in bringing it about. Through shared vision they can move beyond focusing on self, skills and techniques to a more holistic appreciation of organization and work. Semler (1993, p. 51) provides a beautiful illustration of this type of holistic thinking:

> I often thought of the business parable I had heard.
>
> Three stone cutters were asked about their jobs. The first said he was paid to cut stones. The second replied that he used special techniques to shape stones in an exceptional way, and proceeded to demonstrate his skills. The third stone cutter just smiled and said: 'I build cathedrals'.

...Wheatley (1992) also supports the idea that leadership is, essentially, a visionary activity. However, she concludes from her study of chaos theory, quantum mechanics and field theory that vision is best seen in terms of the *intentionality* of individuals and groups who work together to help shape the future. She argues that vision emanates from the good intentions and good hearts of organizational members who want the best for the organization. The view that vision is something outside the group, somewhere in the future, is an outdated one based on a traditional philosophy of science in which vision is like a gravity force dragging us into the future. Wheatley proposes vision as a 'shared energy field' that energizes the group and helps drive them forward together into an unpredictable future. It is shared to the degree that people trust each other and work together to achieve extraordinary outcomes. She states:

> In a field view of organisations, clarity about values or vision is important, but it is only half the task. Creating the field through the dissemination of those ideas is essential. The field must reach all comers of the organisation, involve everyone, and be available everywhere. Vision statements move off the walls and into the corridors, seeking out every employee, every recess of the organisation. (1992, p. 55)

The third element in the authentic leadership framework, *spirituality*, is now discussed.

SPIRITUALITY

The authors make a plea for the restoration of spirituality in leadership. By spirituality a partisan religious view is not meant, but that individuals and groups should experience a sense of deep and enduring meaning and significance from an appreciation of their interconnectedness and interdependency, and from their feelings of being connected to something greater than the self. Authentic leaders are spiritual leaders. Whitehead and Whitehead (1991, pp. 82–3) see spiritual leaders as those who help other people find meaning in their own lives.

> Among the distractions and satisfactions of our ordinary days, daunting questions disquiet us all: Is love possible? Why do the innocent suffer? Does my own life have purpose? Can justice prevail? On our own, these questions are hard to face and harder

still to resolve. We yearn for some way to bring the everyday experiences of our lives, as well as the extraordinary ones, within a context of larger significance. Those who stand with and strengthen us in this search we recognize as spiritual leaders.

Spirituality entails 'living out a set of deeply held personal values, of honouring forces or a *presence greater than ourselves*' (Block, 1993, p. 48); this is necessary to find meaning in our work...

But a commitment to spirituality does not imply naivety or rigidity. Chu (1992, p. 329) sees experience of 'spiritual matters' as providing the inner power and discipline (compassion, sharp intellect, etc.) '*combined with pragmatic worldly skills*...to operate efficiently in our shrewd and competitive world'. In an interesting exposé on work and spirituality, Treston (1994, p. 25) warns that 'work without an *anchoring spirituality* opens the way to exploitation, greed, and global injustice'.

In contemporary organizational life there is a need for the adoption of ethical and moral standards to guide leadership practice (Hodgkinson, 1991; Sergiovanni, 1992; Starratt, 1994). Nair (1994) calls for higher standards in leadership, embracing honesty, truth, trust, integrity, trained conscience, courage and a sense of service (values that underpin authenticity). We share his (1994, p. 91) concern that, 'The majority of our life is spent in work. If our work lacks a moral dimension, is it not likely that the moral content of the rest of our life will decline?' There is another important reason why it would be foolish and undesirable to try to banish spirituality from the workplace. Fox (1991, p. 25) has pointed out that spirituality is inherent in humans and their interactions:

> We are a spiritual species, capable of relating to all things as beauty. And because we are spiritual, we are also capable of destroying all things. Being so young a species on this planet, with immense powers of creativity, we need ways that help us guide that creative energy in directions that allow our passion to mature into compassion.

...So far, we have discussed the concepts of authenticity, intentionality and spirituality mainly from a monocultural perspective. We now ask the question, 'What does it mean to be authentic in multicultural societies?' Terry (1993, p. 142) challenges leaders to deal with human diversity when he asks: 'Are we forever stuck in our own cultural and conceptual envelope, or can we build a universal global ethic that both affirms our human oneness while simultaneously affirming and guaranteeing our differences?' Like Terry, the authors advocate ethical standards that have cross-cultural (even universal) relevance and yet 'protect and enhance diversity' (p. 143). While not aware of any framework that accommodates these seeming contradictory forces, we propose that the elements of the authentic leadership framework discussed so far, together with the fourth elements of the framework, *sensibility*, provide an important starting-point for such a development.

SENSIBILITY

Our world is shrinking quickly with advances in technology, the globalization of commerce, and the movement of people across borders for education and tourism. Many countries – such as Malaysia, Indonesia, Great Britain, Australia and New Zealand – have diverse populations for historical, colonial or emigration reasons. Cross-cultural understanding and recognition of inter-dependence are essential for leaders and managers operating in multicultural settings (Bhindi, 1992; 1995a; 1995b). In our multicultural environments, groups with differing religious beliefs, languages and cultural traditions frequently 'rub shoulders' as they mingle at work, play and in daily life. What are the implications of such multicultural realities for authentic leaders?

... The authentic leader is a sensitive leader. However, as Bhindi (1995b) points out, even at the best of times, multiculturalism is a social mine field.

> Even in the best of times, multiculturalism is a social mine field and leaders have to tread on it very carefully. If overly enthusiastic, you are patronising; if overly cautious, you are tokenizing; if you do nothing, you are a cultural thug. You need to possess crosscultural skills, draw upon the expertise of those around you, extend your own knowledge and experiential base and secure the support and friendship of your constituents.

Authentic leaders operating in culturally diverse organizations promote institutional governance, policies, management practices, and interpersonal relationships which respect the values and sensitivities of all their constituents (see Mead, 1990; Pucik *et al.*, 1993; Magsaysay, 1996; Trompennars, 1996).

CONCLUSION

Whether in a school, church, police or business organization, authentic leaders support people-centred practices and ethical standards that promote meaningful relationships and an organization that is based on authentic values. Authentic leadership is intrinsically ethical. It involves an authentic view of self mediated by significant values (ethical standards) and meaningful relationships. It is also imbued with a sense of spirituality and a sensibility to the feelings, aspirations and needs of others.

Authentic leaders attempt to do what is right regardless of the consequences. They are courageous, standing up for their principles, often at a cost to themselves. Authenticity must be lived in leadership action for a leader to be authentic. The rhetoric of authenticity is insufficient. Terry (1993, p. 138) makes this point quite forcibly: 'Authenticity informs and directs action; action grounds authenticity in life. The abstract and the concrete are joined in authentic action. Without authenticity, action drifts. Without action, authen-ticity remains idle conjecture and wishful thinking.'

The Characterisation and Development of Professional Expertise in Education Management and in Teaching

MICHAEL ERAUT

PART 1: THE NATURE OF EXPERTISE IN SCHOOL MANAGEMENT AND IN TEACHING

1. Introduction

Significant debates about the nature of expertise in management and the nature of expertise in teaching have been conducted quite separately over the last two decades, yet they have been addressing many common issues. For example, what are the respective roles in developing expertise of attending courses and learning on-the-job? What, if any, is the role of theoretical knowledge? How do we take into account the significant part played by tacit and personal knowledge? Less well articulated has been a common ambiguity of purpose: has training been directed towards ensuring competence or promoting excellence? If these debates have sometimes been pursued with limited evidence and analysis, they have at least acknowledged the existence of expertise in teaching and in management. Forty years ago even this was in doubt.

Until quite recently, the expertise of a secondary school teacher was defined in terms of their knowledge of their subject. Teaching itself was not a professional activity but something one learned how to do rather like driving a car. Assuming the role of a schoolteacher was a natural process for a person of good character.

Subject knowledge and character were also important in the appointment of headteachers, together with a talent for self-presentation and public relations, and perceived leadership qualities. There was little attempt to discern or develop what today we might call management expertise. Even at this time, however, conspicuous absence of teaching or management ability was noticed. But agreement on negative examples does not necessarily lead to agreement on positive criteria. As teaching and management became more demanding in a less ordered, more rapidly changing society, the importance of good teachers and good managers became more widely acknowledged; but without much agreement on precisely what constituted a good teacher or a good manager.

... Knowledge of *education* rather than knowledge of the subjects being taught, did not begin to be taken seriously until it could be defined in terms of discipline-based knowledge acceptable to higher education; and the growth of the social sciences in the 1960s and 1970s provided just such an opportunity. Courses in psychology, sociology and philosophy were presented as providing a new theoretical foundation for the profession of teaching; and long-established child development courses at primary level 'upgraded' to meet new academic criteria. Social science-based courses in management began to proliferate at about the same time, though under strong North American influence and with little participation from the education sector. The level of higher education provision established at that time expanded still further during the 1980s as the original dependency on the social sciences weakened and more practice-oriented courses were introduced under labels such as 'curriculum development', 'evaluation', 'classroom research' and eventually 'educational management'. However, one could also argue that the potential contribution of the social sciences was never properly realised. In rejecting the original adoption of an academic approach which failed to deliver direct application in the classroom, there was often only limited exploration of other ways of bringing discipline-based knowledge to bear on practical situations.

As social science knowledge gained in prestige during the 1960s, educational research was dominated by a positivist approach, through which people hoped to discover empirically the characteristics of a good teacher and/or good teaching. While some useful findings emerged from this work, it was generally disappointing. Thus people have come to accept that empirically-based generalisations are likely to be sparse in education because contextual variations and individual differences have so great an effect on transactions and outcomes. Similar trends can be discerned in the research on management.

However, towards the end of this period of social science hegemony, researchers also began to undertake qualitative studies of how teachers and managers think and work. These revealed that 'good practitioners' had an enormously complex and highly personal knowledge base, constructed from experience but used in a fairly intuitive way. Many traces of discipline-based knowledge could he found but not in their original form. Moreover, much of this complex knowledge-base was tacit rather than explicit, so that practitioners could not readily articulate what they did or how they did it. Teachers and managers were pleased to have this confirming evidence of the level of their expertise; but these new research findings were difficult to apply to training in a positive way. It remained unclear how they could be used to promote the refinement, sharing or learning of what came to be called the 'practical knowledge' of teaching or managing.

This issue became more generally recognised with the publication of Schön's book *The Reflective Practitioner* in 1983, suggesting that the problem of personal, partly tacit, knowledge was common to all the professions. Hitherto,

Schön argued, discussion of the issue had been suppressed by two factors: the dominance of codified knowledge within higher education linked to its emphasis on publication; and the prevalence within Western society more generally of a technical-rationality perspective linked to a positivist epistemology. However, while Schön argued his case very convincingly, he did not go very far towards constructing any alternative epistemology.

2. The need for a new approach to characterising professional expertise

There are three main reasons why it is now becoming increasingly urgent to construct such an alternative epistemology. The first is sociopolitical. The more powerful professions, such as law and medicine, have enhanced their status for some time by claiming a complex knowledge base which is unknowable by outsiders; although there are signs that this is increasingly unacceptable to the general public. But the less powerful professions such as teaching have suffered from the opposite problem: familiarity rather than mystery has encouraged the belief that any reasonably educated person could do the job without needing to acquire significant additional expertise. Coming from the university which began school-based teacher training 27 years ago, I cannot help suspecting that its recent adoption by government may have been for the wrong reasons. Instead of getting theory and practice into a better kind of relationship through higher education–school partnerships, the ultimate purpose may be to dispense with the higher education element altogether. Similarly, the recommendations of the School Management Task Force could easily be shifted from a proper emphasis on school-based management development to the abandonment of any formal training. Unless the expertise of teachers and managers becomes more clearly articulated, it will be downgraded; and the social history of the professions suggests that abandoning credible claims to a distinctive knowledge base will lead to a process of deprofessionalisation, accompanied by a rapid loss of status and esteem.

My second argument for developing a new epistemology derives from my interest in professional education. Experience is necessary for developing expertise as a teacher or a manager but it is certainly not sufficient. Until we understand more about how people learn (or fail to learn) from experience, we will have little guidance to offer teachers and managers on how to pursue excellence in their work; and we are unlikely to understand how people learn from experience if we fail to elucidate *what* they learn from experience. Moreover, such knowledge needs to be widely shared. In order to take control over their own professional learning, teachers and managers need to have some awareness of their own personal knowledge base: what is held in common with others, what is purely personal, what is habit, what is intuitive, what is proven, what is fallible, what is authentic, what they know, what they do not know, how they work, how they evaluate their work, what frameworks and assumptions underpin their thinking, etc.

Thirdly, there is the problem of how a whole profession can improve the quality of its performance. Acknowledging that there is a personal and tacit dimension to much professional knowledge does not deny the advantages of sharing what can be articulated and learning from vicarious experience. The profession as a whole can still learn much from pooling experience, reflecting on it critically and conducting appropriate kinds of research. But without a more adequate epistemology these efforts are likely to be overshadowed by current fashion and undermined by political issues.

3. The relationship between professional expertise and different kinds of knowledge

I have approached the problem of characterising professional expertise from a number of perspectives, which I am now beginning to integrate. This paper can be seen, therefore, as a brief review of work in progress.

My first approach focused on the problem of knowledge use, a constant preoccupation of those concerned with curriculum implementation. This incorporates both the issue of how theory or indeed any form of book knowledge gets used in practical situations and the issue of how practical knowledge or know-how gets transferred from one context to another or from one person to another (Eraut, 1982, 1985).

Then looking at the problem in reverse I addressed the questions of how and what people learn from experience. When does this involve the acquisition of tacit knowledge in the form of recognisable patterns, routines or perceptual frameworks and when does it involve theorising, the creation of theory from reflection or practice (Eraut, 1992, 1993a). This raised further issues about both the explicitness and the validity of what was learned from experience.

Combining these two approaches led me to a series of distinctions. First, *public knowledge* is necessarily explicit, whereas *personal knowledge* can be either explicit (and therefore capable of being shared and made public) or tacit (and therefore incapable of being made public without being transformed into some explicit representation). Second, although adopting Gilbert Ryle's (1949) distinction between *propositional knowledge* (knowing that) and *procedural knowledge* (knowing how) I have found it necessary to add a third category, that of *images and impressions*. These are held in the memory but not represented in propositional form, although propositions may be derived from them through reflection. Knowledge of a person, for example, is likely to include images and impressions from a series of incidents held in memory, some public facts and some personal explicit propositions which may well have been first articulated in casual conversation.

Public propositional knowledge comprises facts, case material, concepts, theories, practical principles and conceptual frameworks. It is commonly portrayed as being acquired from books or formally learned on courses; but facts, concepts and practical principles are also acquired informally whenever they are in general use. Such knowledge could be absorbed from one's family and local community or 'picked up' during conversations with fellow-professionals without there being any specific intention to learn about it. Similarly, public knowledge may be used in a conscious, deliberate way or used almost automatically because it has become part of one's normal pattern of thinking. Thus our use of public knowledge is much greater than we usually recognise.

Unless conceptual knowledge is being simply replicated or applied in a routine way, its use is likely to involve considerable thought. Not only does it require thinking about the context of use but also about the particular interpretation to be given to each concept or idea in each particular set of circumstances. As a result of these episodes of use such knowledge becomes personalised. Its specific meaning for any individual depends on this history of use and is also affected by how that person links it into their personal cognitive framework. This process of use incorporates the concept into that person's action knowledge, making it readily available for further use. Whereas public knowledge that has not been used before is unlikely to be used again. Thus both the meaning and the perceived relevance of public knowledge are strongly influenced by the history of its use or non-use.

Personal propositional knowledge can be acquired either by this process of personalising public knowledge or by learning from experience. Most commonly, both sources are interactively involved, but in varying proportions.

Discussion of books will usually draw on a range of participants' personal experiences; and learning from experience usually involves some use, albeit intuitive, of public propositional knowledge. Thus personal knowledge is partly tacit and partly apprehended. A significant consequence of this is that people are not aware of everything they know and only partly aware of their own cognitive frameworks. Hence their personal knowledge is not fully under their own critical control, and they should not be confident of its validity. Since all forms of personal knowledge are used in everyday professional work, the need for both public and personal knowledge to be regularly evaluated is apparent.

In addition to the knowledge use perspective and that of learning from experience, I have approached the problem of the nature of professional work itself. My starting point for this has been that professional expertise is embedded in the quality of the processes that constitute such work; and I have distinguished four kinds of process to facilitate discussion of how the different kinds of knowledge discussed above contribute to professional performance.

- processes for acquiring and interpreting information
- skilled behaviour
- deliberative processes, such as planning, evaluating and problem-solving
- meta-processes, concerned with directing and controlling one's own behaviour.

This classification has the advantage of being common across all person-oriented professions, including education and management. In practice, the performance of almost any professional function will involve processes drawn from several categories; but this does not detract from their usefulness for investigating the nature of professional expertise and the different ways by which it is acquired. In the following sections, I discuss each type of process in turn with particular attention to the nature of the expertise and the ways in which different kinds of knowledge are likely to be involved.

4. Acquiring and interpreting information

Research on perception clearly demonstrates that the acquisition and interpretation of information are linked; and both are significantly affected by pre-existing cognitive frameworks. Such experiential learning occurs both during the normal process of maturation from child to adult, when many schemas for understanding people and situations are constructed (the basis for Kelly's personal construct theory) and during professional practice itself, when further development and modification of frameworks is likely to occur. Similarly, interpretations tend to follow rather than challenge accustomed patterns of thinking; unless some prominent problem or issue impinges upon the attention. This 'conservative tendency' is exacerbated in both teaching and management by the conditions under which most acquisition and interpretation of information occurs.

In educational contexts information is rarely acquired by highly systematised methods of inquiry. Tests, questionnaires and interview protocols represent the most systematic approaches, but even they are rarely developed to a high degree of reliability. Informal marking and short discussions are in much more regular use; and most information is probably picked up by observation and casual conversation, as a result of being present in a particular place at a particular time.

The process of information acquisition also differs according to the mode of interpretation: so it is useful to distinguish between three such modes:

- instant interpretation or pattern recognition, as in recognising a person;
- rapid interpretation; as in monitoring one's progress in the middle of a conversation; and
- deliberative interpretation, when there is time for thought and discussion and even for collecting further information.

...Even in the professional context this learning may be at best semi-conscious, resulting from experience and socialisation rather than any deliberate learning strategy. Such schemas can easily become biased or ineffective because they are subjected to so little conscious reflection. The problem for professionals, however, is not to exclude such experiential learning, they would be lost without it; but to bring it under more critical control. This requires considerable self-awareness and a strong disposition to monitor one's actions and cross-check by collecting additional evidence in a more systematic manner with greater precautions against bias.

5. Skilled behaviour

Skilled behaviour can be defined as a complex sequence of actions which has become so routinised through practice and experience that it is performed without much conscious thinking or deliberation. Thus teachers' early experiences are characterised by the gradual routinisation of their teaching and this is necessary for them to be able to cope with what would otherwise be a highly stressful situation with a continuing 'information overload'. This routinisation is accompanied by a diminution of self-consciousness and a focusing of perceptual awareness on particular phenomena. Hence, knowledge of how to teach becomes tacit knowledge, something which is not easily explained to others or even to oneself.

... If management is not quite as routinised as teaching, it still involves quite a lot of autospeak when what people say follows familiar pathways. Moreover, managers constantly claim that they are so bombarded with messages and calls for actions that they have little time for deliberation; and in such circumstances behaviour will be at best semi-routinised. Like the information gathering habits discussed in the previous section, routinised actions are very difficult to change. Not only does change involve a great deal of unlearning and reconstruction but also the adjustment of a 'persona' which is already known to others and taken for granted.

6. Deliberative processes

Deliberative processes such as planning, problem-solving, analysing, evaluating and decision-making lie at the heart of professional work. These processes cannot be accomplished by using procedural knowledge alone or by following a manual. They require unique combinations of propositional knowledge, situational knowledge and professional judgement. In most situations, there will not be a single correct answer, nor a guaranteed road to success; and even when there is a unique solution it will have to be recognised as such by discriminations which cannot be programmed in advance. More typically there will be:

- some uncertainty about outcomes;
- guidance from theory which is only partially helpful;
- relevant but often insufficient contextual knowledge;
- pressure on the time available for deliberation;
- a strong tendency to follow accustomed patterns of thinking;
- an opportunity, perhaps a requirement to consult or involve other people.

These processes require two main types of information: knowledge of the context/situation/problem, and conceptions of practical courses of action/

decision options. In each case, there is a need for both information and analysis. What does this mean in practice? We have already discussed the wide range of means by which such information can be acquired; and the phenomena of pattern recognition and rapid interpretation. Here, we consider the more cognitively demanding activities of deliberative interpretation and analysis, for which professionals need to be able to draw upon a wide repertoire of potentially relevant theories and ideas. Also important for understanding the situation is knowledge of the theories, perceptions and priorities of clients, co-professionals and other interested parties. While some may be explicitly stated, others may be hidden, implicit and difficult to detect. Thus one of the most challenging and creative aspects of the information-gathering process is the elucidation of different people's definitions of the situation. Few teachers or headteachers are well prepared for this important aspect of their work.

The other information-gathering task is equally demanding, the formulation of a range of decision options or alternative courses of actions. This depends both on knowledge of existing practice and on the ability to invent or search for alternatives.

...If we confine our attention for the moment to processes like problem-solving and decision-making, much of the literature tends to suggest a rational linear model, in which a prior information-gathering stage is succeeded by deductive logical argument until a solution/decision is reached. In practice, this rarely occurs. Research on medical problem-solving, for example, shows that hypotheses are generated early in the diagnostic process and from limited available data (Elstein *et al.*, 1978). Further information is then collected to confirm or refute these hypotheses. Although described as intuitive, the process is essentially cognitive; but it allows pattern recognition and other experiential insight to contribute at the first stage. In less scientific areas, the need for continuing interaction between information input and possible courses of action is even greater. The information cannot be easily summarised and can usually be interpreted in a number of ways. There is also a need for invention and insight when considering possible actions, so new ideas have to be generated, developed and worked out. The process is best considered as deliberative rather than deductive, with continuing interactive consideration of interpretations of the situation and possible courses of action until a professional judgement is reached about the decision to be endorsed and implemented.

Such deliberation requires a combination of divergent and convergent thinking which many find difficult to handle, especially when working in a team. Some find it difficult to focus sufficiently to be good analysts or are too impatient to think things through, while others feel uncomfortable with any departure from routine patterns of thinking. The need for adopting several contrasting perspectives is also increasingly recognised; and this is one of the arguments for teamwork.

7. Meta-processes

The term meta-process is used to describe the higher level of thinking involved in controlling one's engagement in the other processes discussed above. Thus it concerns the evaluation of what one is doing and thinking, the continuing redefinition of priorities, and the critical adjustment of cognitive frameworks and assumptions. Its central features are self-knowledge and self-management, so it includes the organisation of oneself and one's time, the selection of activities, the management of one's learning and thinking and the general maintenance of a meta-evaluative framework for judging the import and significance of one's actions.

The value of this control process was highlighted by Argyris and Schön (1976) who demonstrated that for many professionals there is a significant gap between their espoused theories (their justifications for what they do and their explicit reasons for it) and their theories in use, those often implicit theories that actually determine their behaviour (see also Day, 1982).

This gap between account and action is a natural consequence of people's perceptual frameworks being determined by what they want or expect to see, and by people reporting back to them what they think they want to hear. The solution Argyris and Schön recommend is to give priority not so much to objectives – for then one reads situations purely in terms of one's own pre-planned ideas of how they ought to develop – as to getting good quality feedback. Unless one is prepared to receive, indeed actively seek, feedback – which may be adverse or distressing – one will continue to misread situations and to deceive oneself that one's own actions are the best in the circumstances. However, it is not only obtaining good feedback that matters but making good use of it by being open to new interpretations which challenge one's assumptions.

PART II: THE FURTHER DEVELOPMENT OF EXPERTISE IN EDUCATION

8. The question of quality

One of the most important meta-processes is that of self-development, which provides the focus for the second part of this paper. However, before proceeding to offer some guidance on how expertise might be developed in each of the four types of process, I want to address the critical issue of quality. My definition of professional expertise is *the capability to perform professional roles,* and in Part One I also argued that *professional expertise is embedded in the quality of the processes that constitute professional work.* This link between capability and quality now needs to be made more explicit.

While recognising that for qualification purposes there has to be some defined cut-off point at what the NCVQ chooses to call the level of competence, my underlying model assumes that for most professional purposes:

(a) there is continuum of capability from very low to very high;
(b) capability is partly situation specific and partly transferable;
(c) at higher levels of capability in particular, there is likely to be considerable debate about the relative merits of different kinds of performance.

There is plenty of scope for continuing professional learning, transfer should never be taken for granted and there is no universally agreed model of the best teacher or the best manager.

Quality is usually judged by some combination of:

– stakeholder response, often perceived rather than based on good evidence
– connoisseurship, usually based on observation and interview
– outcomes, such as documents, test results and pupils' work.

However, the formative judgement of quality is one of the weakest areas of school management. The culture of teaching has traditionally emphasised competence rather than excellence and isolation rather than mutual observation; so connoisseurship has not been well developed. Considerable time and energy gets devoted to the assessment of pupils (this was true even before the 1988 Act) but the information is rarely used for feedback on teaching. The collection of evidence from stakeholders is still an unusual rather than a normal activity.

This problem is exacerbated by the prominence of tacit knowledge, which is mainly developed through experience at times when learning is at best semi-conscious and not under critical control. Some perceptual schemas and interpersonal routines are developed before teachers even begin their training, and some during the early years of teaching: only during training is there much chance of receiving any independent feedback. Likewise many of the perspectives and routines of school managers are developed before they take up their posts. While formal learning opportunities for teachers and managers may be important in developing the quality of their contribution to deliberative processes, they are often ill-suited to developing quality in routinised interpretation and action (see Eraut, 1988 for an analysis of the role of management courses). For this it may be better to identify when and where experiential learning is taking place and to try and give it a quality steer. Perhaps the focus should be on new teachers and newly appointed junior managers?

9. Developing expertise in acquiring and interpreting information

The high reliance put by teachers and managers on informal and experiential methods of acquiring information and rapid interpretations with little deliberation gives considerable scope for misinterpretation. Without significant self-monitoring these processes will be out of critical control, based only on taken-for-granted and largely implicit cognitive and perceptual frameworks. Yet the quality of professional action must necessarily depend on the information on which it is based. The following five suggestions for developing this aspect of professional expertise are derived from the analysis made in section 4.

1. Become aware of one's own constructs, assumptions and tendencies towards misinterpretation.
2. Learn to use additional sources of evidence to counteract any possible bias in one's information base.
3. Find out about the perspectives of the other people involved.
4. Expand the range of one's interpretative concepts, schemas and theories.
5. Make time for deliberation and review.

Deliberation is needed both to ensure a good information base for important decisions, and to maintain critical control through reflective self-monitoring of one's own ongoing, largely tacit, information acquisition and rapid, largely intuitive, interpretations.

10. Improving the quality of skilled behaviour

The main constraints on the further development of skilled behaviour are the natural limits on self-awareness during routinised action, and lack of motivation. Presumably for historical and cultural reasons, there is little attempt to treat teaching as a performing art and to work on technique like an actor or a musician. Nevertheless, there are many possible approaches to improving the quality of skilled behaviour.

1. Get feedback from an independent observer.
2. Make recordings and study them, preferably with some friendly support.
3. Use self-monitoring and collect evidence from others to develop awareness of the effects of one's actions.
4. Observe other people in action.
5. Use the information gained from 1–4 to improve the quality of one's current routines.
6. Expand one's repertoire of routines to meet the needs identified above.
7. Use the information gained (and possibly consultancy support) to optimise the conditions for effective performance, e.g. timing, grouping, ambience, resources, flexible planning of introductions/phasing/transitions/conclusions, etc.

Although there is now a tradition, based largely on classroom action research (Elliott, 1991) of seeking to improve skilled behaviour in teaching, no such tradition has yet developed in school management. It should be incorporated into the planning of management development programmes to cover such activities as chairing a meeting, leading a working party, or interviewing a parent or counselling a member of staff.

11. Developing expertise in deliberative processes

Section 6 included a number of suggestions; and the quality of deliberation is clearly dependent on the quality of available information (see section 9).

However, it is also important to understand the nature of deliberative processes and to know how to handle them, either on one's own or in working groups.

The following suggestions are pertinent to developing the quality of professional expertise in deliberative processes.

1. Develop through reading, experience and discussion some knowledge about the various deliberative processes: ways of thinking about them, organising them and making them serve their purpose.
2. Develop appropriate interpersonal skills for contributing to or managing deliberative processes in groups (see section 10).
3. Learn to assemble the appropriate people, expertise and information for production work without incurring too great a cost.
4. Develop a personal and/or group repertoire of concepts, theories, knowledge of practice, thinking skills, etc.
5. Recognise that thinking skills of a high order are needed in tackling practical problems; and get people used to thinking in an action-oriented mode, as opposed to acting in an unthinking mode.

12. Developing the quality of one's meta-processes

Meta-processes have rightly been given a significant emphasis in management education, particularly *self-knowledge* and *self-management*. These last three sections have focused on *self-development*, which critically depends on them both: self-knowledge is needed to give it appropriate direction and self-management to give it sufficient priority. This parallels the need, discussed in the earlier sections, for professionals to make time for deliberation, search for relevant information beyond what has been naturally acquired, and expand their repertoires of routines, schemas, concepts and ideas.

Another important aspect of self-development is understanding the nature of professional knowledge and the different ways in which it is learned. The complexity revealed in this paper should provide a more realistic basis for understanding one's own learning than the gross oversimplifications peddled by many management educators in the name of Kolb.

Also included under meta-processes in section 7 was the conception of a meta-evaluation framework in which values and ethical issues are brought to bear on the direction and control of one's actions. Such a framework is central to any concept of professionalism. I shall conclude, therefore, by stressing two ethical principles which I believe should pervade the meta-processes of any profession (Eraut, 1994). The first is the principle of client-centredness which provides the ethical foundation for the professions; for managers, I would add, the term 'clients' should be expanded to include 'employees'. The second is the moral obligation, with future clients in mind, to improve one's own professional expertise. That principle provides the rationale for this final section, indeed for the whole of this paper.

PART 2

THEORY

Educational Managers' Knowledge:
The Quest for Useful Theory

MICHAEL STRAIN

Three of the five papers included in this section (7, 8 and 9) form part of a continuing discussion. They try to clarify what kind of theory might be most usable and reliable as a basis for education management and its practitioners. Baron's paper (6), the earliest of them, is very different; it sums up, somewhat magisterially, a well-established academic and intellectual tradition and provides a concise and critical commentary on the range and nature of education management research in the UK at that time. The fifth, by Ranson (10), looks to the future, and in a blend of critical analysis and normative theorising, speculates constructively on a key role for education in the Learning Society.

AN EARLIER TRADITION

Baron discusses research in education as concerned with an essentially institutional and political phenomenon, an activity provided by governments, by public demand, in return for votes. This is reflected in his themes for discussion: how civil servants and administrators use research and the implications of incorporating a better understanding of that question in the design and implementation of research itself; how the interest groups and professional associations, the stakeholders as we might say today, interact and bring pressure to bear on what schools and colleges do, or do not do, or at least, not well enough. These concerns are reflected and explored further in Section 1 (Teachers).

Baron is concerned, among other things, with 'boundaries'; those of the disciplinary territories of economics, politics and planning, as well as those established by psychological and behavioural studies, noticeable for being more commonly undertaken in the USA and Canada than in Britain. He remarks on the absence of any 'integrated body of knowledge', and observes that this may have stimulated (European) interest in 'the work of North American theoreticians as a source for conceptual frameworks into which schemes of research can be neatly fitted'. The British tradition is characterised bluntly as 'still, in so many quarters, a contemptuous dismissing of any study going beyond the collection of opinions and facts'. This is a criticism which may still be valid today when one considers the remarkably small number of papers in this field which have been published by *EMA* in the 25 years from 1972 to 1997.

SCIENCE AND SUBJECTS

Greenfield looks back with a missionary's dissatisfaction and undiminished zeal at the results of more than twenty years of 'intellectual turmoil' (Griffiths, 1979) which are said to have characterised theoretical debate among social scientists in that period. He reasserts once again a manifesto, if not a method, one which proclaims that 'Values lie beyond rationality', and fears a 'mindless devotion to technicism ... sweeping the field away into a spuriously scientific irrelevancy, to a technology of claimed but unexamined effectiveness, one that is easy for masses to accept and vastly profitable to those who exploit and merchandise it'. These are serious charges whose force and pertinence is revealed in a new form rather than overlaid or diminished by the scenario outlined later by Ranson. Greenfield insists on the human, wilful origins of social dispositions and human knowledge itself. Neither rationality nor the procedures and rules of 'scientific' enquiry themselves can remove the fragile contingency and constructedness of human knowledge and belief. Like Weber, he reminds us that the 'good' cannot be discovered *for* us by any extraneous device or calculatory apparatus: 'there is no rational way of deciding among the plurality of conflicting possible value commitments. Every rational life, in short, is founded on a non-rational choice.'

Evers and Lakomski are both more modest and yet more ambitious in their aims. They are more concerned, not, as Greenfield so often is, with the *illocutionary* and *perlocutionary* force of what is expounded, the implications and discernible social consequences of a particular theoretical formulation, but with what can be said (Austin's *locutionary* function) about the foreseeable results of what we do and how we do it. Acknowledging 'the very great particularity and contextuality of social phenomena', Evers and Lakomski strive to justify a theory with which the social scientist might avoid having to choose between justifying 'non-trivial' statements about particular phenomena or 'trading in trivial, empirically vacuous, generalisations'.

Evers and Lakomski's *coherentist* strategy aims to bring together in an empirically testable relation the ethological strengths of subjectivism with a number of *super-empirical* qualities such as consistency, explanatory unity, learnability, fecundity and empirical adequacy. Their purpose is to explain and justify the holding of particular beliefs about the consequences of particular actions. Popper's falsificationism is acknowledged as influential both in their writing and in the formal basis of their argument. The qualities they aim for imply that the approach is intended to be of practical assistance to managers and administrators. They intend that it will be capable of formulating principles of verification and of generating propositions of the kind: is this a basis for action on which we can agree? The propositions should also be framed in forms which, through discussion and negotiated consensus on agreed values, suggest practical ways of improving matters.

PRACTITIONER VALUE

But, as Gronn and Ribbins point out towards the end of their probing but appreciative discussion, Evers and Lakomski produce no useful or usable empirical generalisations. Founding their position on the 'black box' of cognitive processes, as the only real fount of 'knowing' and therefore of institutional action, Evers and Lakomski admit, with reluctance, that no empirically testable proposition can be forthcoming until the operations and dispositions of constituents within this 'black box' come to be fully mapped. Their final message, pending full revelation of these mysteries by natural science, is to adopt a pragmatically instrumental approach to 'folk theory', within which category, presumably, we should place the actual historical heritage of teachers' professional and institutional knowledge 'in use'! Put simply, they seem to say, if a particular practice is found to work better, do it, until 'the real story [is] given by the developing theoretical machinery of natural science'. Shorn of their epistemological arguments, the weaknesses in their theoretical claims seem not significantly different from those they identify in the earlier work of Griffiths and Hoy and Miskel, methods yielding generalisations which 'look trivial, or worse, are tautologies'. Perhaps too much theoretical work in education has attempted, in relative isolation from the wider field of social science, to construct ontologies and epistemologies beyond its capabilities and proper function? Teachers seem unable and unwilling to use them and much post-Parsonian social science has redefined its (reflexivising) social role without them.

CONTEMPORARY CONCERNS

At this point it is difficult to avoid reference to a wider public discussion of education research and its relation to professional practice which has recently erupted in the UK. Scepticism regarding continuation of a separate domain for education research (Deem, 1996), scorn for its products (Hargreaves, 1996) and a judicious concern for preservation of its necessary social function (Halpin, 1998) characterise some of the various academic positions. The situation was summarised by Jean Ruddock in her presidential address to the British Educational Research Association in 1994 (Ruddock, 1995). Even an ostensibly pragmatic and benign initiative by the TTA (1996a) is premised upon the perceived irrelevance of much of what is published in academic journals, though acknowledgement is given to the OECD and ESRC view that 'education is relatively thinly researched, particularly in the UK'. The ESRC at least has taken action on this view and announced a £10m programme to investigate teaching and learning at all levels and ages. A recent OECD seminar focusing on the Nordic countries (Denmark, Finland, Iceland, Norway and Sweden) reveals similar concerns (Tuijnman and Wallin, 1995). These include a belief that 'end-users' should be more involved in the design and implementation of research programmes, that education research should benefit practice, and that too little has perhaps been spent on educational research. In contrast to the instrumental preoccupations of our own policy-makers, the Swedish National Board of Education has been criticised for its earlier approach, whose central themes were:

- 'individual cognitive ability and learning...at the expense of a broader social perspective'
- 'an "achievement paradigm"...which accordingly had an inherently instrumental orientation and followed the technocratic R&D model' (Tuijnman and Wallin, 1995, p. 28).

The Board has now been replaced by an Agency whose research rationale, in the words of its Director, 'is intended to encourage the long-term development of knowledge. It should be oriented towards gaining an understanding and new insights as a basis for action.'

> Epistemological considerations must take precedence over organisational issues in the formulation of a strategic research programme. The issue of knowledge use should be considered in an epistemological context before the ramifications of a more administrative nature are considered. According to the principles discussed so far, the use of knowledge should be principally considered in relation to the needs of practitioners. In the same way as education and teaching are conceptualised as an encounter where both teachers and pupils are acting and bringing in previous knowledge and experience, the issue of knowledge utilisation must also be conceptualised as an encounter. This perspective rules out the top-down dissemination of knowledge. Basically, knowledge use is a matter of power, and this draws attention to where the power is situated in the system. (*ibid.*, p. 32)

A NEW ROLE FOR RESEARCH

This epistemological conceptualisation of the research process exemplifies another dimension, too little considered by many of those most closely involved, and reveals awareness of a fundamental shift in the nature of research in contemporary society and in its relation to social change (Scott, 1995). Understood in late modern terms, research no longer directly guides human action, but is reflexively implicated in social processes (Giddens, 1991, p. 20). Today's 'research' will be very quickly sifted and its valued insights transmitted as advice and prescription in popular books, magazines and broadcast media (Giddens, 1992). Correspondingly, much of it is now undertaken outside its traditional location in the universities. The number of sponsors is also increasing; local government agencies, community and interest groups and commercial firms are routinely undertaking and commissioning research, which is increasingly multi-disciplinary and *ephemeral*. The EU also is assuming a more active role in education and training research and is attempting to define research questions and procedures in new ways (Field, 1997, p. 7). It is essential, even in an anthology of past work, such as this, not to lose sight of the relation and value of this work to the clamorous and often discordant anxieties and demands arising from current policies and practice. Reflexivity entails that we interactively become what we disseminate as research and new knowledge. The choice presented by Greenfield and his coherentist adversaries, between subjectivism and science, is no longer a merely scholarly, professional or heuristic option. The kinds of social science that get done will inescapably shape society's structures and characterising activities.

THE LEARNING SOCIETY

There is a growing acceptance that theory formulation concerns power distribution (Tuijnman and Wallin, 1995; Popkewitz, 1997) and that social research increasingly is a medium whereby society reflexively re-orders and adjusts its key institutional structures and processes. It should not be surprising therefore to find good theoretical writing in education proposing, as Ranson does in the extract selected here, not further theoretical refinement but 'organising principles upon which to base education and society for the twenty-first century'.

Ranson is concerned here above all to establish a new relationship between Education and the Polity. This should be one founded on answers to moral questions such as 'what is it to be a person?', 'what is the nature of society?' The relationship envisaged between education and its beneficiaries should be built upon a new moral and political order, embracing values such as 'will support the development of individual powers' and 'create an open, public culture responsive to change'. In this, he is at one with Greenfield when he asked: 'What is the good and how may it be attained? How does education contribute to the social good and to personal well-being and happiness? How should schools be organised to achieve such goals?' Just as Greenfield opposed so much in prevailing theoretical traditions which had operated within a positivistic or functionalistic framework, so Ranson recognises clearly that educational reform, if it is to meet the emerging claims of individuals in advanced societies which have fulfilled or exhausted the possibilities of human productivity inherent in much 'post-war modernisation', must set aside modernity's 'iron cage' of instrumental rationality and seek to 're-enchant the world' with 'learning as inquiry, understanding and discourse'.

THE CHALLENGE OF EDUCATIONAL REFORM

Few have yet confronted, except to withdraw in reaction or discomfort, the deeper challenge inherent in Ranson's conception of educational reform. 'Re-enchantment' can only have effect and 'come into play' when the political and intellectual entailments of the modern era are challenged and replaced by new, socially agreed moral and cognitive criteria. But this means abandoning some central tenets on which modernity was founded and politically sustained. It calls for the rejection of atomistic conceptions of society, of the neutrality of the liberal political order as inherently ordered to promote the public good, of the pervasive domination of instrumental rationality as a prerequisite of scientific, technical, industrial and social progress, and of the domination of professional and provider interests in the processes of defining and providing for the social needs of individuals.

The emergence of new relationships between learner and professional and among professional colleagues, examined later by Dennison in the context of intra-governmental relations and by Ouston and Hall in the context of teacher professionality and school leadership, suggest that the last of these has already been critically re-examined and is coming to be redefined in practice. Parents too, having experienced what was spuriously presented as 'privatisation' of local schools, have become sceptical and more discerning about the limits of teaching, of learning as 'commodity' pre-specified and delivered, without reference to necessary creative experience, and there is some evidence in the recent OECD seminar that some European governments too, through their professional and academic advisers, are now looking for organisational and processual forms within which new kinds of learning can be developed, processes in which 'education and teaching are conceptualised as an encounter where both teachers and pupils are acting and bringing in previous knowledge and experience' (Tuijnman and Wallin, 1995). Ranson's paper, in effect, attempts to construct a structure of institutional values and relationships which accommodate the possibility of individual learning in conditions of 'reflexive modernization' (Beck et al., 1994), conditions in which capability for learning is a prerequisite for full economic and social participation, a Learning Society. Readers may find it constructive and stimulating to consider Ranson's propositions alongside the assaults on the contemporary cult of managerialism and rationality by Smyth, and by Duignan and Bhindi in Part 1. The theoretical and practical agenda implicit in those papers are surely ones with which all education professionals must now engage.

Research in Educational Administration in Britain

GEORGE BARON

THE ACADEMIC/PRACTITIONER DEBATE

The conflict between academic and practitioner arises from each party necessarily inhabiting a different universe. As the researcher develops his approach to his problem, no matter how 'practical' its orientation, he draws on material and ideas from outside the immediate situation to help him in his analysis and his explanations. By so doing he distances himself from the administrator who, when subsequently reading the research report, is alienated by what appears to be irrelevant and extraneous material: furthermore, from his experience the administrator brings to his reading a multitude of questions stimulated by the research but not answered by it. Discussing this conflict Taylor (1973, p. 194) writes:

> The roots of the problem lie in the fact that the knowledge about education that is possessed by all the people who are labelled teachers, administrators, inspectors, researchers and so forth, is to a large and increasing extent role specific knowledge.

This kind of conflict is not between different kinds of people, or even between different types of mind: it is a situational conflict, which occurs even if the researcher is an experienced administrator and the reader a career academic concerned with a practical problem which is the subject of the research ... Other problems arise which can be avoided by greater competence or goodwill on the part of those concerned. Shipman (1976, p. 14) in his capacity as a research worker with the Inner London Education Authority, wrote:

> From within local government the research enterprise based in academia seems to deliver the wrong goods, at the wrong time, without an invoice. It also produces conclusions about education that are subject to gross misinterpretations. The net harmful impact arises from the combination of failure to help in the solution of practical problems, of the promotion of dubious theoretical notions and in recommendations whose implementations are beyond the dreams of even optimistic administrators.

In reply to this, the comment by Brian Simon (1978, p. 2) on the role of educational research in general is apposite:

> The real issue is whether scientists are to operate as scientists, educationists as educationists, researchers as researchers; or whether all are to become service personnel, waiting cap in hand for orders in response to which appropriate methods will be sorted out to produce acceptable results or conclusions.

The tension is further increased when it is a governmental or public body which is the funding agency. The argument put forward some years ago by Lord Rothschild takes the hard line that the funding agency says what it wants and the researcher works within a defined brief. Against this, there is the broader view that research in the social sciences necessarily draws on concepts and knowledge of which the sponsors are not aware and which modify the content of the problem as work progresses.

It is, I think, helpful that the Department of Education and Science is now clarifying its position, by expressing its concern with policy-related research, by identifying specific topics within agreed areas and by seeking early reconciliation between the interests of the parties involved (Kay, 1978, p. 8). Such a stand makes possible a parallel clarification of positions by those primarily concerned with research not directly concerned with policy matters. It is here that the Social Science Research Council has a major role to play and it is to be hoped that this seminar will assist it in establishing the place of educational administration within the total field of educational research.

THE THEORY/PRACTICE DEBATE

To what extent should research in educational administration, whether serving the purposes of the practitioner or the academic, seek to be theory-based? This is the first question which confronts the non-social scientist who encounters for the first time the highly organised teaching and research programmes of American, Canadian and Australian universities. There the place of 'theory' in educational administration is accepted, though its content and its uses and abuses are vigorously debated: here there is still, in so many quarters, a contemptuous dismissing of any study going beyond the collection of opinions and facts.

In a recent book Rosamund Thomas (1978, p. 29) has boldly contrasted the American and British approaches to administrative studies. She argues that in Britain

> doctrines (of administration) remained essentially a philosophy and not a theory of administration, embodying description, subjective attitudes and explanations rather than rigorous systematic analysis.

On the other hand, she argues, in the United States, respect for the expert in administration has led to more attention being paid to academics and more attempts being made to theorise with the result that administration has advanced 'from miscellaneous description to an integrated body of knowledge' (Thomas, 1978, p. 30).

The absence of native-born theory in this country and of anything approaching 'an integrated body of knowledge' explains the fascination felt for the work of North American theoreticians as a source for conceptual frameworks into which schemes of research can be neatly fitted. This has dangers, if it results in our limiting topics to those which can be so treated or in our setting out, once a problem has been identified, to unearth a theory to give it academic respectability. Certainly, the understanding of the researcher should be fortified by a thorough critical acquaintance of the works of the major theoreticians in his field of study. But it would be unfortunate if it came to be a convention that each piece of work must be related to a specific theory or theories. Moreover, as Hughes (1978) has pointed out, research studies describing and analysing current administrative practice do not necessarily require highly sophisticated theoretical underpinnings to be of value.

There is a way of reducing unproductive conflict and of avoiding the reification of theory as being an entity having some kind of existence independent of the world of 'real' events. Glaser and Strauss (1968) advocate the notion of grounded theory, by which they mean the gradual generation and testing of explanatory concepts as a piece of research proceeds. The emphasis is on theorising rather than on theory. Their approach means, of course, that the researcher is not only knowledgeable about existing theories but also has a capacity for theorising. It follows that the training or self-education of the researcher needs to be broad and diffuse: the aim of his reading of theory is to nourish his powers to perceive and to relate, rather than to lead him to work within the confines of the formulated perspectives of others.

THE SYSTEMS THEORY/PHENOMENOLOGY DEBATE

To some extent the issue I have just attempted to present has bearing on the far-reaching debate which followed Greenfield's paper (Greenfield, 1975) in the 1974 International Intervisitation Programme. This debate has been conducted with warmth by many better fitted than myself. I refer to it because it bears so intimately on the uses of theory. One charge made against Greenfield's paper is that he has failed to provide a viable alternative paradigm to that provided by systems theory; another is that he has not shown how research can emerge from a phenomenological perspective. Other charges seem to me to sidestep his argument because implicitly, if not explicitly, 'research' and 'paradigm', in their taken for granted meanings, are within the world of systems theory and the positivist approach. To me, Greenfield's paper made its impact, not so much because it put forward a 'phenomenological perspective' as an alternative to 'systems theory', but rather because it was a first frontal attack on the latter and particularly on the emphasis which much of social science places upon quantification, more complex mathematical models, and bigger number crunchers in the shape of better and faster computers (Greenfield, 1975, p. 86). This explains, to me at least, why Greenfield incurred the wrath of the 'establishment' of research in educational administration within which, at Stanford, Chicago and Alberta, hypothesis formulation has been a prevailing orthodoxy; it also explains the welcome accorded to his argument in Britain by academics uneasy with the formidable research apparatus of the North Americans and reluctant to acknowledge its achievements; and by practitioners happy to seize on any vindication of intuitive judgement.

EDUCATIONAL ADMINISTRATION AND THE SOCIAL SCIENCES

Some years ago, in my contribution to *Educational Administration and the Social Sciences* (Baron and Taylor, 1969), I sought to show how the latter could contribute to our field of study. My thinking was very much influenced by my contacts with American and Canadian scholars and with the work of Professor William Walker in Australia; and it was motivated by the political need to legitimate the study of educational administration in the university world in this country. Certainly, at the University of London Institute of Education, educational studies were and are regarded largely as the philosophy of education, the sociology of education, the economics of education and the psychology of education. Difficulty thus arises in arguing the case for fields of study, such as curriculum development, comparative education and educational administration: in this context it is necessary and appropriate to stress the contribution of the disciplines. I do not wish to quarrel with the position I then took up, although I think I would now incorporate within it the idea of 'squeezing' the disciplines, which Glatter (1972, pp. 48–9, 68) took over from Richard Snyder. But, when it comes to research in educational administration I am much more aware than I was before of the problems which arise when subject specialists are recruited into a field after their primary allegiance has been established. I think that Brian Simon (1978) expresses my concern more adequately than I could myself in a passage relating to general research in education. He writes:

> The study of education has manifestly suffered from subordination to disparate modes of approach and methodologies deriving from fields quite other than education which have simply been transferred into the educational sphere and which, once there, have tended to maintain their distinctive languages and approaches, or pursue their own ends.

...FOUR RESEARCH POSITIONS

What are the various positions from which we can view research? I can identify four, but others may no doubt occur to members of this seminar and readers of this paper.

1. Research for understanding

This, I suppose, is the position of the historian, who is concerned with explaining the past in terms comprehensible to the present. It is also the position of the anthropologist, concerned to explain in terms of his own culture the practices of primitive peoples. The results of such labours may be of use to the politician, the administrator or the professional worker, but this is not their main purpose. The audience for research of this kind is composed of those with similar or closely related interests, able to cope with highly technical and esoteric language.

2. Policy-related research

I am indebted to Brian Kay for this term, which he uses for research promoting 'the formulation of national policies on a more secure foundation of knowledge, and of monitoring and evaluating the implementation of such policies' (Kay, 1978, p. 8). Such research requires specialised knowledge combined with a readiness to work within the frameworks established by political and administrative practicalities. Much work on resource allocation falls within this category.

Policy-related research may precede and help in policy formulation or it may monitor the working out of policies already being put into operation. In either case it is expensive, it is likely to take time and it requires considerable adjustment of attitudes and working habits to be made by both the academics and the administrators involved. Its immediate audience is relatively small, since by design it is directed at the limited numbers concerned with policy-making at national or local level.

3. Research into administrative structure and process

In putting forward this category I am very much aware of the difficulty of distinguishing usefully between 'policy' and 'administration'. But it seems to me to be essential to give identity to that vast area of research concerned with the performance of administrative functions and roles, whether these be in relation to running a school, a college, a department or a supporting service; or with the setting up and maintenance of structures for governing institutions and regulating their relationships with their environments.

This is the area in which I would argue that the maximum effort should be made at the present time; and it is also the area in which all members of the Society are concerned in one way or another.

4. Evaluative research

Evaluation is necessarily a part of any research project. But what I have in mind here is research which is able to stand outside the world of the policy-maker and the administrator and view their intentions and their activities from a variety of political, social and cultural standpoints. It seems to me a main vehicle for research of this kind should be comparative studies, in which scholars and administrators from elsewhere would share in substantial projects in this country. A network of Commonwealth and European agencies exist to foster such exploration and we have our own close and invaluable affiliations with the Commonwealth Council for Educational Administration and the European Forum.

I have spent a little time in presenting these very tentative categories of research for consideration because I feel that it is important for this seminar to consider what should be its focus for future activities and indeed for the efforts of the British Educational Administration Society in the research field. Clearly, we are interested and supportive of all four categories; indeed interest in the one presupposes at least some measure of involvement with the others, since they are interrelated. My own conclusion, however, is that we should at this time pay particular attention to that which I have termed 'research into administrative structure and process'. It is in this area that lie most of the problems which beset those responsible for the conduct of our educational institutions and those with similar responsibilities in other countries. It is also a major aim of this Society to advance the practice of educational administration.

Re-forming and Re-valuing Educational Administration: Whence and When Cometh the Phoenix?

THOMAS GREENFIELD

The fundamental problem in knowing and understanding social reality is what place values shall play in the inquiry. For nearly two decades this question has troubled the theory and knowledge promulgated in the field of educational administration. While some proponents (Pitner, 1988; Willower, 1988; Greene *et al.*, 1989) would by fiat or simplistic analogy declare the issue settled and dead, others (Bates, 1989; Hodgkinson, 1988, 1990; Smith and Blase, 1989) show that it continues – puissant, troubling, and profoundly revolutionary in its implications for the conduct of research and training in the field. The issue runs far wider than educational administration and calls into question, as Geertz (1980, p. 178) points out, the putative objectivity and universality of all the social sciences.

> A challenge is being mounted to some of the central assumptions of mainstream social science. The strict separation of theory and data, the 'brute fact' idea; the effort to create a formal vocabulary of analysis purged of all subjective reference, the 'ideal language' idea; and the claim to moral neutrality and the Olympian view, the 'God's truth' idea – none of these can prosper when explanation comes to be regarded as a matter of connecting action to its sense rather than behavior to its determinants.

Ultimately, of course, it is the science in social science that comes into question. Recognising the value bases of administrative action utterly transforms the standard and previously accepted view of the field, as Hodgkinson (1978b, p. 59) has shown: 'The intrusion of values into the decision making process is not merely inevitable, it is the very substance of decision'. Taking the value dimension meaningfully into account, as does Bates (1989, p. 16), leads to a view of the field that stands in sharp contrast to almost everything that has gone before in the modern era[3], the era in which the field conceived itself as offering

---

3 In administrative studies generally, the modern era dawned with the publication in 1945 of Herbert Simon's *Administrative Behavior*; in educational administration the sun rose upon the new era with the publication in 1958 of *Administrative Theory in Education*, a collection of the 'New Movement' thinking edited by Andrew Halpin (1958).

universal, objective, and theory-based science:

> The starting point for the analysis of educational administration is that it is a socially constructed system of behaviour which is the result of contestation between social groups of unequal power in term of such matters as, for example, class, race and gender. The resulting organisational structures can be seen as facilitating the agency of certain groups and limiting that of others.

The present is a time of dialectical struggle in educational administration and indeed in much of social science generally. In Griffiths's (1979) memorable phrase, the field is in 'intellectual turmoil', and has been for nearly 20 years. To some the established empiricist highroad to truth, objectivity, and control in social organisation is still plain, and as sound as centuries of Enlightenment science and rationalism can make it. To others the empiricist approach is a delusionist dream, a nightmare indeed that needs exorcism to liberate and restore the human and moral perspective before the irrationality of devalued science further misleads us, as we seek to understand ourselves and human affairs. In this view the time left for restorative action may be short. Indeed, the empiricist dream – or nightmare – ultimately threatens to obliterate the human and humane understanding of life in organisations, for it elides the moral complexity that flows inevitably through administrative action. It is now widely accepted in educational administration that some form of renewal or redirection of the field is overdue and necessary. What remains in dispute is how fundamental that rebuilding should be, whether a clear break with the empiricist past is needed or whether a reassertion and improvement of established approaches and assumptions is all that is required. The issue ... is where to find the form and substance of the new phoenix in administrative studies. On the question of newness and how it is to be attained, T. S. Eliot's comment to D. H. Lawrence says it all: 'One can hardly have the phoenix without the ashes, can one?' Some think they see the phoenix reconstituted and already risen intact from the past, from a reassertion and strengthening of old assumptions and approaches. In contrast there are those who say that to hold on to the errors of the past ensures that nothing new can arise. Until the old field lies in ashes, we cannot conceive nor receive the phoenix in its new form.

In these circumstances, we do well first to look back at what has constituted the crisis of knowing and acting in our field over the past two decades. Secondly we need to look ahead to ways that offer the best prospects to take us truly forward, to bring us to moral and valued ends, not just to a fallible and mendacious technical progress.

THE PHOENIX AND NO ASHES?

To understand what is at stake in allowing values a place in the study of organisations and administration, it is instructive to return to the claims of early theory in the field. In his review of the theoretical models developed by Jacob Getzels and others, Lipham (1988, p. 175) makes clear that these models constitute 'a landmark in the application of social-science theories to education'.

In his view, the models provide a set of formulaic and law-like statements to describe, explain, and potentially control all of human behaviour in organisations.

> Behaviour in a social system, therefore, results from the interaction between a given institutional role, defined by the expectations attached to it, and the personality of a particular role incumbent, defined by one's need-dispositions; it can be represented by the general equation $B = f(R \times P)$ (Lipham, 1988, p. 174).

But as Hodgkinson (1983) points out, the tensions between the nomothetic and the idiographic are the tensions between the demands of society and the actions of individuals. The working out of such tensions is the consequence of action by human agents, all of which is chosen, imposed, and existential. Thus it must be seen that the integration of nomothetic expectations and idiographic action requires a judgemental *resolution* of social and personal tensions, not a *calculation* of objective and independent forces. Such a resolution is created and mandated in a dramaturlogical (*sic*) and political context where

> the task of the executive is thus revealed as one of reconciliation, reconciliation of organisation to society and organisation members towards organisational goals, reconciliation of individual and increasingly large collective interests, reconciliations which can, of course, be static or dynamic, creative or uninspired, divisive or harmonious, synergetic or degenerative. (Hodgkinson, 1983, p. 23)

Lipham (1988, p. 181) rejects criticism that Getzels's models ignore 'the very stuff of the humanness of human beings... [their] hates, loves, fears, aspirations, symbols, values, perceptions'. All this he argues is included in the models. What he fails to understand is that such realities make impossible the very calculation of behaviour by formula that is claimed as the models' great achievement. What the proponents of [Getzels's] models do to bring in 'the humanness of human beings' is to make value statements that are denied to be value statements. Instead they are introduced as merely fixed background conditions, as largely immutable contextual factors. This splitting of values from facts permits a view of the organisation as objectified and rational. Thus Getzels *et al.* (1968, p. 134) claim the models make possible a technical superiority in administrators' decisions, for in their view the models express and mirror the putative rationality of the organisation as a whole. That the force and function of values is *exogenous* to the dynamics dealt with in the models is seen in the understanding of values offered in a statement by Guba and Bidwell (1957, p. 75). Drawing on Talcott Parsons' 'suggestions for a sociological approach to the theory of organisation', they explain that

> Parsons... suggests that a major function of the institutional value system is to provide an operating code for decision-making. Values, he suggests, form a structure for administrative and staff decision. In this case the institutional value system would seem to set the limits to the exercise of individual discretion in that the assignment of particular decision-making functions to a given role is itself determined in large part by the nature of the institutional values.

... Defenders of normal science make a noteworthy response to the news that the presence of incalculable values negates their putatively objective and calculable theory of organisation. They offer a two-fold answer to the difficulty. First they call for an expansion of the repertoire of the techniques of observation to include qualitative methods, thought to be the appropriate ones for dealing with values, and secondly they seek the incorporation of qualitative methods within the assumptions of quantitative and statistical analysis. For example, after reviewing powerful arguments against the mixing of methods from incompatible paradigms of inquiry, Greene *et al.* (1989, p. 257) set aside all such fundamental problems and argue for a pragmatic mix-and-match combination of methods that gets the job done. And so they conclude that

> The practical demands of the problem are primary: inquirer flexibility and adaptiveness are needed to determine what will work best for a given problem. Or, in the pragmatic view of Miles and Huberman, epistemological purity does not get the research done.

In a similar approach, Pitner (1988) reviews methodologically diverse studies and finds it easy to incorporate them all into a linear model of 'administrator effects and effectiveness'. That we have at hand a reborn phoenix of administration capable of dealing with all its epistemological and methodological problems without prior ashes is the position taken by Willower. Or rather what Willower asserts in his synthesis of the *Handbook of Research on Educational Administration* is that the old phoenix is still in good shape: it just needs polishing. In his concluding judgement, Willower (1988, p. 730) holds that the phoenix is intact without ashes, its in-built self-correcting mechanisms assuring us that empiricism is not only the best road to truth, it is the only way.

> The norms of inquiry stress the provisional character of ideas and results and the self-corrective nature of science. Hence, inquiry and change are close companions, for a field of study that values inquiry continually seeks new and perhaps better ways of conceiving its subject matter ... Now there is not only an applied social science called educational administration, but it has spawned a number of specialisations and subspecialisations. The *Handbook* is a splendid reflection of that situation.

That a field of scientific inquiry *committed* to an open truth seeking must rest on moral judgements upheld by human fiat, not by rationality or science, is a consideration inconsistent with and therefore ignored, as Willower declares his faith in a self-correcting applied social science of administration. His phoenix is simply the old bird, polished and reasserted.

PARSING THE PARADIGMS

The flaw that surely sinks Willower's summation and endorsement of administrative science is his rejection of the notion that paradigmatic boundaries define and separate sets of assumptions and that these modes of inquiry are quite inconsistent and incompatible with each other. This easy denial of conflicting modes of inquiry is a widely held position in the field. It is used to support a pragmatic eclecticism in methodology, an approach to inquiry that Griffiths (1988, p. 45) acknowledges and tacitly endorses, calling it 'paradigm diversity':

> The idea is emerging that research on organisations should not be restricted to a single paradigm; rather research should proceed in all four (more or less) paradigms.

The mischief worked by this view has already been argued above: it encourages the researcher not just to select *a* paradigm, but to make a patchwork melding of divergent methodologies and conflicting epistemological assumptions. Ultimately it reasserts, as is seen in Pitner's and Willower's arguments, the dominance of the empiricist paradigm of inquiry.

Those who see no fundamental conflicts among the paradigms take the strategic position that the challenge of alternative assumptions can best be met by denying they constitute anything different from that which has gone before in 'normal science'. According to Willower (1988, pp. 743–4) the paradigms simply do not exist. Dismissing Kuhn's *The Structure of Scientific Revolutions*, he reports that Kuhn's use of the concept of paradigm is 'not without ambiguity'. He asserts that the real meaning of paradigm is found in its Greek roots, meaning simply 'pattern, example, or model'. This view leads him to conclude that the meaning of paradigm is adequately conveyed by the concept of theory: 'It does not seem appropriate to talk about paradigm shifts in the sense of a world view or in the sense of the fundamental redirection of a discipline by a new theory and its associated methodology'.

Without attempting to explicate further the nature of the paradigms, I would make some observations on the general idea of paradigm that speak to misunderstandings and unfortunate misconstruals that are all too prevalent in the field and that diminish the value and meaningfulness of the term.

1. The systems-empiricist paradigm is, of course, the one that dominates the field and which some hold to be the best standard of rational and objective truth available to us. It is the view of the world that all those robed with power and authority prefer to take, for it lays claim to and confers certainty, rationality and universality. Those theorists and researchers who support this view are more likely to be serving authority than describing objective reality. This is MacIntyre's point from *After Virtue* (1981), and it profoundly touches the claims of *management science*, revealing them to be 'a moral fable' not an objective view of immutable reality. It is therefore in the interests of both established power and its servants in 'normal' science to disguise their value judgements as objective observations about the world and the conduct of social affairs. To fail to understand and acknowledge this point is not to defend reality, but to defend a view of reality and the prevailing power relations within it.

2. The preferred mode of inquiry in the systems-empiricist paradigm is, of course, the statistical and the quantitative. A common error is to appropriate the putative objectivity and rational force of quantitative analysis to the systems-

empiricist paradigm, relegating all qualitative analysis – words, fuzzy meanings, interpretation, and subjectivity itself – to the other paradigms. There is nothing about numbers that appropriates them uniquely to the systems-empiricist paradigm. As Lord Russell observed, even the apparent and purely factual quantitative statement, $1 + 1 = 2$, has its moral component, for it implies also 'Know that...'. And as Hodgkinson (1978a, p. 272) has said, 'As a philosopher I feel justified in talking about number magic since I have never yet been able to actually find such a thing as a *number* in the empirical world'. And as Weber (1971, p. 19) advised researchers, 'First get the facts', by which he meant all demographic and economic data relevant to the social situation under analysis; then attempt to describe and understand it from the internal perspective of *verstehen*. It is therefore a simplistic and unfortunate error to set qualitative and quantitative analyses in contrast and opposition to each other. Both quantitative and the qualitative analysis may be found in any of the paradigms of inquiry.

3. It is possible, as Bauman (1978, p. 36) points out, to treat people as though they were trees, but trees cannot play the role of people. 'Understanding is re-discovery of myself in thou; I cannot discover myself in a tree, much less can I re-discover myself there'. Or as Schumacher (1977, p. 39) shows, 'the understanding of the knower must be *adequate* to the thing to be known'. The systems-empiricist paradigm may be adequate for certain purposes, but for understanding the intentions, choices, meanings, and the causal links and consequences of people engaged in social action it is clearly inadequate.

4. Smith and Blase (1989, p. 4) note that one of the concerns of empiricist science is to distinguish what 'is' from what 'seems' to be the case. And so it does, and appropriately and necessarily so, in the case of physical phenomena. To the commonsense observer, the sun rises in the east and moves to the west. But physics teaches us that this illusion is produced by the earth moving in precisely the opposite direction. As Weber knew, the progress of physical science requires the scientist's imposition of such an 'is' perspective, for the physical world has no voice to say otherwise. But the social world does have a voice, and it was one of Weber's great contributions to establish how this difference must transform the work of the social scientist and distinguish it from that of the physical scientist. The same issue of 'is' and 'seems' has its echo in the social sciences. While the interpretive social scientist is content to deal with the world of 'seems' in social action, the critical theorist (Carr and Kemmis, 1986) knows that what seems to be the case in social reality appears in the light of true, but external understanding to be false consciousness, ideological repression, and erroneous moral judgement.

For example, Hargreaves (1978, p. 11) highlights the assumptions that Sharp and Green (1975) made about social reality in their noteworthy study of 'progressive primary education' in an English inner-city school. In exploring realities apparent to administrators and teachers in the school, Sharp and Green 'seek to go *beyond* subjective meanings and see an important difference between "things seeming to be the case to the actor and things being the case"'. Thus critical theory appears as concerned to determine the ultimate truth of social reality as does empiricist science. In this light, a further significant implication flows from the structure of the paradigms of inquiry posited by Ribbins (1985). In his typology the systems/empiricist paradigm stands at one end, critical theory at the other of a continuum arrayed from social order to social conflict. Where the systems/empiricist approach establishes what 'is' by eliminating values, critical theory sets out to establish the ought of values, by determining their appropriate 'is'. Thus pushing critical theory to its logical end reveals a continuum bent back upon itself. The critical theory perspective leads ultimately to a certainty as firm as that claimed in systems/empiricism, but now the certainty is not just about factual reality in a value context, but about the values themselves. This too is not science, or at least not an appropriate and adequate social science. It is rather another imposition of values in the name of science.

SPLITTING FACTS AND VALUES

As Hodgkinson (1978b, p. 220) says, 'Values are special kinds of facts; but never true or false'. They are good or bad, but never falsifiable. The question of the divisibility of facts and values continues to bedevil an understanding of the paradigms and issues of methodological adequacy. To begin with Weber recognised that a fact-driven rationality (*Zweckrationalität*) increasingly drives the modern world. What is often called modernity and professionalism calls for such a separation. Thus Weber recognised that, though they are analytically separable, the social scientist faces a world in which facts and values are inevitably and intimately intertwined. Weber's great question was to ask what a value-free social science could mean in a world suffused with values. That he never gave up striving to answer that question should not – and does not – put him on the side of the rationalisers and those who split values from facts. But he clearly saw that much of the modern world is driven by a set of assumptions that does make such split. Those who make the split are often those who set policy, and so a 'subjectively adequate' view of policy-making must take into account the convictions of those who believe that facts can be, and appropriately are, split from values.

VALUES ARE ASSERTED, CHOSEN, IMPOSED, NOT MEASURED

Values lie beyond rationality. Rationality to *be* rationality must stand upon a value base. Values are asserted, chosen, imposed, or believed. They lie beyond quantification, beyond measurement. They are not 'variables', though they may be treated as such. Simply and clearly Hodgkinson (1978b, p. 220) puts the fundamental quality of values, the essence that distinguishes them from facts and lets us understand their force and meaning: 'The world of fact is given, the world of value made. We discover facts and impose values.'

Again it is Weber who helps us understand the relationship of values and rationality. As Weber argues, a technical or narrowly scientific rationality asks only what means best fosters an end. It assumes the end is unquestionable and clear and that the means to attain it rationally and efficiently are equally clear and available...For Weber, the technical spirit of modernity exists in a disenchanted world, one bled of values. Brubaker (1984, pp. 80 and 98) demonstrates Weber's view that modern science

> 'disenchants' the world by construing it as a rationally calculable and manipulable causal mechanism...It is intellect that rules the disenchanted world, a world in which 'one can, in principle, master all things by calculation'. The truly human life is one that is guided by reason. To live a life informed by reason, an individual must become a personality. To become a personality, he must commit himself to certain fundamental values. But this commitment...cannot itself be guided by reason, for in Weber's view there is no rational way of deciding among the plurality of conflicting possible value commitments. Every rational life, in short, is founded on a non-rational choice.

The impossibility of the empiricist dream, or rather the impossibility of ever assuaging the empiricist anxiety for certainty and control, is mocked with trenchant irony in Julian Barnes's *Flaubert's Parrot* (1984). Though the book is a novel, it is also a *tour de force* evoking Flaubert's moral vision, his despair over the technology propelled by 'democracy' that reshaped the nineteenth century in the name of progress and transformed our own...The targets [Barnes] aims at through Flaubert reveal a blind science that destroys people while insisting it is morally neutral, while insisting it is only helping people to live better, to achieve *their* goals more fully.

What does constitute progress? What is the good and how may it be attained? How does education contribute to the social good and to personal well-being and happiness? How should schools be organised to achieve such goals? What are the moral choices that face educational administrators? Such questions are hardly asked any more. Instead the field seems bent upon implementing a uniform, but undefined 'effectiveness'. Decisions are obviated. Training in procedure, mouthing the accepted answers is all that is required. This will not do. But this mindless devotion to technicism could engulf us, sweeping the field away into a spuriously scientific irrelevancy, to a technology of claimed, but unexamined effectiveness, one that is easy for masses to accept and vastly profitable to those who exploit and merchandise it.

Justifying Educational Administration

COLIN W. EVERS AND GABRIELE LAKOMSKI

Educational administration, in common with many branches of applied social science, is nowadays characterised by considerable theoretical diversity. Logical empiricist models of behavioural science, which dominated the scene for so long, now compete with a range of alternatives; for example, varieties of subjectivism, values oriented approaches, critical theory, and cultural perspectives. And a recent Special Issue of the *Educational Administration Quarterly* (Griffiths, 1991, pp. 262–451) on 'Nontraditional Theory and Research' canvasses further possibilities.

Although sometimes associated with 'intellectual turmoil' (Griffiths, 1979, p. 43), we agree with Hughes (1988, p. 671) that such developments in the field should be viewed 'as a strength rather than a weakness'. This is because traditional science approaches (usually lumped together under the label of *positivism*), in being based on a very narrow account of knowledge and its justification, end up ruling out much that is of value to administrative theory and practice. Indeed, methodology of science as traditionally conceived by logical empiricists rules out much that is of value in science. (The classic criticisms are in Feyerabend, 1975; Hanson, 1968; and Kuhn, 1974.) It would be fair to say that, in response to both concerns about narrowness, and debates in the philosophy of science over the weaknesses of positivism, educational research methodology in general can now be described as post-positivist, at least in the specific sense that a number of different so-called research 'paradigms' have found acceptance alongside traditional methods of acquiring and justifying knowledge (Keeves, 1988). To the extent that educational administration reflects these broader trends in educational studies we have grounds for approbation.

Amid all this good cheer, however, lurks some gloom. For just as positivistically construed science of administration sought to exclude non-science from administrative theory, so the main theoretical alternatives which developed in opposition to positivism show an understandable but equally regrettable tendency seriously to limit, or even exclude, science from

95

administrative theory. The tendency is regrettable because scientific knowledge is also of great value, and the resulting exclusions are methodologically suspect because the knowledge used to justify them may be less reliable than the knowledge denied. It seems to us that both kinds of attempts to exclude knowledge stem from a failure to distinguish sharply between positivism and science (e.g. Maddock, 1991, pp. 96–8). But once we see positivism as a philosophical theory, or better, a cluster of philosophical theories, about the nature and methodology of science, it is a further issue as to whether such theories are sound. In our view, the philosophical theory, or version of positivism, which underwrites traditional science of educational administration, namely logical empiricism, is systematically flawed, especially in its epistemology. We think educational administration is best served, not by the current fragmentation into relatively distinct 'paradigms', but by moving ahead to a particular *post-positivist* theory of science that is broad enough to incorporate considerations of ethics and human subjectivity. We think that such a theory should be justified by a *coherentist epistemology*, which we see as the major alternative to the foundationalist epistemological assumptions shared by positivism – and some of its critics (Williams, 1977, 1980; Bonjour, 1985; Lycan, 1988; Lakomski, 1991).

Knowing Educational Administration (Evers and Lakomski, 1991) defends and applies this coherentist epistemology to offer a perspective on a number of important recent methodological debates in educational administration. Since theory of knowledge shapes both the structure and content of substantive theories the perspective, although preliminary, has fairly systematic consequences for theory and research in the field. One consequence is a shift towards naturalism, because there is a premium on administrative theories cohering with natural science. Another is a more generous view of what counts as evidence and a resulting holism that shuns partitions on knowledge. (For more on the philosophy see Quine and Ullian, 1978; Quine, 1960, 1981, 1990; P. M. Churchland, 1979, 1988; P. S. Churchland, 1986, pp. 239–400.) The discussion which follows is a brief introduction to some more specific consequences and also to some select features of the epistemological machinery which figures in their defence.

THE THEORY MOVEMENT: PAST AND PRESENT

... We can easily identify the main features of traditional scientific theories of educational administration:

1. There is a premium on generalisations couched in an abstract theoretical vocabulary.
2. Theories should be testable.
3. All theoretical terms should admit of operational definition.
4. Ethical claims and reports of 'inner' mental episodes should be excluded from administrative theory (except, perhaps, where the relevant vocabulary

admits of exhaustive operational definition, say in terms of preferential and other behaviours).

We now know that this package of requirements is too strict, even for such well-structured bodies of knowledge as physics. [Yet] the sheer durability of the programme in mainstream educational administration, and the skill with which it has been implemented, are therefore, ironically, all the more impressive. For example, the advice on theory building contained in Griffiths's (1959) remarkable little book *Administrative Theory* remains largely unchanged nearly thirty years later in Hoy and Miskel's (1987) *Educational Administration*, perhaps the most widely used introductory text in North America.

Even without the benefit of a systematic alternative it is easy to be concerned over the very heavy demands logical empiricist criteria of theoryhood make on available epistemological resources....Given the very great particularity and contextuality of social phenomena, the demand for high level generalisations places further burdens on evidence. For true, non-trivial, law-like, empirical generalisations are in short supply in social science. So much so, that in practice the methodological choice is stark: one can say something non-trivial, over a very limited domain and thus abandon the traditional ideal of scientific theory, or one can keep the ideal and risk trading in trivial, empirically vacuous, generalisations.

We think that the influence of systems theory in current educational administration reflects the second option, and it is partly for this reason that we see systems theoretic behavioural science of educational administration today as particularly continuous with the Theory Movement initiated in the 1950s. We are not in general opposed to the systems metaphor as an heuristic device; complex, feedback-driven, self-regulating systems are ubiquitous in nature. And whether open, closed, natural, or even rational or loosely coupled, they are amenable to close causal and empirical analysis. Rather, it is in the explanatory value of the big picture – when it comes to schools, bureaucracies, and organisational life in general – that weaknesses emerge.

Without going through all the supposed properties of systems (given, for example, in Hoy and Miskel, 1987, pp. 16–21; 55–83) we can generalise our methodological concerns as follows: inasmuch as the notion of a system and its properties is thought to be widely applicable, the relevant generalisations look trivial, or worse, are tautologies. Not all the news is bad, of course. Logical empiricism extolled the touchstone virtues of precision and explicitness in the formulation of theory, and the metaphysical virtue of supposing there was an actual world of social and organisational reality which constrained the boundaries of what could legitimately be said. However, just the worries we have considered concerning operationalism and generalisation are serious, even for natural science theories, and warrant a breaking of the alleged nexus between positivism (a poor cluster of theories about the nature of science) and science itself. In our view, what successes traditional science of educational administration has enjoyed, have been due to the implicit use of further, more flexible, coherentist criteria of knowledge and its justification. (Donald Willower's pragmatist approach reflects some of these criteria. See Willower, 1988; 1992.) An important aim of a new science of administration is to make these criteria and their application more explicit.

THE GREENFIELD REVOLUTION

The above problems were well known, even by the early founders of the Theory Movement. The provisional solution was (and still is) to hedge and qualify, pending more systematic developments of theory. In 1974 Thomas Greenfield launched a critique of the traditional science approach that raised fundamental difficulties threatening the whole point of the enterprise. Drawing on arguments developed in the philosophy of science by Kuhn and Feyerabend, he challenged the alleged *objectivity* of science. And drawing on arguments from a long interpretive tradition in social science he challenged the *applicability* of science to a big range of social phenomena (Greenfield, 1975).

Turning to the matter of objectivity, Greenfield's epistemological arguments strike at both the supposition of an epistemically privileged observation base, assumed necessary to secure objectivity, and the logic of testability, assumed necessary to transfer the objectivity of observations back up the layers of theory.

Consider, first, the question of an observation base. The language in which observation reports are formulated needs to be sufficiently theory neutral to be able to figure in the adjudication of rival theories. But as Greenfield (1979b, p. 173) notes: 'That we require ideas to understand our experience and to perceive reality is generally accepted as a principle of epistemology'. And so it is, for what Greenfield is referring to is the nowadays widely acknowledged point that all observation is *theory laden*, or more precisely, that all observation reports invoke the theoretical language of some theory or another. Experience, when it functions as empirical evidence, is always interpreted experience, whether of the humdrum, like chairs or tables, or the more arcane, like voltage drops dimming the lights, or a particular choice being a good decision. For the humdrum is relative to commonsense, or some other widely accepted theory, while the arcane invokes more remote or perhaps controversial theory. The effect of theory ladenness, for Greenfield, is to diminish the value of appeals to some 'objective' standard of evidence 'out there'. Rather, the standard is no more objective than the theory under test.

We may note, in addition to Greenfield's point, that the problem is even more severe, once it is recognised that the business of identifying an epistemically secure foundation for knowledge, of distinguishing sharply between theory and observation, is itself a theory driven task, and one that draws on quite modest theories of human learning and perception. Since accounts of human cognition are not themselves epistemically privileged, the whole structure of justification is problematic for logical empiricism.

Greenfield's attack on the logic of testability comes in two parts corresponding to the components 'confirmation' and 'disconfirmation'. Against traditional views of confirmation, he applies Kuhn's (1974, p. 150) claim that different theorists live in different worlds, asserting that there are multiple, possibly orthogonal, realities. This thesis underwrites Greenfield's (1983, p. 298) anarchistic theory of organisations, where following Feyerabend (1975), he urges a proliferation of perspectives for human empowerment:

> Language is power. It literally makes reality appear and disappear. Those who control language control thought, and thereby themselves and others. We build categories to dominate the world and its organisations. The anarchist wants to let the reality of people within the categories shatter them and thereby to reduce the control.

The basic epistemological idea here is that all theories are *radically underdetermined* by all the empirical evidence that is ever available; or equivalently, that any number of theories can be compatible with the same evidence; or again, that an arbitrary number of different curves can be drawn through the same finite set of data points. However, under these conditions an obscurity invests the notion of confirmation, for it is now not clear *which* scientific theory is being confirmed from among all the empirically equivalent alternatives.

Retreating to disconfirmation, or falsification, is no help either, for as Greenfield (1979b, p.170) argues:

> A long and well accepted logic in research requires researchers first to have a theoretical view of the world and then to test it stringently against reality by collecting empirical data through operationally defined procedures. In contrast, Kuhn and Feyerabend argue that theory is never disconfirmed by empirical research. If findings are inconsistent with the theory, we are likely to disbelieve them or to search for other data that fit better with the theory.

He illustrates this argument with the example of factor analysis: 'Typically, researchers keep rotating their factors until something interpretable emerges' (Greenfield, 1979b, p. 170). What Greenfield is drawing attention to (in addition to the problem of theory ladenness) is the *complexity of test situations*. It is whole theories, including the machinery of data interpretation, that are tested, not isolated individual hypotheses. The question of which hypotheses we should revise is not therefore settled by the disconfirming data.

To sum up, we think that Greenfield has identified three principles which tell powerfully against traditional views of scientific objectivity: the theory ladenness of observations, the underdetermination of theory by observation, and the complexity of test situations. From these principles, we offer the following reconstruction of Greenfield's case for subjectivity in administrative science:

1. If all the objective evidence there is for a scientific theory is empirical evidence, and
2. if empirical evidence is never sufficient for choosing among competing theories, then
3. choosing among competing scientific theories of educational administration

is ultimately a subjective matter, a matter of human will, intention, and values. (See Greenfield, 1991, pp. 202–4.)

Our response to this argument, in keeping with our coherentism, is that we deny the condition expressed in the first premise. We think there is more to objective evidence than empirical evidence. We think that theories should also enjoy a number of *super-empirical* virtues; in particular, consistency, simplicity, comprehensiveness, coherence, explanatory unity, learnability, and fecundity (Churchland, 1985). On our usage, justification which invokes these criteria in addition to empirical adequacy, is called *coherence justification*. Moreover, we think these are objective criteria in the sense that they are common, or touchstone, among rival theoretical perspectives which place a premium on the *explanation* of phenomena. Greenfield's attack on narrow versions of empiricist science is therefore successful, but misses the mark against broader post-positivist versions justified by coherentist standards.

Greenfield's criticism of the applicability of traditional science models to administrative phenomena proceeds somewhat independently of his critique of scientific objectivity, since he adopts Taylor's (1979) distinction between brute and nonbrute data. Science may deal with brute facts, but in the social world what counts as a fact depends on interpretations, and interpretations of interpretations:

> the important factors of organisational life call nonbrute data into play...there is therefore no ultimate reality in the understanding of organisations. (Greenfield, 1984, p. 151)

For Greenfield, organisations exist only by virtue of the interpretations people give to each other's behaviour:

> They have no ontological reality, and it is no use studying them as though they did. They are an invented social reality of human creation. (Greenfield, 1986, p. 71)

On this view, organisations are cultural artefacts, and the appropriate aim of social science is to understand and interpret the meanings of human action, meanings which make an action the nonbrute social fact that it is:

> The basic problem in the study of organisations is that of understanding human intention and meaning...Action flowing from meaning and intention weaves the fabric of social reality. (Greenfield, 1980, pp. 26–7)

The details of this interpretive position are sufficiently well known not to call for further elaboration by us. Suffice it to note that any systematic science of administration must offer some alternative account, some way of overcoming the implied bifurcation between natural science and social science. Greenfield is on strong ground here as alternatives are sketchy and programmatic. Nevertheless, utilising some substantive science, and the coherence criteria of justification, we have some constructive suggestions.

Note first that all the cultural and interpretive skills a person possesses must be *learned* in some way from experience. On our best natural science of learning, this will involve the development of relevant brain states from the ongoing processing of neural inputs from sensory receptors. So barring clairvoyance, the acquisition of language and culture is a physical process. The interesting question is which conceptual framework, or theory, ultimately best describes it: the language of meaning, intention, belief and desire, or the more austere language of natural science.

A second point to note is that the social behaviours to be understood and interpreted are the non-random, or patterned, behaviours. Drawing on information theory, we can define patterned data as data which are *compressible* (see Chaitin, 1975). Roughly speaking, data are compressible if there exists a description of the data, or a formula, that contains fewer characters (if written down) than any description, or listing, of all the individual data items. The true law-like generalisations of natural science thus count as superb *compression algorithms*, compressing a vast number of individual data descriptions into a single formula, or collection of formulae, such as a theory. But from this information-theoretic perspective, the same principle applies in social science. The terms 'intention', 'meaning', 'belief and 'desire', for example, are no more than basic theoretical terms of the *folk psychological theory* embedded in the age-old ordinary commonsense we use to explain, predict, and interpret our social world. To be sure, the folk-theoretic framework of understanding human (social) behaviour in terms of the rational coordination of a person's hypothesised beliefs and desires, admits of lots of exceptions and counter-examples. But despite this 'noise', folk theory is a very powerful compression algorithm, abstracting ruthlessly from the vast ensemble of causal data behind every thought, every word, and every action (Dennett, 1991). In fact, so impressive is folk theory that, like Greenfield, we may even think we have understood a decision, or an action, if we have located it as a point, reasonable by our own folk-theoretic lights, between the axes of belief and desire. (Indeed, the decision theory mathematical apparatus of utility maximisation is essentially an elaboration of this basic idea.)

Despite the elegance and empirical success of folk theory, the noise, or exceptions, are troublesome. For example, most of the phenomena dealt with in special education outrun the model's modest resources, inviting explanation instead in terms of brain processes – the causal machinery of behaviour. More seriously, it has little to say about human learning, a theory of which is clearly presupposed if it is to be able to account for the acquisition of language and culture. Since brain processes underlie all cognitive phenomena, not just those of special education, simplicity, comprehensiveness, and the explanatory unity that comes from coherence with a causal/neural theory of learning suggest that deep accounts of human social behaviour will come ultimately from the natural sciences.

The advantages of compressibility (which might accrue from a compartmentalised treatment of phenomena) for creatures of modest cognitive resources living in a complex world, are not to be denied. However, as compressibility reflects mainly the theoretical virtue of empirical adequacy, we recommend the following pragmatic methodological approach to science and interpretivism in administration. Adopt an instrumentalist stance towards the categories of folk theory, freely utilising them where they enjoy most empirical success, but see the real story as being given by the developing theoretical machinery of natural science...When it comes to justifying administrative knowledge, we see the systematic advantages of global theoretical coherence that a meshing with natural science offers, as eventually overhauling the more local, or compart-mentalised, empirical adequacy of folk theory that interpretivism offers.

The Salvation of Educational Administration: Better Science or Alternatives to Science?

PETER GRONN AND PETER RIBBINS

Evers and Lakomski's *Knowing Educational Administration* (1991) is a tough and uncompromising but important book. It seeks to examine the merits of traditional science and its alternatives as a basis for educational administration as a field of study....

Greenfield states the nub of [his own and Hodgkinson's] differences with Evers and Lakomski. 'Free will exists in some measure at least,' he wrote, 'and that is where the struggle with Evers and Lakomski begins. They deny mind and free will, reducing everything to matter, arguing as Evers has, that it is easier to physicalise the mental than to mentalise the physical. In opposition to that dehumanising proposition Hodgkinson and I are united' (Greenfield and Ribbins, 1993a, p. 265). These are views which we take up below but we want to stress at this point that if Greenfield felt that some of the ideas advanced by Evers and Lakomski were dehumanising, he nevertheless cherished them as honourable opponents. As he has written: 'I take great satisfaction from what they have said, not just because it is appreciative...but because they pay attention to the text of what I have written. They pay attention to what I have said, even though their view of it is rather selective. They don't look at all of my writing over the last twenty years and I wish they had looked at some of the other things. But what they look at, they look at squarely and carefully.' He goes on to acknowledge that Evers and Lakomski are critical of those who do not do this 'and that is something which has aggrieved me most over the years. Too often I have been personally attacked rather than attacked on the basis of what I have written.' Accordingly, it was 'satisfying at this juncture to find critics with whom I may disagree, but who will understand what I've said and deal with it' (*ibid.*, p. 263).

REFLECTING UPON 'THE GREENFIELD REVOLUTION'

In their opening statement Evers and Lakomski (1991, p. 1) suggest that from following mainly models of theory and research associated with more traditional views of science, the field [of educational administration] has moved to a position of much greater diversity.' This shift was made possible by the development of 'alternative philosophical perspectives on the nature of knowledge which could function as frameworks for rival systematic conceptions of administration' (*ibid.*). From such a perspective, it is ideas about the nature of knowledge, or 'the structure of justification, as specified by epistemology', which 'determines much of the overall framework in which theorizing in educational administration can take place' (*ibid.*, p. 3). Evers and Lakomski cite three major developments to illustrate this point. The first and second have already had a considerable impact within the field and the third underpins their own proposed new direction: logical empiricism, the paradigms approach and coherentism.

The discussion of Greenfield's subjectivism to be found in *Knowing Educational Administration* is, in many respects, unsatisfactory. In part this is understandable given that Evers and Lakomski adhere to a theory of the administrative world which is incommensurable with that proposed by Greenfield. As is implicit in the title of their book, as far as Evers and Lakomski are concerned, one can only ever *know* administration. It follows that to ask other kinds of questions about administration or administrators is meaningless. If knowing is all, then it is hard to see any point in asking how an administrator feels about the world, or what the right and proper way is for that administrator to act in regard to that world. Nor is there much sense in recounting how actual administrators might construe such issues for themselves.

In particular, we make six main criticisms of Evers and Lakomski's thesis in general and its implications for their discussion of Greenfield's position in particular. The first general point is that in their search for a 'better science', rather than 'traditional science' and its logical empiricist base, they, in effect, leave untouched the core of Greenfield's main position. Indeed, they can be said to jettison it. Unlike Evers and Lakomski, and despite his rather teasing subtitle, 'Towards a Humane Science', Greenfield argues for an alternative to science or, at least, for a definition of science which does not exclude a serious concern for feelings and values. This may, in part, explain why Evers and Lakomski neglect three key aspects of his work. Firstly, the primacy which he accords to values: in particular his claim that all statements about science and values are themselves valuational, that in a sense theories are really moral versions of the world, is nowhere addressed by Evers and Lakomski. Secondly, and arising from this point, whilst they recognise that Greenfield believes organisations are non-natural, socially constructed entities, the substance of his most recently developed view that they entail a moral order, is likewise ignored. Thirdly, the idea that such a paramountcy of values for organisations may have implications for the role of the administrator as a kind of entrepreneur of values who wilfully constructs the social world for others, is given no credence at all (Gronn, 1996).

There are many ways in which these ideas can be illustrated with reference to educational practice. For example, there are a number of studies which have been undertaken into the English public school and their imperial variants (e.g.

Gathorne-Hardy, 1979; Honey, 1977) which emphasise its purposes in terms of the notion of character building and the creation of a political and administrative élite through the paraphernalia of the boarding house and fagging and buttressed by conceptions of a headmasterly tradition going back to Arnold of Rugby and Thring of Uppingham. If this represents a particularly striking case in point it should be stressed that the ideas which underpin the approach can be used to give an account of any school at any time in its history. Thus, for example, the study by Best *et al.* (1983) of continuity and change at Rivendell draws on similar ideas to describe the three regimes of headship which existed at the school between the 1960s and the 1980s. This case study offers an excellent example of the merits of viewing the school as a moral order and the headteacher as an entrepreneur of values.

These are points which Greenfield has developed in many of his papers and most notably in his last, known as 'Science and Service' (1991), where he concludes that a central issue in management science generally, and in educational administration in particular, is the place that facts and values have in shaping an administrator's action (p. 221):

> many who struggle in the arenas where theory is still debated can be divided into two camps: those who see the central administrative issue as all fact and those who see it as all value.... In a sense both camps offer a pure science, one focused on facts, the other on value.

In the latter camp he sees the critical theorists, the deconstructionists and the post-modernists, and in the former the coherentists. A brief examination of the latter position can be used to show the weakness of attempts to force science to deal only in pure values or pure facts. The problem, Greenfield argues, has been economically presented by Lakomski (1987, p. 71, original emphasis):

> If attending to our values helps us make *better* decisions, then we need specific criteria to help us to decide *between* competing values. In other words, there has to be a way to *determine* if value X is better than value Y in some specified way. But if values are merely non-cognitive or affective and subjectivist, then we cannot determine rationally which of two conflicting values is better.

It might well be asked: what is Lakomski's answer? The clue, as Greenfield suggests, lies in the phrase 'if values are *merely* non-cognitive [emphasis added]'. The answer, he says (Greenfield and Ribbins, 1993b, p. 222), is 'to make values cognitive, to turn them into facts. [Lakomski] notes that even subjectivists will defend their values with arguments... defending or acting on personal preference implies that *in practice* not all values are considered equally acceptable or worthy. When people actually defend their preferences, they admit a modicum of rationality and objectivity by admitting that some preferences or values are better than others.' Perhaps. But, as Greenfield asks, what would convince one individual of the validity of another's value position? And why *should* we be rational (Greenfield and Ribbins, 1993b, p. 222)?

What Lakomski fails to recognise is that an appeal to argument is an appeal to values. Rationality itself is ultimately a value position... To be rational or to decide to look for the 'coherence' of evidence is to make a value choice. Such a choice may be one that many people make or that many scientists make, but consensus about a value does not transmute it from the value realm to the cognitive and rational. If we are to ask what values are better than others, we must look in a domain other than rationality or coherence.

For such reasons, Greenfield chooses to take the middle ground, 'the position that argues the central questions of administration turn on an interweaving of fact and value' (*ibid.*, p. 221).

Our second general point follows from the first. As we see it, one important implication of this refusal or inability to consider Greenfield from within his own terms is that it is just not clear where values and questions of moral choice fit in Evers and Lakomski's coherentism. Their long-term project seems to be to naturalise ethics and to do so in part by attacking such notions as the 'is'/'ought' dichotomy and the naturalistic fallacy. It could well be that these ideas are false. This view has been put forward by Quine and by Alasdair MacIntyre in his *After Virtue?* (1981). But we do not find the examples Evers and Lakomski give to support their case (for example: either snow is white or we ought not to kill – 1991, p. 168) very compelling. More importantly, we are unclear about the meaning or place which they give to values in their model. Exactly where do right and wrong, justice and fairness, equality and freedom, etc. fit in a pragmatic problem-solving approach geared to finding the 'best' theory? In any case, what does 'best' mean? 'Best' for whom, given that there are usually contending interests involved in the resolution of any value conflict? What might, for example, 'best' mean in the context of disputes which are currently taking place in the United Kingdom with regard to the appropriate levels of pit closures or over the level and structure of pay for teachers during a period of economic recession? And what happens if what is thought to be best is deemed to conflict with other considerations? A contemporary example is the way in which market theories are driving or justifying various macro and micro-level economic reform measures in Western economies. Suppose a coherentist could demonstrate that a particular rational economic doctrine (or 'theory') of, let us say, 'the withering state', is 'best' then what happens if the price to be paid is severe economic dislocation, injustice and hardship? What does a coherentist position advise an administrator to do?

Our third point refers to what Evers and Lakomski describe as the 'extra-empirical virtues' upon which the coherentist can draw in the resolution of disputes over the determination of what counts as 'best' theory in a specific instance. It is not clear where these virtues come from. Nor is it clear exactly what, in this context, 'coherence' means? Words like 'fecundity', 'simplicity', 'consistency', 'elegance' and 'comprehensiveness' are sprinkled throughout their text, and they seem to be very important to the coherentist position which Evers and Lakomski advance. But how are we to understand them? There are references to the work of Lycan (1988, p. 130) and his five rules for guiding the comparison of two theories which are equal in other respects. What it is for theories to be 'equal' is not discussed further but, following Lycan, they propose that in such cases Theory 1 is to be preferred to Theory 2 if it is simpler, explains more, is more readily testable, leaves fewer messy unanswered questions and squares better with what is already known. Evers and Lakomski (1991, p. 38) accept that 'terms like "simpler" and "explain" await more detailed elaboration' but they claim, nevertheless, that 'at least we have a framework for moving towards critical judgements'. Yet none of the terms which underpin the rules identified above is closely defined in the text. And their meanings are far from self-evident. On the contrary, most of them appear to be 'essentially contested'. Nor are we told if these 'rules' constitute a comprehensive list of coherence criteria and if so, why just these particular rules? And what if in making such comparisons, Theory 1 is better than Theory 2 on some criteria but not on others? What kind of a calculus do we use then? Are some of the rules prior to others and if so how are they to be weighted? Are all of the criteria of equal epistemological status? Again we simply do not know because no answer is given to this issue. These are intriguing, interesting and suggestive features but they have travelled some distance from Greenfield's values.

It could be that there is no way out of the difficulties of applying the coherence criteria discussed above. Where problems exist of choosing between theories on coherence grounds these can be resolved by a process of arbitration against the relevant community of scientists. Greenfield believed that Evers and Lakomski were committed to such a view and he argued that 'to me [this] puts it on a social basis' (Greenfield and Ribbins, 1993a, p. 238). If this is the case then to do so might create more difficulties for them than solutions. For example, what is a scientist and who is to be defined as a scientist in this context? In thinking about such questions, an attempt by Carr (1964) to define 'history' and to determine who has the right to be described as a historian might be instructive. In effect, he concluded that history is what historians say it is and historians are those who other historians say are historians. Not only does this entail circular logic but practical difficulties. As Greenfield points out (Greenfield and Ribbins, 1993a, pp. 238-9) we need only 'think of the fate of Galileo and other heretics who were right but forced to say their theories were wrong'. And their theories applied to the physical world. If there are difficulties with the application of Evers and Lakomski's ideas in this context then

> their argument becomes shaky indeed when it is applied to the social world. There truth is defined, as Szasz says, not by scientists looking into test tubes and telescopes, but by "experts" who go not to their laboratories to observe, but to make judgements... whether schizophrenia is a disease, a sin or a wilful and moral choice.

The fourth point concerns the issue of causality. Even if, for the sake of argument, it were to be conceded that Greenfield does not consider the question of the causes of human action, this is not necessarily fatal to his thesis. What causes someone to adhere to and pursue particular values is certainly an important question. This is so because an answer to it might lead us to form judgements about the appropriateness or otherwise of a particular set of social arrangements as, for example, in the case of the socialisation of the young. However, it is one thing to point to the significance of causality, another to argue that Greenfield glosses over it and still another to fail, as Evers and Lakomski surely do, to reveal to their readers what a causal account of an organisation might look like. In any case, what does it mean to 'cause' something to occur? Does it mean that if humans are disposed to doing something (that is to say their genetic dispositions propel them to) that they simply learn over time to do so? Or does it mean that they are in some sense innately made to act in spite of whatever they might want to do? How much of what anyone ever does is done because of, as opposed to in spite of, what they themselves choose to do? To what extent is their behavioural repertoire an act of free choice on their part or determined for them?

Fifthly, we want to consider how much credence can be attached to Evers and Lakomski's reduction of explanatory terms to the language of brain states and the central nervous system. Is it just wishful thinking to claim that, because somehow so-called 'folk' explanations elsewhere are crumbling before sophisticated scientific theories, explanations of human behaviour within the field of administration will do likewise? This sort of thing is asserted, in the sense that it simply must follow what is happening in the so-called hard sciences. Beyond this, little evidence and no proof is offered. Instead, the reader is given a promissory note. The assumption seems to be that if the proof does not exist now, then it will emerge in due course. Such a claim appears to be 'properly scientific' in the sense that it seems to be potentially refutable. But is it? In this, it is remarkably similar to the claim structural/functionalists make of the notion of 'function'. They hold that the existence and persistence of any part of the system is to be explained in terms of the contribution it makes (its functions) to the needs of the system as a whole. Given this, how can such a theory cope with persistent deviance? As Best (1977, p. 72) points out, 'this highlights a fundamental weakness in the ... functionalist paradigm'. Indeed,

> there is a circularity here ... for there appears to be no way we can refute the account it gives of society: to cite instances of persistent and apparently dysfunctional phenomena is merely to invite the answer that, if it persists, it must be functional and the only puzzle, is to establish the exact nature of the function.

Best goes on to point out that phenomena like 'ignorance, crime and social inequality have all to be explained as functions' (*ibid.*), in so far as, and in the final analysis, they all contribute to social cohesion. In both of these cases, coherentism and functionalism, therefore, how long are we going to have to wait for the evidence? As long as it takes, it seems, which might be forever.

However much we might like to believe that the stability of organisations is due to relatively enduring dispositions encoded through learning in each person's central nervous system, can it be proved? Until it can be what we have is merely an interesting hunch like any other. Whilst Evers and Lakomski (1991, p. 94) note 'the lack of any really useful empirical generalisations in social science', they miss their chance to provide their readers with one. Instead their audience has to take them on trust when they say that the causal story 'as it would be currently told, is too complex to be of any general use' (*ibid.*), and claim that even a simple administrative action like issuing an order presumes 'such enormous networks of causal regularities that we could hardly begin to describe them in engineering terms [!!]' (*ibid.*). If this extraordinary sleight of hand is to be believed it surely invites an amazing leap of faith and, ironically, a very long wait on the part of practising administrators for a pragmatic theoretical standpoint (coherentism), dedicated to the goal of problem-solving, to be able to deliver on its promises to come up with solutions.

Towards the Learning Society

STEWART RANSON

INTRODUCTION

Education has, once more, become a national issue and priority during a period of great social, economic and political change in our society. The intention of this paper is to identify the argument surrounding education, to develop an analysis of its needs, and to propose organising principles upon which to base education and society for the twenty-first century. My purpose is to argue for the centrality of education by tying it into the large and unique issues of the time....

ANALYSING THE DEEP STRUCTURES OF UNDERACHIEVEMENT

The cause of underachievement lies in the long cultural tradition of educating a minority. Only a few succeed because that is what our society has preferred. Any analysis of the dominant characteristics of the educational and political systems reveals the institutionalising of underachievement.

1. *Characteristics of education*: young people fail to fulfil their potential, develop their powers because of principles and assumptions which are constitutive of the education system.

(i) *Assumptions about who education is for*: boundaries typically surround the process of learning. Education is too often regarded as a stage in life: to be in education is to be young, to be successful academically, and to be located within an institution – traditionally a school because colleges specialised in 'training'. Such boundaries express a narrow conception of who education is for, excluding most people and limiting the possibilities of achievement.

(ii) *Assumptions about the learning process*: traditional conceptions of teaching and learning – insisting upon the didactic transmission of knowledge to passive and solitary individual pupils – have almost certainly diminished rather than enhanced the motivation of most young people, inculcating anxiety rather than joy at the prospect of learning.

110

(iii) *Assumptions about the curriculum* have usually involved the introduction of unnecessary barriers into the experience of education: organising learning into bounded subjects (Bernstein's 'classification code') and bifurcating knowledge between theory and practice, defining an 'education' in the former as the accumulation of abstract understanding. More recently, a curriculum has been imposed upon the majority of voting people which reverses this traditional emphasis and now insists upon a narrow concept of vocational preparation for work determined instrumentally by the needs of the labour market.

(iv) *Assumptions about educational institutions*: not only has education been 'institutionalised', the schools and colleges have typically been conceived as enclosed institutions controlled by their professional communities. Parents or employers or the wider community – the sources of complementary support and motivation – have usually been held at bay. The organising rules and structures of educational institutions have, moreover, rarely been responsive to the needs of the clients they are designed to serve. As Aitken (1983) argued, they have been rigid systems: 'we need to break away from such a rigid delivery system of fixed entry points, of hours in the day, terms, academic years and self-contained levels and entry qualifications'.

(v) *Assumptions about the organising principles of the system*: the determining principle of the education system is, paradoxically, more accurately described as a system of failure rather than of enabling, recording and celebrating achievement because it has been designed primarily for the purposes of differentiation and selection... It has been a race because an education has been a privilege from which most are excluded. The dominant instrumental assumptions are tied to the labour market and the education system has provided mechanisms for 'cooling people out', or down, from 'education' to 'training' to 'work'. Society has set limits on the numbers it has been willing to educate, passing off the failure of the majority in terms of their failure (blaming the victims) or the inescapable limits of resources. Thus an education has denied what the conditions of learning require – a sense of purpose, commitment to and responsibility for personal development – generating instead for many a pervasive sense of futility. The assumptions of social selection are deeply inscribed in society and polity.

2. *Characteristics of the polity*: determine and reinforce those of education because, as Weber (1978) argued, social structures come to exhibit a 'dominant order' of beliefs and values which legitimate a pattern of power and organisation. Thus the source of underachievement and lack of motivation lies in the underlying structures which have characterised the post-war polity, providing neither the purposes nor conditions to empower most people. While the period of liberal democracy provided services and opportunities that were indispensable for many, it was also a meritocracy which measured the numbers it wished to motivate. The programmes of post-war modernisation and reform in time ran up against the limiting beliefs informing that dominant order:

(i) *The belief in the essential atomism of society* composed of private and self-sufficient individuals (this is the ontology of the dominant order). This doctrine seeks to oppose and undermine the belief that human nature is essentially social and that our distinctive capacities and potential can only be realised through collaborative endeavour within society (cf. Taylor, 1985). Thus the welfare state identified with and served the needs of individual clients rather than enabled the collective development of whole communities.

(ii) *The belief of a liberal order in being neutral about the good*: moral values are to be a matter for private reflection and choice and the state should eschew any prescription of virtue in the public domain. Thus the development of the welfare state was bereft of any moral foundation that articulated the public good, apart from an exiguous utilitarianism.

(iii) *The dominance of instrumental rationality* of scientific knowledge, in any understanding of the world (the epistemology of the dominant order). This 'positivist' ideology created an overdetermined account of reality, that resisted the possibility of alternative constructions of meaning or action. The world, and knowledge of it, is given to members of society rather than created by them (cf. Habermas, 1972). The hidden curriculum of the welfare state expressed determinism and dependence rather than agency and emancipation.

(iv) *Professional domination*: the handing down of knowledge was part of the more general vision of how society was to be developed. Liberal democracy believed that the just and open society could be *provided* and, as it were, handed down to a passive public by professionals and administrators, the controllers of knowledge.... Post-war social democracy arguably atrophied because of its limited conception of the public domain. An educated public cannot be delivered by specialists. It can only emerge from the meaning and by the agency of the people themselves.

These interdependent values defined the dominant mode of organising the relationship of people to their society; lack of motivation reflected unequal opportunities and power. The polity did not provide the purposes and conditions to motivate all as equal members, making some active members, most passive dependents, depriving the majority of the motivation for learning, to achieve more than a menial job, to become something more than an instrument in the labour market. This order, of the professional society, has been in doubt since the mid 1970s. There is a need for a consensus about a new political and moral order in which solutions to problems of underachievement will reflect broader conceptions about the nature of power and purpose in society...

THE TRANSFORMATIONS AND THE CHALLENGE

The economic, social and political transformations of our time are altering fundamentally the structure of experience: the capacities each person needs to flourish; what it is to live in society; the nature of work and the form taken by polity. The changes raise deep questions for the government of education and for the polity in general about: *what is it to be a person?* Is a person a passive being or possessed of powers that define his or her essential agency? *Is there any such thing as a society* and what is it? An aggregation of individuals or some form of social and linguistic community? *What should be the nature of the polity?* What is it to be a member and with what rights and duties? What distribution of power and wealth is consistent with justice and freedom? Who should take decisions and how? What forms of accountability and representation define our democracy?

Any effective response will require a capacity for renewal, for learning, from the institutions of our society as much as from each individual confronting the changed circumstances in private life. From either perspective, the problems of the time are public, require public solutions, and yet it is the public institutions which are being eroded.

There is an urgent need for fundamental change, to create a common purpose and the conditions for individuals and their communities to flourish by empowering the sense of agency and responsibility for the future. The foregoing analysis suggests that to realise such aims will depend upon the creation of a new moral and political order both to support the development of individual powers and to create an open, public culture responsive to change. The defining quality of such a new order, and the key to change, is a society which has learning as its organising principle. There is a need for reforms that will rescue us from the mistakes of the past and prepare us more adequately for the future. Our priority must be both to change the purposes of education and to embody, in the reform of social and political institutions, the organising principle of learning.

During the past decade there have in fact been two principal strategies for reforming education. The first, emanating from Whitehall, has promoted a philosophy of the administered market; the second has reflected the analysis of local professionals and members, striving to create a context for learning that will revive motivation in disadvantaged inner-city dwellers. Both have some of the conditions which prepare the basis for a model that can promote the learning society.

STRATEGIES FOR RECONSTRUCTION

Model 1 – From Whitehall: The Market Solution

The 1988 Education Reform Act created the most radical recasting of the government of education since 1944, now further reinforced by the 1991 White

Paper on *Education and Training for the Twenty-First Century* (DES, 1991a). The intention of those at the centre is not only to redefine the roles and responsibilities of the partners in education but to do so as part of a broader reconstituting of the social and political order. They present a vision of an active consumer democracy which is intended to replace the purportedly weary assumptions of the liberal democratic state.

While aspects of both reforms are to be commended and would probably survive electoral change, nevertheless as a whole their underlying organic principles are flawed responses to the needs of the time and contradict their own objectives. Firstly, the preoccupation with instrumental vocational objectives for education provides too limited a vision of the needs of individuals and society for the twenty-first century; the commitment to 'parity of esteem' between vocational and academic routes only serves to confirm the intention to stratify them into separate channels.

Secondly, the government's avowed commitment to empower the public in its relationship with state bureaucracies expresses tendencies which have a broader appeal. However, the belief in market competition as the principal vehicle for public choice and accountability not only appears to contradict other more traditionally 'universal' objectives, such as entitlement, which are internal to the legislative plans, but also creates a mechanism which can only disempower many. The market is formally neutral but substantively interested. Individuals (or institutions) come together in competitive exchange to acquire possession of scarce goods and services. Within the marketplace all are free and equal, only differentiated by the capacity to calculate their self-interest. Yet of course the market masks its social bias. It elides but also reproduces the inequalities which consumers bring to the marketplace. Under the guise of neutrality, the institution of the market actively confirms and reinforces the pre-existing social order of wealth, privilege and prejudice. The market, let us be clear, is a crude mechanism of social selection and intended as such. It will provide more effective social engineering than anything we have previously witnessed in the post-war period. The effect of the market mechanism in education can only be to create a social, and selective, hierarchy of institutions.

Model 2 – From the Inner City: A Model of an Empowerment Curriculum

This model for reconstruction was developed by local professionals and their councils, who were required very directly to address the issues of disadvantage and hopelessness in 'the inner city'. The distinctive characteristics of such entrenched disadvantage and underachievement caused these LEAs to turn away from the post-war model, of putting their faith solely in increased resources, towards recognising the need for a more fundamental review of the purposes and conditions of learning. They defined the problem as an entrenched loss of self-esteem, dignity and confidence. In this context, the task was understood as 'the long-term process of transforming the way people think about themselves and what they are capable of and of shaping our methods of implementation accordingly'. Initially, the LEAs perceived the management challenge as one of clarifying their vision of education, in the direction of enabling local people to develop the confidence and capacity to handle their own futures. Subsequently, they attempted to articulate this vision in development plans that could both manage change and help to regenerate education. Such plans often began by expressing the new values and principles which would shape the reform of provision, teaching and learning, the curriculum and relations with parents. I shall summarise these in turn.

1. *Valuing Capacity*

Values were carefully chosen to celebrate a distinctive vision about the reservoirs of capacity in individuals – the purpose of education being to create active rather than passive learners, empowered with the skills to make responsible choices about the direction of their own lives as well as to co-operate with others to improve the quality of life for all in the community. The LEAs believed in:

(i) *Valuing the identify and dignity of each*, to develop the self-esteem which is a precondition for learning. Education helps young people to form positive attitudes to themselves as well as others and thus to dissolve prejudice.

(ii) *Belief in individual capacity and achievement*: 'that no limit should be assumed to the individual's capacity for achievement: this must be the basis of expectations of all children and voting people from all backgrounds'.

(iii) *Valuing agency, assertiveness, self-confidence*: to learn is to reach out, to examine something beyond the self, to encounter a different environment and the strangers within it. The value of self-confidence is especially important for those groups – girls, the black and ethnic minorities – which have, traditionally, been disadvantaged by education.

(iv) *Agency: empowerment for autonomy and responsibility*: enables children to become independent learners: they manage what they are doing, make decisions about the best way of doing it and have access to resources.

(v) *Responsibility for others and the wider community*: the LEAs wished to encourage an outward-looking education: 'schools and colleges should help young people to form constructive and co-operative attitudes to each other, to their work and to the community so that they can play an active and responsible role in society'. There was also some movement towards active citizenship and an understanding of the importance of taking decisions.

2. *Provision for entitlement*

A number of values established objectives for schools and colleges: what is offered in terms of opportunities, resources and facilities. Thus it was argued that provision should enable the principles of: *entitlement* to a comprehensive and continuing education for all to achieve personal growth throughout their lives; *responsive* to the expressed educational needs of all in the community; *accessibility* to enable members of the community to take up learning opportunities, which require *flexibility* of provision in schools and especially in further and higher education to enable students to transfer courses and maintain *progression in* learning. *Resources* remain a vital condition for educational quality and these LEAs invested considerably in staff development; indeed they strove to protect expenditure in the face of pressure to contract it. A belief in *quality development* was expressed in the growing commitment to the monitoring and evaluation of provision. Teachers and advisers sought to develop principles which would encourage a **comprehensive curriculum** that would be *relevant* to learners, enabling them to draw upon their experience of living within the community. This proposed curriculum should be broad and balanced in the learning offered, *modular* in its form, though ensuring *coherence* and integration across the experience of learning, enabling *continuity and progression*, and supporting young people with *formative and positive assessment* to help them understand their achievements and progress.

3. Active learning

If learning is to be effective it should motivate young people by engaging their interests and by relating to their experience. The process of teaching, moreover, should seek to involve students in, and negotiate with them, a process of active and collaborative learning: 'we must shift from a teaching approach to a learning approach'. The values emphasised:

(i)   *Student-centred learning*: education should begin from the needs and strengths of the individual and not merely the benchmarks of preconceived standards; 'learning should be appropriate to the needs of individual pupils and provide a challenge to each one'...'We must take time and involve students, to share the ownership of learning. It is no good if the "problem" is ours and we tell the answers. It is only when the child owns a problem in learning that they will really want to learn "to write" or "to read". We need to listen to children.'

(ii) *Participation and dialogue*: motivation is more likely if learning grows out of a process of agreeing with pupils the tasks to be undertaken.

(iii) *Active learning*: there is a strong belief amongst educators in disadvantaged LEAs that if the learning process is to be involving it needs to be a more active experience than it has proved traditionally in most schools. Active learning can encourage students to *take responsibility* for their own learning experience and that of others.

(iv) *Learning can serve others*: learning, even within the traditional subject curriculum, can be given purpose by serving the needs of others in the community.

(v) *Collaborative learning*: if students are to achieve the educational value of respecting other persons and cultures, then the very process of learning must encourage collaborative as well as individual activity. Pupils need to be given responsibility for developing projects together so that they decide the ends and plan the means: 'learning is most fulfilling as a co-operative activity rather than a solitary or competitive enterprise'. Your ideas and knowledge provide the spark to my discovery, your progress is necessary to mine.

(vi) Learning as enjoyment: 'learning should be interesting and challenging, it should be an exciting experience: it should be fun: too many schools are still boring environments'.

4. Partnership with parents and the community

Partnership with parents is regarded as the key to improving pupil motivation and achievement, while service to and involvement of the public reflects the broader responsibility of school and college to promote education within the community. Characteristics of partnership for improving learning quality include:

(i) *Welcoming parents into the life of the school as partners*: establishing a new style in which schools will listen to and respond to parents – 'as teachers we need to listen, learn and respect: the great mystique about teacher autonomy needs to be unmasked'.

(ii) *Parents as complementary educators – in the home*: parental contribution to schemes of reading is encouraged because of its acknowledged influence upon motivation, confidence and attainment scores; and – *in school*: they increasingly recognise the wide range of skills and experience amongst parents which can support the learning process.

(iii) *Developing shared understanding of the curriculum*: establishing a closer match of understanding within the partnership takes time, given the differences of perception, but 'teachers, pupils and parents as well as others need to know what is intended, how it is to be pursued and achieved'.

(iv) *Dialogue in curriculum design*: listening to parents and members of the community about how the curriculum, enriched by local knowledge and experience, can enhance a school's multi-cultural and anti-racist understanding.

(v) *Partners in assessment of learning progress*: establishing regular communication with parents about the progress their child is making; involving the parent in assessment and in agreeing a strategy about future development.

(vi) *Partners in evaluation and accountability*: schools having the confidence to report to parents about performance, to listen to the 'accounts' of parents and to involve them in evaluating achievement.

What we learn from the strategies pursued by disadvantaged authorities is that however important resources are, and they are very important, how much more significant it is to hold a new conception of the purposes and conditions of learning. That we cannot learn without being active and motivated; without others (i.e. the support of society); and without shared understanding about justice and rights to equal dignity. This suggests that if we are to establish the conditions for all to flourish, to be motivated and to take their learning and lives seriously, then reform needs to address the wider public purposes and conditions of learning. The challenge is vast: it implies no less than the re-enchantment of the world with the learning society whose principles can dissolve and supplant the dominant paradigm of instrumental rationality, the drive to competitive self-interest, prejudice, accumulation and bureaucracy that embody Weber's iron cage of icy darkness stifling the conditions for most individuals and communities to flourish. Our task is to re-enchant the world with a moral and political order, the defining principle of which is learning as inquiry, understanding and discourse. This could provide the possibility – which Rorty (1989) denies – of linking together a morality of personal development setting out principles about how we are to live, with a just polity which can constitute how we are to agree a future.

PART 3
POLICY

Education Policy (1972–97):
The Emergence of the 'Independent' School

BILL DENNISON

RATIONALE

To interpret the journal's response to 25 years of rapid, unpredictable policy changes by means of five articles is no easy task. From the perspective of English schooling (and some limitations are necessary to ease selection) there is, though, a single theme that runs through so many of the contributions. In some it provides the dominant item; in others, it remains a powerful influence even when no more than a sub-text. This key motif can be summarised in two words: institutional independence. It spawns so many crucial questions. What freedoms ought to be awarded an individual school? How much autonomy is best? What are the consequences for other partners? What are the effects of independence on school performance, or on issues related to equity? Some are picked up initially in a discussion of the consequences of the Taylor Report (1977) on school governance.

GOVERNING BODIES

It is difficult to appreciate, only twenty years on, the radical nature of so many of the Report's recommendations, given the then prevailing orthodoxies. Take the proposal for a separate governing body for each maintained school. In many urban areas, the Education Committee continued as the Board of Managers (note the name) for all primary schools. Indeed, as Barnes and Humble make plain, while many LEAs might have accepted the concept of a separate board fairly readily, any moves to give the boards increased independence through the abrogation of LEA powers would have been stoutly resisted. Hence their reluctance to contemplate parental and teacher membership, not so much because they necessarily rejected the notion but in case it might diminish their control, and the power of individual councillors. A handful of LEAs had made moves towards wider representation but with caution bordering on tokenism, focusing on the composition of governing bodies rather than the award of decision-making powers.

The same criticism can be made of the Report itself. Its main proposal for filling the individual governing bodies, through four constituencies with a stake in schools (LEA, parents, teachers and the local community), did little more than reflect both the spirit of the time – the emergence of consumerism, the calls for more accountability from public institutions – and specific educational developments – the widespread establishment of comprehensive schools (lobbying for their own governing bodies as a matter of status), the strengthened governing bodies in FE colleges (following the Weaver Report), and the growing confidence of primary schools after Plowden and the disappearance of the 11+.

Yet as Barnes and Humble indicate, Taylor was intent on achieving more powerful, more influential governing bodies. Indeed, they highlighted three factors that propelled the Committee towards its vision of enhanced autonomy: to generate a sense of independence in each school, to grant more freedom for the headteacher to exert leadership, and to provide greater opportunity for teacher and parental involvement. But two other, associated themes – highly significant in terms of subsequent developments – were also pursued. The first related to the curriculum. It was argued, quite powerfully, that a vital aspect of school independence, and the exercise of headteacher leadership, derived from curricular freedom. Second, the issue was raised (admittedly, not in a substantive manner) of the likely effects on school performance of governor reform.

Essentially, Taylor was a contribution to the debate, ongoing since 1944, about power and influence. Where should it reside among the partners – government, LEAs and schools? Was the system of checks and balances working? Did it avoid awarding too much control to one partner? Was one consequence of dispersed responsibilities that no partner could function adequately? Taylor tried to transfer the balance more towards schools. However, by concentrating upon structural and procedural issues, by failing to specify what these new bodies might do, what powers they would need and, therefore, what others would have to concede, its own influence on school autonomy was minimal. Little was to change for a further ten years.

CENTRALISATION–DECENTRALISATION

As a consequence, Fiske, at the start of the 1980s, when reviewing the checks and balances equation, could report a creeping nationalisation, but without reference to the consequences for school autonomy. Of course, he was writing as someone steeped in the LEA tradition. For him, the significant agenda was the continuation of a long debate: whether education was better placed in or outside of local government. As such, he described a service in a state of drift, casting doubt on the post-1944 nostrum of a 'national system locally administered'.

Yet, he pointed not so much towards an actuality of creeping nationalisation but more to factors contributing to the need for greater powers to be held centrally. He detailed a better informed, more mobile population (geographically and socially) demanding greater uniformity of provision and a better quality of service. He noted the emergence of powerful lobbies, impelling the DES to be more directive. He itemised the criticisms of the Department, for lack of planning and absence of clear guidance on major issues (by OECD), and failure to consult sufficiently widely (by a Parliamentary Select Committee). By contrast, he described the minimal powers available to the centre to intervene in the running of LEAs (and schools), other than through section 68 of the 1944 legislation – to combat unreasonable actions. And the courts had already placed severe limitations on this power.

Little wonder, then, having established such a scenario, and given the constitutional power of the centre over local authorities, that Fiske's interpretation of a re-negotiated 1944 settlement was a national system. He drew a historic analogy with gas, electricity and water supply, in each case beginning as local undertakings but under pressure for uniformity of provision and improvements in quality being nationalised: up to the 1970s (even when he wrote in 1980) the preferred solution for governments. A solution made more likely for education, according to Fiske, by the demands of contraction – demographic and financial.

The analogy he did not pursue – and why should he as it was so low in the consciousness of those in the public sector? – was with larger, dispersed private sector organisations. There, better communications, facilitated by developments in IT, was sustaining major change, with the centre taking a strategic view, establishing the parameters within which the business functioned, but with individual managers, in the operating units, awarded greater freedom over day-to-day issues, though held fully accountable for performance.

Significantly, Fiske made no reference to the operating units: the schools – and governing bodies. He did, though, speculate as to why, in the absence of centrally held powers, the system appeared so uniform. His answer was teacher mobility – the total freedom, without any employer intervention, with which teachers could move from job to job. For secondary schools, the consistency of the examination system could also be added.

Yet was the system so uniform, not to Fiske perhaps, but to individual parents and children? There were conspicuous differences: the continued existence of grammar schools in some areas, transfer ages at 11, 12 and 13, sixth form colleges, nursery places available in one part of town but not in another. But it was the more subtle variations that were becoming more significant, building in the public consciousness: schools developing good reputations, other places best avoided by those families, albeit a minority, that had the wherewithal or the knowledge to exercise choice. Long before the publication of performance tables, ahead of the impact of effectiveness studies, a realisation was building that improvements in the quality of service had to come primarily through the schools. Any rewrite of 1944 had to be much more than some readjustment of the checks and balances between DES and local authorities.

In fact, contrary to Fiske's interpretation, financial retrenchment, far from making nationalisation more likely, had an inverse effect. Commercial organisations soon learned about exporting problems from the new strategic centre to the periphery. Naturally, it was argued that such arrangements made eminent sense: decisions could be made by those closest to the problem; straightforward, easily understood, transparent, accountability mechanisms could be established. At the same time, though, the centre had also introduced mechanisms for deflecting criticisms to the periphery, for ensuring that unpopular choices – decisions affecting scarce resources, for example – were seen to be the responsibility of local representatives.

The political attractions of such thinking appealed to a right wing administration intent on achieving value for money in public services. Hence, the twin-track approach of the 1988 legislation: the centralisation (of curriculum and testing) to control schools, to raise public confidence in what they were trying to do, to ensure that their activities were more consistent, and their outcomes could be compared through reliable measures of pupil performance, was accompanied by decentralisation (of powers to schools over finance, staffing and buildings) in an attempt better to align their increased accountability to their powers over day-to-day matters.

PRIVATISATION

Writing at the time of the legislation, Pring was concerned less about the detection of changes in the balance of power, more to gather evidence of privatisation. After describing a number of relatively small-scale examples, he distinguished between individuals paying for education services within the state system (as for individual music tuition) and the purchase at public expense of education services provided by the private sector, when (say) the whole of a music service was put out to tender.

Essentially, his main concerns were twofold: first, an anxiety about the government inspired culture of the 1980s and early 1990s (anti-union, anti-local authority, pro-private enterprise) that had not only made the legislative proposals practicable but also created a harder, competitive edge to many aspects of the service. In his view, shared by the vast majority of academic commentators, there was no place in the public sector for practices involving overt competition between schools or for headteachers and governors forced into decisions on staff redundancies. Indeed, such practices undermine the key values that shape the provision of a public service.

His second concern, intensified by the first, was pressure on public finances, sustained by the apparent unpopularity of higher taxes and the ineluctable upward rise of spending on other services, notably health, social services and pensions. Education, shorn of demographic growth (except in HE), unable to argue for extra spending to cover technological innovation (compared to the health service, for example) and, until 1997, lacking a powerful sponsor, continued to be squeezed. By contrast, expectations still grew. The route to the expanded HE, the new skills required for entry to, and success in, the labour market, the availability of school choice, the enhanced knowledge this generated about the merits of particular schools, served to heighten what parents, pupils and employers thought the system ought to be achieving.

One view, therefore, of the privatisations identified by Pring would be as a range of ameliorative measures to help bridge the gap between the state's capacity to supply and burgeoning private demand; particularly as the measures were on so small a scale, representing a tiny fraction of overall educational expenditure. There is, though, an alternative view, much less palatable to Pring, but more in line with government ideology at the time he was writing. This would characterise these developments as a first, significant step towards a substantial privatisation of the service; or, to develop Fiske's analogy, the route pursued with gas, electricity and water. And one interpretation could be used to support such a stance: deprive the public sector of resources; assist the search for private funding (as with the introduction of City Technology Colleges); help parents become more discriminating, ask them to behave like consumers, encourage them to regard education as a private good, thereby avoiding the need for increased taxation.

Of course, an affluent minority do take this a stage further and choose private education. For them, but only for them, this is real privatisation. The state could, to some extent, mirror such arrangements: licensed schools, charging fees, paid for by parents, with either schools or families subsidised by the state. But even in 1988 such ideas failed to surface as viable propositions.

State schools did, however, become significantly more autonomous. A minority elected to leave their LEAs for Grant Maintained status; all began to be funded on the basis of pupil numbers, and were given (via the governing body) real power over staffing and buildings; all were directed to control their own budgets as cost centres. In essence, they were asked to exhibit many of the characteristics of private businesses, not least to behave as independent entities, accountable for their performance to a range of stakeholders. But they were not privatised.

AUTONOMY AND EQUITY

Davies and Hentschke turned their attention to the consequences of the new independence for schools. In effect, a new system of checks and balances had been forced upon them. As such, it is pointless to speculate whether they would have chosen, of their own volition, the new relationships – with government agencies, with LEAs, with pupils and parents. The associations with pupils and parents might have changed least, yet even here schools still had to come to terms with the need to attract enough pupils to sustain funding; pushing them towards both the superficiality of glossy brochures and marketing campaigns and also, more significantly, better harmonisation between pupil and parental expectations and their satisfaction.

At the same time, increased autonomy was accompanied by major changes in the concept of accountability. For example, while a school is free to attract extra children and benefit from additional funding, it is also held responsible if numbers fall. Yet in this case, and in so many others, severe limitations are placed on the freedom. A significant role continues for the LEA, setting limits for pupil numbers, defining admissions policy, determining which schools stay open – establishing the funding levels. There is also crucial DfEE involvement: devising the curriculum, organising pupil testing, overseeing school inspections.

Schools find themselves implicated in a complex system of checks and balances. They have more independence but that has exposed their accountability; and for most teachers much of the new freedom is illusory. Few are associated with choices about finance or staffing or buildings. And even among those that are, the time when such decisions were made by a largely anonymous LEA have become a distant memory. More important, much of the autonomy becomes still more illusory, when so many choices a school might want to make are rendered unrealisable by resource shortages.

But it is the accountability for school performance that epitomises the new arrangements so starkly. In the old system, government and LEAs were understood to be responsible for how well the service was faring. It was assumed that all schools were making reasonable progress, offering most children a decent standard of education but with few procedures for checking the accuracy of either perception – certainly not in any systematic way. A management by exception principle obtained. Under-performing schools were sometimes, but not always, detected as a result of complaints, chance visits or random inspection. Arrangements to assure improvement or to establish rigorous monitoring procedures were rudimentary. There were no formal procedures for detecting, never mind correcting, poor quality teaching.

The new system, however, by granting schools more autonomy must accept also that independence will encourage difference; indeed it assumes that each school will make unique progress. The imposition of the National Curriculum does not obviate this tendency. Unquestionably, without it, schools would have become even more different. So a principal role of the curricular framework is not so much to erode independence but rather to provide a base for inter-school comparison, as demonstrated by the freeing of primary schools from statutory curricular demands, but only in those subjects not included in national performance tests.

Indeed, it is the performance tables of pupil achievement and the outcomes of OFSTED inspections (and the emphasis placed upon them by government, parents and the media) which confirm each school as an independent entity. It is in this context that both the school as an institution, and individual teachers, feel most exposed. They are concerned about the methodologies employed to collect the data, about the mechanisms by which the data is interpreted and publicised and, more generally, their lack of control over the whole process, whether it be the backgrounds of their pupils or the lack of a clear technology linking specific teaching approaches to intended learning outcomes. As for the commercial model, problems have been exported to them but without the commensurate authority or means to deal with them adequately.

For the other partners in the changed relationships, the centrality of performance to school autonomy also raises critical questions. For the centre: are its measures of performance reliable, are they valid; by making them so important are other fundamentals – creativity, social skills – which cannot be assessed so readily being driven out? For LEAs: how do they promote performance in unique enterprises; do they know enough about the characteristics of every school to feel confident when identifying which are under-performing (and why), and the most appropriate means towards improvement? Indeed in many respects, they find themselves in a similar position to central government (as Fiske described in 1980): expected to raise overall performance and to ensure its consistency but denied most of the means for direct intervention.

In fact, with the revised arrangement for checks and balances, the same dilemma faces both central and local authorities. Simkins highlights the issue that granting schools more freedom encourages them to be different and to become more unequal. However, unlike the organisations from which the model was developed – the dispersed commercial organisation – inter-school equity constitutes a major issue. In a firm, an under-performing unit is liable to be closed; conversely, only the best performers receive investment. An LEA, even if it wished, is denied such tactics. There exists an obligation to the taxpayer: that every school is providing value for money. There is also an issue of supply. LEAs must ensure there are available sufficient school places reasonably close to where children live, with enough spare to facilitate parental choice. As a result, even if a school is closed for poor performance, there is often no alternative other than to open a new school in the same premises, employing many of the previous staff. Effectively all that has happened is to suspend the school's autonomy for a brief period.

So on logistical grounds, or to satisfy the democratic processes of lobbying (by councillors, governors, parents), a minimum level of fairness in the relative treatment of schools is essential. Simkins takes the issue further to consider what constitutes equity. There is a financial dimension: is equity guaranteed by the same expenditure per pupil? If so, what about those with special needs, or schools with high numbers of children from deprived localities? Or should the criterion relate more broadly to the quality of education? But how can this be satisfactorily, and objectively, assessed? And how can the range of quality offered even to a single cohort of children in one school be understood?

Probably the best that can be achieved is a rough approximation to an equity of financial input. But this, in itself, produces major problems. The piecemeal development of funding mechanisms has ensured gross disparities. How much is spent on a child's education is heavily dependent on where the child lives. Without exception, every child receives more during secondary schooling than primary (without a defensible explanation) while a host of apparently irreconcilable issues surround the funding of particular needs. In addition, any agreement to eradicate the grossest disparities would take years to implement without forcing some schools into closure while providing others with an excess of resources.

Achieving an equity of provision, ensuring that schools are offering a similar quality of education, is made even less likely by school freedom. The old system did no more than disguise the fact. The new arrangements give further opportunities for schools to become unequal. All that a strict inspection regime and published performance tables can hope to achieve is to smooth anomalies, particularly by identifying the worst performers but not, as an archetypal bureaucracy might have done, by holding back the best.

Tension between the equity and effectiveness functions remains inevitable. Over its first twenty-five years, the journal has chronicled the emergence of the school as an autonomous, highly significant partner with government and LEAs, particularly in the pursuit of improved performance. That pursuit stands to become still more important as the links between schooling and success in the labour market develop still further. The independence of the school appears confirmed as the main route to improved effectiveness. The role of the other partners over the next twenty-five years will depend heavily upon how much importance is attached to inter-school equity.

Governing Schools: Has the Taylor Report Got the Balance Right?

ALAN BARNES AND STEPHEN HUMBLE

1. ALAN BARNES

The 89 recommendations of the Taylor Committee seem to rest upon three principles, two conservative and one innovatory, which should be warmly welcomed. First, the committee have declared themselves firmly in favour of each school having a board of governors to which its local authority should delegate significant powers: only such a body can ensure the degree of institutional autonomy necessary in the English tradition for the protection of professional freedom, the encouragement of innovation and the preservation of a variety which has been a source of strength in our schools too valuable to be foregone in order that a child may move from Penrith to Plymouth without changing his textbooks. It would have been easy in the present climate to suggest in panic the elimination of an impediment to detailed direction and control by politicians or officials local or central.

Secondly the committee recognise that the success of schools depends heavily upon the leadership provided by their heads, whom they clearly intend should be left free, in their exercise of day-to-day managerial responsibility, from unreasonable interference whether by lay governors or by Weaver-style academic boards. The report stresses that governors should not mistake themselves for inspectors and resists the temptation, stronger no doubt in 1977 than now, to saddle schools with an elaborate, cumbersome and potentially divisive staff committee armed with legally protected powers to make professional decisions which only the governing body could veto, though limits have properly been set to the authority of heads both by the wide-ranging powers suggested for governors and by the particular duty which it is suggested should be laid upon them to satisfy themselves that satisfactory consultative procedures operate.

Thirdly, the committee support the representation on governing bodies of parents and teachers. This, of course, is an innovation except in so far as the recommendation has in a number of areas been anticipated in recent years, partly because its desirability was so generally agreed.

Despite these sound foundations, however, the committee's proposals seem to lack realism or judgement in some important respects. It does not seem likely that the controlling parties in the local authorities will be willing both to allow governing bodies significant powers and to rest content with a power to nominate only 25 per cent of members. That parents and teachers should be represented is clearly right: the proposals as to scale may be inept.

The reasons advanced for requiring headteachers to be governors of their schools are unconvincing. Many heads, as the report recognises, will be reluctant governors: they need a right to attend and to be heard but the power to cast a vote will be inadequate compensation if it imperils their standing as the principal professional advisers to their masters. Moreover, there is little logic in making heads members of bodies to which they should in the first instance be accountable.

With regard to the powers of governors, the committee's suggestions represent no very dramatic change from the 1945 model articles. The Auld report on Tyndale and the current desire of the DES to reduce schools' autonomy have had some effect and it is suggested that governors should operate within a framework provided by national and LEA policies, though the report offers little indication of what this might mean in practice. There is no explicit recognition of the fact that at present many LEAs can scarcely be said to have any curricular policies beyond the views of individual advisers but the need for many authorities to strengthen their teams of general advisers is recognised.

In the peripheral but important matter of dealing with disruptive pupils, the report suggests that the powers of governors vis-à-vis the LEA should be restricted. Rightly concerned that pupils should not, having been suspended from school, be left to languish indefinitely beyond the educational pale the committee propose that the right of expulsion and the duty of hearing appeals should be reserved to the LEA and that heads' powers of suspension should be limited to three days. Certainly, there are matters here which need sorting out but on this issue as on others, the committee's report mixes the sensible with the vague and impracticable. A high level committee should not after two years' deliberations produce anything as woolly as (in 9.10): 'We have heard of instances in which this power appears to have been used ...' and one wonders whence came the figure of 3 for the number of days for which a head might suspend. It is hard to see any sense whatever in a limit which might be reached before the head could see the parents or talk to his chairman and would certainly not allow for the calling of a governors' meeting. The most debated parts of the report are likely to be those dealing with the division of powers between the governors and the head and staff, especially with regard to the curriculum. The committee's proposals in this area have already incurred the predictable displeasure of the NUT. Many professionals, however, would accept that the curriculum cannot be divorced from organisation and management and that ultimate authority should lie with governors, partly because they see a need for firm action in an extreme Tyndale-like situation and partly because they recognise that they must be responsible to someone and would prefer a body committed to the school to an individual or committee which thought first of the LEA.

Unfortunately, the influence of those who take this view is likely to be reduced by the failure of the report to distinguish clearly between the ultimate (within the school) authority of the governors and their normal *modus operandi* and by its suggestions that governors should play a more active and positive part in policy formulation and decision-making than realists will think at all likely. The prospect of the committee's proposals being willingly accepted by the profession would have been much enhanced if there had been a recognition that the normal role of lay governors must be responsive rather than creative. In the future as in the past, lay governors will surely be reactionary, not in the sense of being hostile to new methods and illiberal about discipline (though they often may be) but in that they will react to proposals coming from the professionals and to particular situations and problems as they arise.

Over a period, they can in this way exercise piecemeal a considerable influence on the ethos and general policy of the school in an atmosphere of consensus, inducing in the professional a greater responsiveness to public opinions and needs in ways analogous to those by which a historian head influences a competent and respected head of physics. There are passages in the report which suggest that something of this sort is what the committee has in mind but others which convey a different impression. In particular, the stress laid upon the part of governors in defining a school's aims seems badly misplaced: broad planning *ab initio* is precisely what laymen can least be expected to do well. They can usefully tell teachers that they do not prepare pupils for job interviews but, asked to decide how best to prepare them for work, they are likely to produce at best laborious statements of the obvious and, at worst, a confusion between the desirable and the possible leading to frustration and disillusion.

2. STEPHEN HUMBLE

The Taylor Report is an immensely important document. Its central concern is who shall have power and responsibility over our children's learning in schools. Any report on that subject ought to be welcome and for my part I give a qualified welcome to Taylor's recommendations. But though Taylor takes an important fresh look at the subject it is worthwhile considering that Taylor is only one of several perspectives that are now being brought to bear upon the debate on the education system in this country.

Taylor is grounded in the Department of Education and Science. This is not to say that it toes the DES line but its focus is on the school – school government and school curriculum and the accountability of schools. The important feature of the composition of the committee is not its heterogeneity (teachers, parents, local government officers and members) but its overriding homogeneity: they are all educationists. Its considerations are essentially of school activity and of school and local education authority activity, and not of school and LEA in relation to the rest of the local authority. The local authority is part of the changing environment that is now pressing in on the LEA. Taylor does not get to grips with the issue of the changing environment because its remit was a partial response to a problem seen in isolation. The DES finally acknowledged that there was something wrong with the government of our schools and its make-up and set up a committee to review just that. Thus Taylor could not help but provide what is essentially a mechanistic solution to the farce of present school government.

Taylor appears in the midst of a turbulent education world. Educationists, especially teachers and education officers, are seriously questioning whether education should be in or out of local government. The local authority is seen to be making undue claims on the LEA through corporate planning. Yet both local authority and LEA are themselves falling victim to a pressure far greater than a mere managerial innovation. A dramatic fall in birthrate and public expenditure coupled with the admission that both can hardly be planned for from one year to the next, have meant that the ground has been swept from under everyone's feet. By way of practical illustration let me cite the example of one chief education officer who, short of money, described this week the agonising decisions he was involved in, in having to issue short-term contracts to teachers, redeploy them, redeploy pupils and close schools. I asked him how he would reconcile these ever more central and authoritative decisions with the decentralising tendencies of Taylor. Not surprisingly he replied that the local education authority is the authoritative voice and has to act as such. Taylor can expect short shrift from hard-pressed local education authorities.

Demographic and economic forces are not the only ones at work in this period of Taylor. Quite inside education, but related to these forces, there is upheaval in the school curriculum. Piecemeal innovation in this area has been gathering momentum for years. The setting up of the Schools Council in 1964, effectively under teachers' control, was intended as the answer to opening up the 'secret garden' of the curriculum without jeopardising teachers' autonomy. It has not worked to the satisfaction of Government and has been overtaken by the call in the Great Education Debate for a relevant curriculum and a return to standards.

Some sort of centrally co-ordinated core curriculum is almost bound to result. This, and the establishment of the DES Assessment of Performance Unit, accompanied by widespread testing (overtly of pupils, covertly of teachers), must be seen by teachers' unions to constrain the teacher's professional judgement in the classroom and (paradoxically) call him to account for the results of his action there. Coming on top of all this Taylor can expect short shrift from this quarter.

Taylor takes representation away from local authorities, which is not likely to please them. It gives representation to the teacher. But with its concessions to the parent and the community it drives a wedge into the relationship between him and his school and the LEA advisory service – which is not likely to please them.

There are tremendous entrenched interests opposing the implementation of

Taylor. Taylor moves in the direction of the parent and the community. It is the direct result of the rise of consumerism, including greater clamour for the accountability of the public services, and stronger parents' and neighbourhood movements. The greatest argument against Taylor is that it diminishes the control of democratically elected members. This is the argument contained in the Fulton Minority Report on Taylor. The Minority Report reflects the concern of our chief education officer quoted above, that in the face of the pressing demands of the present 'the centre' (though they are not very definite about what this means) needs more control, not less. In a letter on Taylor to *The Times* (23 September 1977) another chief education officer writes rather persuasively:

> Yes; much more parental involvement and head, teacher and officer accountability is needed, but it will be achieved by the growth of the systems of opening schools to parents and holding regular meetings for all parents and teachers on the things they all want to talk about, not by the setting up of many new committees restrictive in membership and confined mainly to non-elected and therefore non-accountable membership.

Yet this correspondent says nothing about how this growth is to be achieved. Taylor is a response to the long historical inability of the education system to achieve such growth. It suggests providing statutory backing so that all four quarters of its representative school governing body – including parents and representatives of the community – have an assured base from which to operate.

The counter argument is that legislation will not bring potential governors forward: Taylor's argument is that they will not begin to come forward and participate meaningfully without statutory backing. (I would myself like to have seen proposals specifically to increase the participation of low-income parents and ethnic minorities.) The Report covertly recognises that its proposals are not the solution to participation but a necessary springboard to it. One member of the committee, for example, wrote a book which was published simultaneously with the Report to plead for the implementation of the Report and proper follow-up (Sallis, 1977). Taylor sees a fundamental, statutory reordering of the composition of school governors as the only way out. Given the intransigence of local education authorities, what other way out is there?

Education – Going National?

DUDLEY FISKE

I want to take advantage of this occasion to reflect on the way in which we run the education system and to examine some of the things that have been happening to its administration and management. Some of the matters on which I shall comment are current and controversial but others have occurred over the years almost without anybody taking much notice. My purpose is to bring out ways in which power and influence have been moving significantly since 1944 from the local scene to the national stage. We now seem to have reached a most peculiar position where the local education authorities have the responsibility to their electorates for the condition of the education service in their areas but are effectively denied the powers necessary to deal with those responsibilities. If power without responsibility has rightly been branded as corrupt, what are we to make of its opposite – responsibility without power?

The conventional shorthand description of our system since 1944 has been that familiar phrase – 'a national system locally administered'. The Act of 1944 effectively brought to an end what was essentially a local system operating under national supervision, and the question for us now is whether the skilful balance of powers then introduced to replace it has outlived its usefulness. After thirty-five momentous years it would not be surprising if it had. I do indeed believe that within the next few years we shall need to re-examine the whole basis of the central/local government relationship so far as the running of the education system is concerned. I put it this way deliberately and without immediate reference to the wider local government scene where a similar appraisal may also be necessary but where of course many services are still on the model of local provision under very loose national supervision – the pre-1944 model as far as education is concerned. My priority tonight, however, is the needs of an education system and I can do no better than repeat the words of the evidence of the Society of Education Officers to the Layfield Committee in 1975 – 'We are local government men but not at any price' – one of those haunting comments that refuses to go away whether you are an educationist threatening divorce or a local government man seeking to attack the separatist stance of education

134

officers. It is not, however, my purpose tonight to argue that all or part of the education service should now be removed from local government to some other kind of government structure. I want to diagnose rather than prescribe.

The theory behind our system is dispersal of powers, with a careful balance worked out on broad lines in 1944 and refined by thirty-five years of experience that seeks to protect rights. The rights of central and local government in their dealings with one another, of local government in its management of institutions and in turn of those institutions and within these of such different interests as Headmaster, staff and parents. The reality now surely is that such a balance is failing the acid test of accountability – who precisely is responsible for what. It has become so confused that often that seems to be a question we cannot answer. Hence, for example, the current debate about the school curriculum which is much confused by uncertainty on this point. Local government has apparently the formal responsibility but central government is determined to be in on the action.

As far as a local education authority is concerned it is essential to remember those important elements of the education system for which it has no direct responsibility.

Even worse in some ways is the impression over the years that local government is something that one outgrows with time and maturity. Thus we have created ad hoc authorities for such services as gas, electricity and water that began as municipal enterprises but were eventually organised on a specialised and national scale, with subordinate regions or areas that are separate both geographically and administratively from the local authority network. We have had the Health Service separated since 1974 though here the critical factor has always been said to be the pressure of the medical profession. Within education we had the decision in the 1960s to create the colleges of advanced technology as fully-fledged universities. This indeed was a breakaway from local government that clearly arose from a belief that something can become too big, too important or even too expensive for local government to handle. The campaign of those who seek to take polytechnics down the same road is of course based on precisely the same argument.

We live in a small country and one that is exceptionally London-dominated so it can come as no real surprise that the steady increase in public interest in the education system should have focus that is increasingly national. Despite all the efforts made to promote regional awareness and all the money invested in local radio the fact remains that the national aspects of the education system are repeatedly emphasised and the local administration aspect is played down save perhaps when blame is to be apportioned.

Moreover our population has become more mobile, partly from choice and partly from necessity, and as families move about the country usually at a time when the children are of school age the nature of the education that is provided is a crucial factor to them. They will expect a great deal of uniformity. In what is a largely urban society the significance of a local authority boundary line that may appear to have absolutely no geographical logic is baffling and adds to a sense of frustration with local authorities that are not always prepared to be flexible.

My point here then is that there is a wide and widening gap between the balance of powers as laid down in the statutes which on the whole still favour the local authority and the public perception of where power really now should lie. When the law and the regulations are so out of line with what is perceived to be the position it may be time to look again at the statutory position.

The rise in influence and activities of the teacher unions and professional associations is another factor in shifting the focus to the national stage. While recognising that internally they often have their own problems in reconciling the rights of local branches with national policies the total impact of their efforts is to reduce the amount of discretion that remains at local level. Let me say at once that I do not believe that the answer here is a return to some kind of locally negotiated salary scales as has apparently been floated recently in some places. The effect, however, of the annual Burnham round, of the current difficult, protracted but crucial tails on better defined national conditions of service for teachers, of campaigns on such issues as class sizes and class contact hours is obvious. The local authority as an individual employer is left with very little discretion indeed and often may not even attempt to negotiate some local variation outside very clearly defined agreements. If we add to this that in the area of teacher training the role of the local authority has broadly in recent years been little more than that of agent for the contraction determined on by central government, that the Burnham scales prescribe the salary of each individual in much greater detail than in the rest of local government.

To the unions as the most obvious and important example of those whose work has an increasingly national focus must be added a host of other pressure groups that have emerged in the past quarter of a century. Many are small in number and in resources but their total effect in challenging the right of a local authority to run its own affairs and where necessary in seeking to appeal to national level is considerable. These include the broad area of consumer interests represented by such bodies as the Advisory Centre for Education. Each organisation has a specific defined purpose but whether or not intentionally their combined effect is to emphasise the national system and to urge that within it the amount of room for local discretion should be restricted. Often in their own ways the Select Committees of the House of Commons and the other activities of Members of Parliament will, it seems to me, add support to this view. The fact that locally people might want and have something different, even something less, is a cause of public criticism in national media and even of appeals for national level of intervention. Nor are national politicians reluctant to get involved.

During the past five years we have seen the emphasis in education switch from expansion to contraction. Inevitably this means that a system with plenty of initiatives pressing in from the edges onto the centre is largely replaced by one where the centre tends to set the pace. Intervention of all kinds has become the order of the day and there is a steady flow of unwelcome and sometimes irreconcilable messages coming from the centre to the local authorities and on to the schools and colleges. A contraction in terms of numbers to be educated might reasonably be catered for. One that is accompanied by reductions in resources that aim at contraction in the ratio of expenditure per head is much harder to handle. Thus though there are attempts to move power in the other direction, most notably the Taylor Report's prescription for new and more effective governing bodies, it seems most unlikely that anything meaningful can or will in practice be given as powers to these bodies. Indeed the Education Act 1980 is deliberately and significantly silent on the matter of powers. The appearance of decentralised control is to be of greater significance than any attempt to make it meaningful.

Now through the Local Government Planning Act we are to have a significant increase in the powers of central government in matters financial. Much has been made elsewhere that this will mark the end of local government as we know it, with local authorities becoming little more than local agencies of Whitehall. The right of central government to determine the total amount of grant that is given is not at issue but significantly local authorities are now to be prevented from seeking to balance their local books by bridging the gap with a rate locally determined.

Not that local government can complain too loudly. At the recent AMA conference the paper given by Professor Foster very clearly brought out the extent to which the finances of local government have changed. He showed that the proportion of expenditure met from the domestic rate payments has fallen steadily throughout the century to the point now where it accounts for no more than 10 per cent of the total. The balance is made up by some 60 per cent from the Rate Support Grant and 30 per cent from the rate paid by commerce and industry. The significance of these figures is very great for when only 10 per cent of your budget comes from the rates paid by the householder it is not easy to justify the claim that local authorities are truly accountable to their local electorate. In no sense can we now talk of independent local authorities even today when in theory at least they have the right to levy a rate of whatever size they judge appropriate to balance their books. Moreover the response of those who claim that their rates were put up and few electoral reactions were met needs to be treated with some caution for my impression is that those who pay 75 per cent of that raised locally (namely the commercial property owners) have indeed made some very determined noises of protest in recent years. In short, the basis of income now for local authorities is such that as Professor Foster suggested there are grave doubts about its moral authority in dealings with Whitehall.

I have deliberately spent most of my time on this analysis of some of the relevant factors because I wanted to bring out the extent to which there are already forces at work that tie the hands of individual local education authorities. Some are, as we have seen, the positive actions of government. Others arise more subtly from less easily identified forces such as the work of pressure groups or the activities of press and television. Taken together, however, they represent formidable pressure in a national direction.

If I am right that we need to review the balance of powers and attempt to clarify responsibility so that each level is clearer about what it is doing, in which direction might we seek to move? You may be surprised to know that very tentatively I am beginning to think that power at the centre may well need to be positively strengthened and that local education authorities should not approach such a review of functions in a wholly defensive mood. Creeping centralisation of the kind that we have been experiencing in recent years seems to me a great deal less desirable than an open and proper study of what is now needed for the running of the service in the last twenty years of the century and beyond.

All of which brings me to the Department of Education and Science and the suggestion that in some respects it needs more not less powers. The theory is still that clearly enunciated by Edward Boyle in 'The Politics of Education' of partnership. But at one point after defending that arrangement he added: 'I would like to keep this concept of partnership going quite a bit longer'. My question therefore is how long is 'quite a bit' − because ten years after he recorded that view the time may be approaching for a redefinition of powers.

It happens that the latest issue of the BEMAS journal has a long and interesting article by David Howell based on the book published last year by Sir William Pile, a former Permanent Secretary, about the Department of Education and Science. Howell rightly in my view says that there is a good deal more to be said in favour of the Department and its activities than one might glean at first sight from, say, a reading of the weekly educational press. My complaint is not that the Department is too interventionist or too active but rather that it often seems to have the emphasis wrong − much concern, for example, about the minor details of building projects or articles of government or individual cases, but little or no clear guidance on major issues. It may be that the other interests on the educational scene, and in particular the local authority and teachers' associations, frighten off those in the Department who are minded to take initiatives. On the whole, however, my view is that we could often do with a clearer and firmer lead than we get. Moreover all the forces that I have been examining should tend to make that task easier to those minded so to act.

If that is a possible development there are, however, (two) particular aspects with which I should like to deal briefly. The first concerns the legal and financial powers of the Department. Should these be positively strengthened? The answer really depends on one's interpretation of section 1 of the 1944 Act which specifically gives the Secretary of State the duty to control and direct the execution by local authorities of national policy. If you believe that this is a very wide reaching provision that does equip the Department with a formidable array of powers, albeit so far little used in practice, then you may conclude that no further legislation is needed. If on the other hand you prefer a milder interpretation based on the custom and practice of thirty-five years of minimal rattling of the sabres, then it could be that some deliberate increase in statutory powers is needed. One of the difficulties, and it is at once a strength and a weakness, is that there has over the years been a tendency to wait for consensus to emerge before taking action. While that was fine in an age of broad consensus, I am not sure that it will serve us now and in the future when agreement is much harder to find. There are now issues where broad agreement is probably never going to emerge but where nevertheless some kind of decisions are needed. On balance I incline to think that it is more a matter of nerve and willingness to lead than lack of adequate legal weapons, but I could be wrong.

The second aspect is openness of government and of the processes that lead to the making of a decision. Here the comments of the 1975 Select Committee of the House of Commons are relevant still. They, you may recall, said that the Department tended to consult 'too late, on too narrow a base and with too closed a mind'. The point surely is that little or nothing of the business that is handled by the Department of Education and Science needs to be regarded as in any way secret. There is indeed much to be gained and little to be lost by a much more open attitude and the contrast to the day-to-day work of a local authority really is very striking. It is normal for the reports of a chief education officer to an education committee to be public documents, for meetings often now including those of sub-committees to take place in public and for officers to go through a series of public meetings in which any questions can be asked. It really should not be impossible as part of a move towards more active national leadership to include more openness in the procedures of government of the education service.

Privatisation

RICHARD PRING

INTRODUCTION

Twenty years ago, the issue of privatising education was not seriously being addressed. It would have seemed nonsensical, so firmly embedded in our commonsense understanding of the social world was the idea of a free and public education service that met the educational needs of all youngsters – eventually up to the age of 16 – according (in the words of the 1944 Education Act) to their age, ability and aptitude. Of course there were private schools, but in no way were they seen as a threat to the expanding public sector. And, indeed, such was the feeling of confidence in the future of the public sector, that (with few exceptions) the private sector could be expected to wither away – there being no point in paying for what was freely available.

This confidence in the public sector was felt as firmly by those responsible for running the system (including civil servants and political leaders of both parties) as it was by the general public. It was an era of expansion, of hope, of confidence in the public sector. Such confidence, however, was gradually eroded and certainly did not survive the 1970s – not only in Britain but in America and elsewhere. Schools, it was claimed, did not really make a difference, and access to higher education of working class children (just one significant statistic) seemed to bear that out.

Nonetheless, it is only very recently that there has emerged the more radical solution to the problems as they are perceived, namely subjecting the system to the same kind of market pressures as any commercial commodity would be subjected to. Quality requires choice, and choice requires private enterprise.

I was alerted to these possible changes six years ago whilst attending a meeting in London of RICE – the Right to Comprehensive Education. At that meeting a very distinguished Chief Education Officer forecast the privatisation of education. He argued that such a view was deeply entrenched within Treasury thinking and that shortly we would see, under various guises, the gradual transformation of a public sector into a private one. This, only six years ago, was greeted by disbelief. Key words here are 'under various guises', because, in attending to the privatisation of education, either to measure the extent to

140

which it has taken place or to examine critically the ideas that underpin it, we must not be limited to any one model. We may not be talking simply about the transfer of public sector institutions to the private sector, something that is easily measurable. Nor may we be debating simply the educational merits of public and private schools. Indeed, following that meeting, I was given the task by RICE of 'mapping the territory', trying to establish a suitable framework within which privatisation might be understood and examined. Privatisation takes place on many fronts and in many different ways, and the ideas that underpin it are equally complex. What is certain is that the old, simple and clear distinctions between public and private no longer hold. There has been a conceptual shift which reflects new economic and social perspectives and it is these which need to be explored before a clear empirical account can be given of what is happening, or a critique of these developments be mounted.

LOCAL OR COMMUNITY RESPONSIBILITY

There has always been, and there always will be, some tension between, on the one hand, national and regional attempts to ensure fair distribution of resources and equality of opportunity, and, on the other, responsiveness to local demand as schools link more closely with the communities they serve. And this tension can only increase as the demand for education from a more highly educated public does itself increase. For are there no limits to what one can expect from the public purse in meeting unlimited demands? And if there are such limits, should the community itself be prevented from making its own contributions to what could be an inexorable demand? What sense can be given to community involvement and to community responsiveness, unless the community itself can in some way affect the direction of the school, shape its curriculum, and make up for whatever is lacking in the resources required to meet its own particular if not idiosyncratic demands? The rural comprehensive school, for example, with the help of local farmers, finds the resources for more practically based prevocational courses in agriculture that otherwise would be denied to the new CPVE intake. It has been pointed out to me that the head of a rural comprehensive school of 1200 pupils will have roughly 800 parents with a disposable income of about £2 million, that is, an income where there is genuine choice to be exercised between such things as holidays, extra clothes, hobbies, leisure activities – and education. Might not (should not) the schools I have been talking about (cost centres with responsibility for their own marketing, budgeting, and financial arrangements) start off from a base-line identified in the public budget as necessary for proper opportunities for all, irrespective of class or religion, and then put to those parents the various options they have, and thus hope to secure increased benefits for its pupils? Is this privatisation? Clearly not in the sense of there being private schools. But the schools are in receipt of private funds, which affect the quality of education and they would certainly be talking the language normally reserved for the private sector – a blurring of concepts and thus a blurring of boundaries.

Let us take one step further. One school in Avon (and many others are following suit) enhances its capitation by asking parents to covenant so much per year. Through the covenant schemes, it receives about £13,000 per year. An enhanced curriculum certainly. Community involvement certainly. But privatisation? Private means were not a necessary *condition* for there being public education at this school, and as far as I know pressure was not put on parents to dip into their private pockets. But certainly the curriculum, as it was enriched, depended on private means.

Or, again, links with the community can mean an enrichment through sponsorship. One town in the South West is dominated by one firm and its factories, local houses have been built by the firm, the town's bypass has been partly financed by it and some teachers' salaries in the public sector are paid by it. The conditions for their so doing have been agreed with the LEA and the firm's contribution to staffing must be over and above what would be provided by the LEA – that is, in no way is the publicly funded provision affected. The context for this is as follows. The town is not the liveliest place to live. And yet, evidently, lively executives are required if the firm is to compete successfully in the manufacturing race. It is, I believe, a well-known fact that lively executives have gifted children. Hence, to attract them to this town, the firm needed to assure potential employees that the local schools have the number and the quality of teachers to meet the needs of their gifted offspring. The comprehensive schools, therefore, did receive private help, extra teachers in maths and languages, so that special tuition could be given to able children. Furthermore, feeder primary schools received extra help for the same purpose.

Privatisation? The curriculum of these schools is different, is enriched, as a result of private funding or sponsorship to meet the needs of a local employer. But it is still a public school. On the other hand, is it entirely? Are not the firm's extended family on the governing bodies of all the local schools, and may not the continued injection of private funds be conditional upon educational aims as they are evolved in the board rather than the staff room?

As I mentioned earlier, there must be some concern, amongst those responsible for forward planning, over the resource implications of meeting a rising demand for health and education services. Presumably a revolution in the ways that services are provided will require a reappraisal of the division between the private and the public responsibilities. We have seen this in the health service – the private contribution to prescription charges or to dental treatment or to spectacles. Why not therefore something similar in education? Guarantees might be forthcoming of a basic service to all, irrespective of financial or social status, but the *enrichment* of that service could come to depend on private funding. And indeed parents could be expected to contribute to that enrichment according to their financial means. And the dilemma of those who resent this encroachment upon a fully funded public sector is that, if one fails to support and to liberalise such encroachments (with a clear distinction between basic education and its enrichment), one might actually dig deeper the public/private divide as it has been traditionally understood. In Exeter (perhaps not typical) over 15 per cent of the secondary age group go to private schools, making one maintained school vulnerable to closure and certainly (as teachers are withdrawn in line with falling numbers) impoverishing curriculum provision. Half the outgoing population of one local primary school is going on to private education. One regional tertiary college has an active music department, populated, however, almost exclusively by the products of the pre-16 private system – it would have to close if it were dependent on pupils from the secondary maintained sector so poor is music provision there. How long can one complain about inadequate resourcing, and not indeed subscribe to private financing (in one way or another) of the public sector – if that sector is to remain a viable alternative to the private one for those who are demanding even higher standards of provision?

The national conditions – viz. less money available to meet an ever increasing demand for services – that generate this soliciting of private support can, of course, have a more ideological force than the pragmatic one of taking the collection box to a wider audience. There is, for example, the belief that a service is appreciated more when it is clearly related to private means expended upon it. At times this is given a certain moral force as when Mark Carlisle (1982), shortly after relinquishing office as Secretary of State for Education, spoke at the prize giving of an independent school:

> I am old fashioned enough to believe that not only is it one's own responsibility rather than that of the state to provide for one's own family, but that, if one is fortunate enough to do so, it is one's right and duty.

But, more sinisterly, the motive could be that only a certain number of children ought to receive the level of education that more and more aspire to and that requires the increased funding. Stewart Ranson's (1984) research revealed ambivalent attitudes amongst higher civil servants over meeting the aspirations of those who pursued higher standards of education. Contrary to popular myth, so it was stated, education has been too successful – we can cope with the Toxteths and the Brixtons, but we may not be able to manage future unrest. Once again we must teach young people to know their place.

DISTINCTIONS

I have given several examples of what could be classified as privatisation but towards which I am, for practical reasons, feeling increasingly ambivalent. I feel that, in adopting too dogmatic a stance against all forms of privatisation, I may be reinforcing a divide between public and private that can, under present circumstances, only reinforce the advantages of the private, thereby exacerbating the impoverishment and thus the disillusionment within the public sector. I don't feel (reluctantly and sadly) that I can be so exhaustively condemning of privatisation in all its forms as I was when I wrote the paper for RICE in 1983 (Pring 1983).

To develop this point, however, I need to repeat the distinctions which I made there. The chief distinction was between (a) privatisation in the sense of purchasing at *private* expense educational services within the *public system* and (b) privatisation in the sense of purchasing at *public* expense educational services from private means to enhance the public sector. And I have tried to show, as charitably as I can, reasons why the former should not be condemned outright – namely, that this may be the only way in which one can ensure the kind of curriculum enrichment that a more sophisticated and educated public wants from the public sector at a time when less public resources are available. Such a charitable acceptance of some privatisation in *that* sense would, of course, have to be conditional upon a range of safeguards – against the proportional removal of public resources, against the pressure upon parents to make contributions from their private purse for basic education, against the reduction of publicly funded education to a minimum safety net level, against the restriction of access at any one school, against undue influence over the curriculum by private contributors and against the promotion of commercial products in return for favours given. All that will be difficult, but not impossible. I have also, in talking about the former (namely using private means to enhance the public sector) drawn attention to the shifting conceptual framework within which we are increasingly asked (or forced) to consider the merits or otherwise of privatisation in this sense. In particular I referred to the way in which a whole network of concepts (previously confined to the private business world) enter into our descriptions of the public sector – selling one's product, getting the best buy on limited funds, becoming a cost centre, responding to market forces, meeting demands, and delivering quality goods. I don't think we have realised how pervasive this way of thinking has already gone. No longer does it appear so odd or so contrary to the ideals of a public education.

I have made the distinctions between (a) privatisation in the sense of purchasing at *private* expense educational services within the *public sector* and (b) privatisation in the sense of purchasing at *public expense* educational services in private institutions. In the latter case the Government or the local authority is promoting the private at the expense of the public sector – it is a shifting of resources, an alteration of the overall structure of education, a policy development that cannot be defended as an enrichment of the curriculum. On the surface, it is part defended in terms of securing the educational welfare of the gifted – enabling able youngsters from impoverished homes to benefit from the qualitatively superior education of the private sector. Or again it is one element in the provision of choice – enabling those of modest means to exercise choice between schools, thereby putting those schools (on each side of the private public divide) under pressure to improve the quality of education – a direct relation is assumed between quality and choice.

Therefore, these two different senses of privatisation are related. The dominant image is of the market, the need to create therefore competitive market conditions, the idea of schools as entrepreneurial cost centres relating cost to quality. Putting money (under certain conditions as in the case of the Assisted Places Scheme) into private schools helps create those conditions – or so we are led to understand.

There are other ways – significant in financial and social terms – in which private education is supported out of public funds: the payment of fees of Government personnel (children of parents within the diplomatic corps or within the armed forces, for example); contributions of LEAs to fees in private schools of children with special needs; tax allowances on covenanted fees or on trust funds that support the private sector. But the Assisted Places Scheme and the proposed voucher do more than any other to reveal the deeper ideological base for privatising the educational system. In the first place, there is a moral purpose. It is seen to be morally preferable to shift the responsibility for learning from the state (or teachers employed by the local authority) to parents. There is a stress upon individual responsibility which (so we are told) has been undermined by too much reliance upon a welfare state. The virtue of self-help is once again proclaimed. In the second place there is the close link presumed between choice and quality, and thus the need to create appropriate market conditions for proper choice to be made. This idea of consumer power as a route to improved quality of life does, of course, go beyond education to health, to energy, to every aspect of our public life. But the assumptions behind it are, to say the least, questionable.

First, our society is more than an aggregate of individuals. The power, rights and authority that individuals have are derived in large part from the social context in which they find themselves; the complex network of institutions, law and persons bestows those rights upon individuals as well as providing the intellectual and cultural nourishment that enable them to grow as individuals. The individualising of choice leaves out of account those wider social responsibilities, that promotion of social cohesiveness which the educational system is in part seeking to promote.

Secondly such educational changes embody a very undeveloped sense of choice because educational facilities are not the kinds of things that can spring up or die in accordance with mercurial popular demand. And mobile classrooms are not the solution. Quality schools grow bit by bit: they depend upon a team of staff that, often against the odds, builds up its curriculum and its relationships unrecognised maybe by its media. And it can be destroyed by inaccurate or misleading media coverage. Some people will have the insight and access to make wise and well-informed choices. But the majority will not, thereby losing out on what could easily become a surreptitious form of selection – certainly a form of reinforcing advantage amongst those already advantaged.

POLITICAL AND SOCIAL BACKGROUND

The privatisation of education in its various forms is taking place against a background of increasing criticism of the achievements of the public sector.

Many of these criticisms are ill-informed. Nonetheless, there is a disillusionment and little is left of that optimism of the 1960s. Privatisation therefore is to be understood as a part solution to the problems as the critics identify them. It will, in one of its two senses, mean increased resources for a system that, dependent entirely on public funds, will never meet the increasing demands upon it. Or, tied to public institutions, schools will, in the view of many people of influence, never be as responsive as they should be to community or parental interests.

On the other hand, privatisation in the second sense incorporates a more radical social philosophy – one which sees the idea of market forces to be the key to educational improvement, and in which virtue is identified with freedom from public provision. To sort out where one stands in relation to privatisation requires a clear distinction between the two senses. Pragmatically, I can see good reasons for supporting limited privatisation in the first sense. Indeed, unless one does so there is a danger of exposing the public sector to yet further impoverishment with the consequent flight to the private sector of those with resources to do so. But privatisation must be hedged around with the conditions referred to so that public responsibility for an essential public service is not undermined.

The second sense of privatisation, however, is a different matter. The inappropriateness of the market metaphor needs to be exposed. It is a dangerously misleading analogy for understanding educational processes and for directing educational policies. *All* children matter, not just those whose parents have learnt to play the market effectively. And the improvement of schools requires long-term planning – not the quick alteration of a commodity to meet changing fashions. Furthermore, the stress upon individualism – upon individual preference – at the expense of social responsibility and cohesiveness must be a matter of concern as we become ever more closely interdependent rather than less so. A complex society such as ours needs an educational vision and a policy to match – which in turn requires accountable rather than independent and private institutions to deliver essential public services. And there is the rub – and possibly the greatest weakness in the plans to privatise in the second sense. For it will not be long before those in receipt of public money will be asked to take on board public responsibility – to make their contribution to the educational needs of all as they have been determined by those who provide the financial support. An independent school that has 50 per cent of its pupils on the Assisted Places Scheme cannot remain independent much longer.

School Autonomy: Myth or Reality – Developing an Analytical Taxonomy

BRENT DAVIES AND GUILBERT C. HENTSCHKE

INTRODUCTION

Developments in school autonomy have received enthusiastic promotion and support. But has anything significantly changed in the performance of schools? Early research has focused on describing what has happened, identifying perceived initial managerial improvements and hoped for future benefits. In England and Wales HMI reports on LMS and GMS schools fail to identify, at the early stages of these reforms, specific improvements in teaching and learning directly attributable to delegated school management. Very little research has tried to identify the fundamental shifts (or lack of them) in decision-making in schools that could lead to significant improvements in school performance.

This paper seeks to provide a framework to examine whether any fundamental changes in decision-making have taken place. It puts forward the view that a clearer understanding of the nature of managerial decisions in general, and decision-making in autonomous organisations in particular, is necessary before an analysis of decentralised schooling is undertaken. To do this the paper establishes a taxonomy of managerial decisions to provide the necessary theoretical framework.

THE MOVE TO SCHOOL AUTONOMY

Throughout many parts of the world governments and educators are promoting the benefits of significantly increased autonomy for those who work in local schools. These arguments for increased autonomy in schools are echoes and modifications of similar arguments directed at all but the very smallest organisations in society. Get the decisions about how to run the firm down to the people who know best what needs to be done. Current arguments about changes in school governance and management all aim in this one direction, although they travel under a variety of names: 'local management of schools', 'school-based management', 'shared decision-making', 'self-managing schools', 'self-determining schools', 'locally autonomous schools', 'devolution' and 'restructured schools'. Regardless of the specific label applied, the terms are meant to describe a school in a 'system of education where there has been significant and consistent decentralisation to the school level of authority to make decisions related to the allocation of resources' (Caldwell and Spinks, 1992, p. 4).

The justifications for this move are several and persuasive in their logic, at least if the premises are accepted. The political justification for decentralisation – the argument that the closer government is to 'the people' the more likely it is to be responsive to their demands and interests – assumes the worthiness of people getting what they want for themselves from government. The economic arguments for decentralisation – that decentralised units foster necessary competition in sheltered monopolies and are more likely to produce offerings in line with the preferences ('needs' and 'desires') of local, more homogeneous, groups of consumers/citizens – add efficiency and effectiveness to the other worthy goal of public sector responsiveness. Thomas (1987, pp. 224–234) makes the point that decentralised unit managers are better able to make choices to maximise efficiency because:

> The unit managers are (i) closer to the clients and (ii) better able than more remotely sited managers to identify the needs of the clients. In addition unit managers (iii) will give primacy to satisfying these needs; and (iv) will also know the best, i.e. most efficient, way of combining available resources to meet as many of these needs as possible. Finally, in making decisions on resource combinations the unit managers will vary the proportion of resources as (v) production requirements and (vi) relative prices change.

These propositions about the improvements of increased school autonomy are part of similar propositions about the benefits of decentralisation in all organisations. These, again, include the benefits of increased flexibility in response to changing circumstances, enhanced effectiveness, greater rates of innovation, higher morale, greater worker commitment, and greater productivity. Such arguments tend to exist without qualification, without a sense of the inherent limits of the concept (if any), and without formal enumeration of any 'down side' or 'dark side' features.

Although the intensity and variety of arguments for decentralisation in general, as well as the scope of associated legislative activity over the last half dozen years, is impressive and compelling, it does not seem to follow automatically (to us at least) that these arguments point to an effective degree of decentralisation that provides sufficient autonomy in decision-making that could significantly affect the input/output equation of educational productivity and lead to an enhancement of the teaching and learning process.

We have researched the experiences of two countries, the United States and England (in general terms, both are heading toward increased autonomy for schools but are doing so in ways which appear to be fundamentally different) in order to assess the degree of decentralisation and subsequent real autonomy in decision-making. In our attempt to understand the variety of changes within and between both countries we have sought first to gain some sense of the shift in management rights. What managerially has really changed? More specifically, our goal has been to examine what decisions have, in the past, been made outside of the jurisdiction of the educators in publicly funded schools which, with increased autonomy, now reside somewhere with educators at the school site and if these changes in managerial rights at the school level are, in some absolute sense, 'large' or 'small' or, more importantly, are significant in affecting school outcomes.

UNDERSTANDING INCREASED SCHOOL AUTONOMY IN THE CONTEXT OF OTHER ORGANISATIONS

In order better to appreciate the relevance of those specific changes in schools, we have sought to place them in a broader context of management decisions and management rights in all organisations. This, for us, has meant asking two other questions. What might be the taxonomy of all major management decisions within which we might locate 'traditional, i.e. non-decentralised' as well as 'restructured, i.e. decentralised' schools. And, then, in the context of that taxonomy, are 'restructured' schools in some fundamental way different from 'traditional' schools, and if so, by how much?

We are using 'management decisions' as a variable for placing schools on a continuum of organisational autonomy. We felt that if we could identify the major categories of managerial decisions made in organisations and then ascertain whether managers inside or above the organisation had the right to make those decisions, we would have some sense of how realistic and useful are the current arguments for, and changes in, school autonomy. At one extreme of this continuum is an organisational unit such as a division of a larger company in which, in theory, all of the major management decisions reside with the 'parent organisation', i.e. authorities above and/or beyond the organisational unit. At the other extreme is an organisational unit which is essentially an autonomous business, wherein those same major management decisions sit within that organisational unit. All organisational units, including US and English elementary and secondary schools, would fall somewhere within the boundaries of totally autonomous organisations at one extreme and, at the other extreme, totally 'dependent' organisations.

The concept of using management decisions as a variable is a slippery one for several reasons. Firstly, managerial decisions may be 'sector bound'. Some of the decision rights which describe the autonomy of an organisation are exclusively associated with one economic sector and not others. The following generalisations which characterise differences between public and private sector organisations are not uncommon.

Government and business are fundamentally different institutions. Business leaders are driven by the profit motive; government leaders are driven by the desire to get re-elected. Businesses earn their income from their customers.

Governments get most of their money from taxpayers. Businesses are usually driven by competition; governments usually use monopolies. Because politicians tend to be driven by interest groups, public managers – unlike their private counterparts – must factor interest groups into every equation. ... All of these factors combine to produce an environment in which public employees view risks and rewards very differently than do private employees (Osborne and Gaebler, 1992, pp. 21–2).

Secondly, managerial decision rights have numerous interdependent dimensions. Regardless of the sectoral location of an organisation, the full impact of decision rights is often only understood when their interdependencies are considered. A given decision right will be 'different' when seen in the context of other decision rights.

Thirdly, managerial decision rights are inherently complex. Managerial decisions that can be easily identified as 'simple decisions' are, in fact, complex webs of many smaller decisions about rights and procedures, all of which make up the 'simple decision'. It is the composition of these many smaller decisions that, in the end, describes how the 'simple decision' is made and how 'real' it is.

Fourthly, management decisions are owned and can be delegated via a wide variety of relationships. Stated another way, we tend to think of delegation as taking place when a manager 'above' an organisation says to a manager 'in' an organisation, 'You have the authority, subject to various constraints, to decide about (fill in the blank)'. While this is perhaps the most commonly understood sense of the term delegation, there are a variety of alternative forms of this relationship between the manager 'above' and the manager 'in'.

These 'problems' with thinking about a taxonomy of specific types of managerial decisions are really reasons to seek to pursue it. If organisational autonomy is so largely shaped by sector location, then the debate about school autonomy should shift to include more consideration of alternatives to public sector schools. If managerial decision rights have numerous interdependencies, then it would be useful to understand, through a taxonomy, which types of management decisions are mutually dependent. If managerial decision rights are complex and made up of many small decisions, then 'the devil may be in the details', i.e. the devil of successful school reform may be in the details of clusters of small decisions, not in the generalities and abstractions about school autonomy. Finally, if decisions can be delegated via a variety of mechanisms, then the form, as well as the content, of school-based decision rights may determine the impact of school autonomy.

So, even (or especially) in the face of these confounding circumstances, we think it helpful to attempt to identify the range of possible management decisions that can be decentralised, if only because so much has been claimed for the benefits of increased autonomy in general. What are the natural limits to that logic, and what special circumstances, if any, refine or actually refute that logic?

MANAGERIAL DECISIONS: A TAXONOMY

It is important to develop a taxonomy that will allow an analysis to take place of key management decisions in autonomous and non-autonomous organisations. Items to be considered in the comparative analysis are those which vary in terms of whether they are made by the larger organisation for the unit or whether they are made within the organisational unit itself. Although there is a wide variety of such decisions, we think that they cluster around five broad issues which an autonomous organisation would have to confront:

1. decisions about the business to be in
2. decisions about how to organise and operate the production process or service delivery of the organisation
3. decisions about the kinds of labour to employ and how that labour is compensated
4. decisions about the customers or clients to be served
5. decisions about the categories of revenues to pursue in order to operate the business.

These 'decisions' are really large bundles of many, more specific decisions, which themselves are complex and interdependent. It is difficult to separate, for example, people who make decisions about growing and shrinking a business from people who have the authority to raise revenues for the business. However, we believe that this five-part taxonomy is a useful analytical approach and we now propose to examine each part in turn.

APPLYING THE TAXONOMY

While there is a wide variety of specific management decisions which can be moved up or down in an organisation, it seems to us that these five broad categories capture most of the major decisions of this type. Although it may be useful for analytical purposes to distinguish among the five clusters of management decision rights, the clusters are themselves highly interdependent, each almost defining the others. It is difficult to imagine, for example, extreme autonomy in mission direction and pursuit of financial revenues coupled with extreme dependence with regard to decisions about clients, labour and work processes. It is also difficult to imagine extreme autonomy in organisation of work processes coupled with extreme dependence with regard to decisions about employee compensation.

The issue of autonomy v. dependence is not a discussion of how the organisation is managed, e.g. 'top down' v. 'bottom up' management within the organisation. That kind of issue, the 'how' of management, can and does take place in all kinds of organisations, including those that are largely autonomous and those that are largely dependent. What we are describing here is, instead, a discussion of the basic decision rights that exist within a particular organisation, regardless of how it is managed.

This is not to suggest that there is not a great contribution that can be made to improving school management by looking at how to manage schools. It is to suggest that 'good management' as a concept can be separated from the concept of 'which managers have which decision rights?' In fact, to focus only on how well one manages without considering the decision rights of managers is, we think, to miss much of what can be done to improve schools.

What we now want to do is to describe the extreme 'right-hand-side' of the continuum, i.e. the organisation which has the highest degree of autonomy with respect to major management decision rights. Following that we contrast that with the extreme 'left-hand-side' of the continuum, the totally dependent organisation. Finally, we discuss how each of these pure types interacts with the external environment.

AUTONOMOUS ORGANISATIONS

Senior managers of an autonomous organisation determine the business it is in, when to modify the business it is in, and when to get out of that business. They make decisions about how to organise the business and how to produce its goods/services. They organise and reorganise themselves whenever they see fit, and determine both the categories of labour they wish to hire (by skill, degree, certificate, experience, etc.) as well as the individuals within those categories. Of course, they design and implement the services they provide and determine the wide range of 'conditions of labour' that they employ, including the nature of job security, compensation, benefits, bonuses, non-monetary incentives and the physical amenities surrounding labour.

They not only determine the market in which they seek to sell, they are free to seek the market niche and the market share that they desire. The 'flip side' is also true in that senior managers in an autonomous organisation can choose not to serve a particular category of market and choose not to serve a particular customer ('no shoes, no shirt, no service').

Closely associated with markets for the organisation's services (but not identical) are decisions about markets for the pursuit of revenues. If the individual pays for the service then the client and financial markets are identical. If, instead, there is a third party payer, the markets are different. One form of third party payer is government, which can choose a variety of ways in which to subsidise service. It can provide money to the consumer who then finds a producer; it can provide money to the producer on behalf of the consumer once the consumer has chosen a producer; and it can provide money to the producer in a lump sum appropriation, not tying compensation to any specific client. In an autonomous organisation a variety of potential financial markets are pursued or at least able to be considered.

Finally, senior managers of an autonomous organisation can acquire and dispose of the net worth of the organisation. They can decide to reinvest cash reserves in the organisation and enhance its infrastructure or take those cash reserves as personal compensation and 'milk' the organisation. The 'flip side' is also true here: the autonomous organisation is exposed to all of the demographic, economic and political vagaries of the external environment and can fail. It can be either liquidated or taken over by another management team. Among many examples of service-producing organisations that approximate to the autonomous model are small law offices, non-chain restaurants, single-site private schools and privately-held health complexes.

DEPENDENT ORGANISATIONS WITHIN A LARGER ORGANISATION

In one sense, the dependent organisation is merely the 'opposite' of the autonomous organisation. The basic mission of the organisation is determined by an external body, e.g. the parent organisation, and decisions about modifying the focus of the business it is in, including when to get of the business, are not the domain of individuals in the dependent organisation. The basic production processes are determined by the parent organisation. Examples such as Kinko's Copiers, H and R Block Tax Services, Travel Lodge, and MacDonald's Restaurants come to mind.

The categories of employees to be hired are determined outside the dependent organisation, and the individuals who are hired into that organisation are chosen outside the organisation and assigned to it. Although supervisory and other personnel responsibilities may reside with individuals within this organisation, basic decisions about compensation levels, the composition of compensation packages, and changes in compensation associated with changes in performance are made outside of that organisation. Examples of organisations that approximate these practices are some branch banks, police, and fire substations.

Dependent organisations do not determine their clients or markets. Those are assigned to them either as individual clients or by geographic location. There is little if any authority within the organisation about who may be excluded from service within the organisation. If, by virtue of geographic location and personal characteristics, a client fits within some minimum bounds of eligibility for service, he or she must be served by the organisation. The capacity of the dependent organisation is determined by the parent organisation.

The dependent organisation really does not pursue external financial resources, except through the parent organisation. Because work (services/goods) and the means for production (labour/capital) are provided elsewhere, individuals within the dependent organisation are not required to seek revenues by pursuing financial markets in order to sustain their organisation.

Finally, individuals in the dependent organisation do not have the rights to dispose of the net worth of the organisation, in particular the organisation's fixed assets. They cannot buy and sell pieces of the organisation. The rules for the disposition of revenues are confined to an annual operating budget which is tightly controlled and monitored by the parent organisation.

CONCLUSION

The proponents of the decentralisation of decision-making argue that, by giving schools real autonomy, decision-making at the school level will have a significant impact on the teaching and learning process, leading to measurable improvements in outcomes. The key hopes for this reform may depend on whether we are witnessing real autonomy in decision-making or merely a degree of managerialism that decentralises administration rather than decentralising autonomous decision-making.

To analyse the effects of decentralised or autonomous management, we believe it is first necessary to understand the complexity of managerial decisions. Secondly, it is necessary to formulate key elements in autonomous decision-making that allow an analysis of whether decisions in the management of autonomous organisations lie within the remit of school managers. Only if managers in schools have the control over those key decisions can we expect the benefits of decentralisation to accrue.

To that end we believe that the taxonomy established in this paper will be of value to those working in schools and to those researching in this area. It will enable them to assess the success or failure of the decentralised decision-making movements against criteria about the real degree of autonomy that was present in the process.

The Equity Consequences of Educational Reform

TIM SIMKINS

The education reforms of recent years in England and Wales, commencing with the Education Reform Act of 1988 and continuing with a number of further substantial pieces of legislation, embody a strategy to pursue the Government's 'five great themes' of 'quality, diversity, increasing parental choice, greater autonomy for schools and greater accountability' (DfE, 1992, p. 2)

These themes have been pursued through four interconnected sets of measures. First, giving a high degree of autonomy through school-based management schemes: 'local management' schemes for the majority of schools which remain with their LEAs and 'grant-maintained status' for the minority who choose to 'opt out'. Secondly, all schools are being made much more explicitly subject to market pressures, through a significant increase in the opportunities for parents to express preferences about the school they wish their child to attend and through the funding of schools on the basis of formulae tied to pupil numbers. Third, however, this market is being firmly controlled through the implementation of the National Curriculum and a national system of testing for pupils aged 5–16. Finally, much more public information is being made available about schools. Examination and test results and other information – for example, about 'non-authorised absences' – is to be published regularly in a standard format on a school-by-school basis; schools are required to publish for parents a range of information about their philosophy and provision; and all schools are to be subject to inspection every four years with the results published.

Taken together these reforms represent a radical and multi-faceted attempt to address concerns about the quality of schooling in England and Wales. How far they will succeed depends on a number of complex factors (Simkins, 1994). However, it is important to recognise that the reforms also have important equity implications. Indeed, it could be argued that, despite the Government's strong emphasis on the objectives of increasing quality and choice in the school system, it will be equity considerations which are likely to dominate the debate

155

as the consequences of the reforms begin to work through.

This paper attempts to provide a framework for considering the reforms within an equity perspective. It begins by exploring the meaning of the term with particular reference to its uses in relation to resource distribution. It then explores the central aspects of the reforms from an equity perspective before drawing some conclusions.

THE MEANING OF EQUITY

As a starting point, the term 'equity' may be broadly equated with 'fairness' and 'justice' (Le Grand, 1991, Chapter 2). A distinction can also be made between 'procedural' and 'distributional' equity – the former concerning fair treatment in terms of rules and procedures, the latter concerning fairness in the distribution of resources and opportunities. Formula funding, for example, can be argued to be more procedurally equitable 'in that it is based on objective criteria (in the sense that the criteria are set out as common rules and not determined by administrative discretion)' (Levacic, 1992, p. 27). More challenging and complex questions are raised, however, when the issues of distributional equity are addressed, and these will be the focus of this paper.

Distributional equity can be treated in a number of ways, with terminology often confusing and inconsistent. A useful starting point is the distinction between horizontal equity (the equal treatment of equals) and vertical equity (the unequal treatment of unequals). For those who value equity as an objective this distinction is relatively uncontroversial, and it highlights some key questions. For example:

- How are 'equals' and 'unequals' to be defined? What categories are to be used and what criteria will distinguish between them?

- What does 'equal treatment' mean? Does it mean 'identical' or 'equivalent' for example? And should it be conceived in terms of access to resource provision, of the nature of the educational experiences which the resources provide, or of the outcomes or benefits which result for the individual?

- How should treatment vary between unequals and why?

These questions are addressed in part by Wise (1967, Chapter 2) and Monk (1990, Chapter 2) who discuss a number of definitions of 'equality of opportunity' which embody differing approaches to 'distributional equity'. Drawing on their work, we can divide definitions of distributional equity into two broad categories.

The first category, which defines equity in terms of resource inputs, comprises:

- the 'equal expenditure per pupil' definition

- the 'maximum variance' definition: placing a limit on the permitted variance in expenditure per pupil

– the 'foundation' definition: a prescribed minimum level of expenditure provided for all pupils

– the 'classification' definition: treating equally all members of specified categories, whether these be defined in terms of need, ability to benefit or some other variable.

In policy terms such expenditure-based approaches to funding for equity are attractive, not least because they can be put into operation fairly easily. Admittedly, the more sophisticated foundation and classification definitions do not of themselves resolve the questions outlined above arising from the concepts of horizontal and vertical equity, but they do make clear that the focus of attention is on the central policy concern of expenditure levels. Viewed in economic terms, however, they leave a good deal to be desired. In particular, they do not address the issue of the relationship between expenditure, educational processes and learning outcomes. In other words, they do not account for the fact that the distribution of resources in a particular way does not in itself guarantee that educational opportunities, let alone outcomes, will reflect this distribution.

Divergence may occur for a number of reasons. For example, pupils may be unwilling to utilise the resources offered or teachers and others may not have the capacity to make the best use of the potential which the resources provide. The first possibility raises a conception of equity which relates to 'deserts' or 'merit'. Why should those who are unwilling to make good use of the resources provided receive them at the expense of those who are willing? The second draws attention to the importance of the qualitative dimension of resource allocation which may be embodied in such variables as teacher motivation or qualifications or school climate. Equal expenditure does not guarantee equality of provision in these terms.

To overcome such qualifications it is necessary to consider definitions of equity which incorporate some view about the outcomes to which the resources are intended to contribute. Wise (1967) suggests four such definitions.

– the 'minimum attainment' definition: sufficient resources should be provided to enable all pupils to reach a minimum level of attainment

– the 'full opportunity' definition: resources should continue to be provided until the marginal gains of all pupils are reduced to zero

– the 'levelling' definition: resources should be distributed so that the least advantaged are favoured most and variances in achievements are minimised

– the 'competition' definition: resources should be provided in proportion to the pupils' ability to benefit.

EDUCATIONAL REFORM AND EQUITY

How can these various concepts of equity be related to the educational reforms in England and Wales? As has already been indicated, the reforms are complex, comprising a number of components, some of which may be in tension. Their consequences for 'distributional equity' are, therefore, difficult both to untangle and to predict. Broadly, however, such consequences will arise through the ways in which the reforms influence the allocation of resources among schools and individuals. The main mechanisms for this are formula funding, increased parental choice of school and school-based management.

The prime determinant of the block budget of the school which a child attends is the funding formula which the relevant LEA is required to use to allocate resources among schools. The consequences of formula funding for an individual school, however, depend not simply on the design of the formula – an essentially static concept – but also on the nature of the school's 'market' where choices made by parents and other factors influence the size and composition of the school's pupil body. The formula and local market circumstances interact to determine the distribution of resources among schools in a particular area and how this changes over time. Resource distribution needs to be considered broadly; clearly budgetary levels are important, but any full analysis of the resource position of a particular school – and hence of the degree of equity between schools – should also take account of other factors. These include the quality of resources a school can attract (in terms, for example, of teacher experience and qualifications, and the state of its buildings), and the characteristics of its pupil body, considering evidence about peer group effects on achievement (Monk, 1990, pp. 364–70).

The formula and local market circumstances, however, only determine the degree of equity between schools in the system and hence place constraints on the opportunities which schools can provide for individual pupils. The *actual* opportunities provided to any pupil within these constraints depend upon a school's internal resource allocation policies and, in particular, upon how the school chooses to use the freedoms given to it under the school-based management component of the reforms. Such policies will reflect the school's philosophy and objectives, including an explicit or implicit understanding of equity issues. Increasingly, however, they are also likely to be coloured by school managers' perceptions of the effects of particular school policies on its market position.

The rest of this paper will consider in turn each of these variables – the funding formula, the 'market', and resource allocation within schools. Some reference will be made to empirical evidence about the consequences of the reforms, but the main concern will be to unpack the equity issue and to identify the questions which need to be addressed if the debate about equity is to be carried forward.

FORMULA FUNDING

It is a requirement of the legislation that all schools be funded by formulae which are 'simple, clear and predictable in their impact' and are 'based on an assessment of a school's objective needs, rather than on historic patterns of expenditure in order to ensure that resources are allocated equitably' (DES, 1988, para. 104). It has already been noted that there is a sense of procedural equity here. In addition, some clear ideas about distributional equity are built into the rules to which all formulae must conform. At least 80 per cent of the budget must be allocated on the basis of the number and ages of pupils, with the remaining 20 per cent (or less) available to compensate for pupils' special needs and circumstances, and for the diseconomies associated with small schools.

The importance given in the legislation to funding schools by formula gives both the Government and LEAs the opportunity to express key values and policies through the details of formula design. Thus, the Government gives primacy to horizontal equity of inputs among pupils of the same age with some vertical differentiation between pupils of different ages and – in so far as the 20 per cent limit allows – among those with different needs irrespective of age. LEAs, however, have the opportunity to exercise discretion – and hence pursue their own values – in a number of ways.

Formula funding, then, raises a number of equity issues. For example, how appropriate is age as the prime determinant of need? If it is appropriate, do formulae adequately reflect the needs of different age groups? And how far do differences among LEA formulae lead to inequity among pupils with similar needs living in different parts of the country (Bullock and Thomas, 1993)? These questions are not easy to answer, but two points can usefully be made. First, it seems clear that the majority of formulae interpret the requirement for 'objectivity' relatively narrowly in terms of unambiguous quantification of the components and relationships in the formula rather than in terms of a clear definition of the needs of pupils in various categories. It is this which biases the formula approach towards procedural rather than distributional equity.

There appear to be two reasons for this. First, the constraints imposed by the Government in its search for simple formulae have precluded the design of formulae based on any complex assessment of need. Second, and probably more important, LEAs in designing their formulae have generally attempted to reflect earlier patterns of resource allocation.

Some studies have begun to explore the issue of need from first principles. For example, Kelly (1992) develops a model based on assumptions about curriculum provision, maximum group sizes, required contact time for teaching-related activities and for management, and provision for special educational needs. This generates an increased funding requirement for both primary and secondary sectors, but with a proportionately greater increase for primary schools. Other LEAs are now undertaking similar studies and reaching similar conclusions (e.g. Sheffield City Council, 1992; Jesson and Levacic, 1993). The basis of such conclusions, of course, derives from professional judgement about the resource needs of particular pupil groups rather than from any empirically established relationship between resources and learning. In terms of our earlier discussion they embody input rather than outcome-based definitions of equity. They do, however, take us beyond analysis based simply on historical expenditure patterns, to a debate about need-based funding, especially in relation to the relative needs of the primary and secondary sectors. Any resolution of this debate, however, seems a long way off in a climate of tight public expenditure control which makes any substantial redistribution of resources among age groups difficult to achieve.

A second set of questions about formula funding concern the allocation of that proportion of the budget which is not allocated on the basis of pupils' ages. How do the rules for this relate to particular definitions of need? And how far does the restriction of such allocations to 20 per cent of the budget affect the distribution of resources among pupils with different needs? LEAs differ considerably in the ways they treat these factors, as indeed they do in their age-weightings and in the amount spent per pupil unit. Furthermore, the ability to meet differential need adequately is limited by the requirements to allocate the bulk of the budget on the basis of AWPUs and to make the formula simple and objective (Lee, 1992).

Formula funding, therefore, both embodies certain Government assumptions about equity – in particular the importance of procedural equity in allocating resources to schools – and concepts of horizontal and vertical equity which give primacy to classification of pupils by age. On the other hand, it leaves room for considerable variations in the resources which similar schools in different parts of the country receive, because LEAs differ in the amounts they allocate per pupil, in the relativities they establish between resourcing levels for different age groups and in the ways in which they treat other variables relating to need. An important determinant of the resources available for the individual child, therefore, remains the place where he or she lives. Allowing for this, resourcing levels are made more predictable – although not necessarily more equitable – by formula funding. The design of the formula, however, is only part of the story.

INCREASED PARENTAL CHOICE

Analyses of the assumptions underlying formula design are helpful, but they are also limited in that they take an essentially static view of funding formulae. They do not really get to grips with the dynamics which formula funding linked to increased parental choice sets in train. The main reason, of course, why the Government has chosen to tie formula funding so closely to pupil numbers is to make schools more responsive to parental wishes. Popular (and hence 'good') schools will grow, while unpopular schools will contract and eventually close. This raises two equity issues. The first concerns the consequences of unplanned changes in school size. As has already been noted, formula design is essentially a static affair, which assumes that schools of a particular size have particular needs. Most formulae attempt to protect small schools through a variety of devices. For example, some give additional lump sums to small schools; some use sliding scales of additional resources related to school size; and some give a degree of protection against the consequences of employing staff whose salaries are higher than the average. Such protection is limited, however, and must compete with other needs – compensation for disadvantage, for example – which must also be funded by the 20 per cent of the budget which need not be driven by pupil numbers. The question needs to be asked then whether, as schools expand or contract, the quality of opportunity which can be made available to pupils will remain the same. A number of points are relevant here:

- as schools expand or contract, how will scale economies and diseconomies affect the range of curriculum areas which can be offered, per-pupil resourcing levels (including class sizes) and the opportunities for teachers to have adequate non-contact time?

- how will changes in school size, especially if these are perceived to be associated with school quality, affect the ability of different schools to attract high quality staff?

- how will perceived changes in the market position of schools affect the composition of their pupil bodies and hence the peer group effects which are known to have an important influence on achievement?

The introduction of open enrolment and increased competition increases the likelihood that the more 'popular' schools will try to become more selective in their intake. Initially the Government was cautious about such a development, since the concept of schools selecting pupils rather than parents selecting schools seemed inconsistent with the rhetoric of a policy of parental choice. The position is subtly changing, however. Research on grant-maintained schools (Bush et al., 1993) has found that schools which are oversubscribed are able to influence the socio-economic and/or academic composition of their intake without using formal entrance examinations or tests, although the local market effects of the existence of grant-maintained schools can be quite complex (Power et al., 1994). One small-scale study of LMS schools shows how some schools may actively attempt to change the composition of their pupil body in order to improve their market position (Deem et al., 1993). There is growing evidence, too, that the number of exclusions of children with behavioural difficulties is rising (Stirling, 1992; Imich, 1994), although it would be premature to link this trend to the effects of increased competition, and the Government has recently discouraged exclusion except in exceptional cases.

The effects on equity among schools of the increased 'marketisation' of education has been widely commented upon elsewhere (e.g. Jonathan, 1989, 1990; Ball, 1993c) and evidence is emerging only slowly. The issues are important and this is the arena in which the debate about the balance between quality and equity is likely to become sharpest, with the question 'Quality of what and for whom?' becoming a major issue. It should not be assumed, however, that the broader school system is the only arena in which these issues will be played out. Much less researched and debated – yet also of considerable importance – is the 'internal arena' of the individual school.

SCHOOL-BASED MANAGEMENT

According to the Government 'effective schemes of local management will enable governing bodies and head teachers to plan their use of resources to maximum effect in accordance with their own needs and priorities, and to make schools more responsive to their clients...' (DES, 1988, para. 9). This will 'increase the quality of education by making more effective use of the existing resources for teaching and learning' (ibid., para. 23). Whether school-based management will indeed achieve improved quality of schooling is an important empirical question which cannot be addressed here (see Simkins, 1994). Freedom to allocate resources internally in relation to their own perceived needs and priorities, however, also has potential implications for equity. Whatever the systems-level equity consequences of the reforms, school-based management gives individual schools the power, at least to a degree, to reinforce or mitigate these through the internal resource allocation policies which they pursue.

Very little has been written about the values, priorities and assumptions which underlie such policies. However, there can be little doubt that in most schools equity considerations play an important part. To explore such issues in more detail, a number of questions could be asked. For example:

– Which groups of pupils and which aspects of the curriculum are resourced most favourably, through smaller class sizes or other forms of additional resourcing?

– What factors determine the ways in which teachers are allocated among groups?

– How are special needs defined and resourced? What is the balance between provision for pupils with different levels of ability or differences in socio-economic background?

– How are choices about the allocation of resources discussed? Is the emphasis on need (particularly in relation to relative disadvantage, however defined) or in terms of the contribution which particular resources can make to increases in achievement? If the latter, whose achievement is emphasised?

CONCLUSIONS

As was pointed out at the beginning of this paper, the Government's rationale for its reforms makes no explicit reference to equity. It is the twin issues of quality and choice which are claimed to drive the reforms. Yet the very comprehensiveness of the changes makes it inherently implausible that they will be neutral in equity terms. Predicting their equity consequences, however, is far from easy. The concept is many-faceted, and the reforms provide a variety of mechanisms through which equity might be enhanced or reduced. This paper has focused on a number of dimensions of the reforms which impinge in particular on equity conceived in terms of resource distribution.

Formula-funding clearly embodies the concept of procedural equity but it has consequences for distributional equity too. At the heart of the formula-funding system is an input-based definition of equity with pupils classified primarily on the basis of age. The relative values applied to pupils of different ages seem to relate more to historical patterns of expenditure than to detailed specifications of need, although an increasing amount of work is suggesting that primary pupils are disadvantaged by traditional expenditure patterns especially when these are related to the requirements of the National Curriculum. Additional provision is made in formulae to compensate for other factors, especially diseconomies arising from small size of school and the requirements of children who have special educational needs or come from disadvantaged backgrounds. However, a maximum of 20 per cent of the funds distributed to schools may be used to compensate for such factors and it is far from clear that this is always sufficient to ensure that the needs of vertical equity are fully met.

The implications of formula-funding become more complex when placed within the context of increased parental choice of school. Parental decisions and other factors in a school's 'market' will determine whether a school's roll increases or declines. Changes in school size in themselves may affect the range and quality of opportunities which schools can offer their pupils. However, beyond this, perceptions of a school's present and prospective market position may affect its ability to attract and retain high quality staff and may also have an effect on the social and academic composition of its pupil body. The equity consequences of these qualitative factors may be considerable.

Formula-funding within a context of increased 'marketisation', then, presents school managers with considerable challenges. The policies which they develop internally to address the issue of equity cannot be conceived in isolation from the changing environmental pressures to which the school is subject. These pressures include the particular funding formula applied to the school, the degree and nature of competition in the local arena of parental choice in which the school is situated, and the National Curriculum requirements which apply to the age range of the school's pupils. Little evidence is yet available to predict how schools will adjust their internal allocation policies to the new situations in which they find themselves.

A comprehensive discussion of equity within a context, for many schools, of increasing resource constraint and increasingly complex and challenging environmental pressures will bring to the surface difficult, yet fundamental, questions about their core values and the degree to which these can, and should, be defended in an increasingly hostile world. Ball (1993b) argues that the empowerment of schools under school-based management and the parallel disempowering of the LEA is having the effect of 'privatising' to individual schools the means by which social values are translated into educational policy. One result of this could be that the degree of equity or inequities in the educational system as a whole becomes little more than an aggregate product of the individual policies of many thousands of independent 'schools in the market place'. Such a diagnosis would be premature, but it raises considerably the stakes attached to schools' internal resource allocation policies and the ways in which they choose to respond to the increasingly complex and demanding challenges with which they are faced.

PART 4

LEADERSHIP

Challenges and Dilemmas:
A Journey Through Twenty-Five Years
of Leader-Watching

VALERIE HALL

FINDING A GUIDE

My starting point for identifying four key articles about managing and leading in education was easier than the journey itself. Given the relatively *tabula rasa* status of this theme in the early 1970s, Meredydd Hughes' proposal for a research-based model of headship provided a signpost in uncharted territory. He started a debate about the nature of educational management and leadership which others have continued, by challenging and refining the embryonic understanding his account of leader-watching represents. Indeed, the clarity of his signposting was so sharp that it almost closed down more adventurous explorations in the 1980s, when the continuing emphasis was on establishing the precise dimensions of the job (see Hall and Southworth, 1997, for a summary of developments in leader watching during this time). The discussion between Peter Ribbins and Brian Sherratt which provides the second reading in this selection represents a deliberate attempt to stray from the straight and narrow (and managerialist) path followed by researchers and commentators on headship in England and Wales in the 1980s. Instead, it tackles some of the unfamiliar features of the leadership landscape, looking for illumination in the untried territory of a headteacher–researcher partnership. Ribbins and Sherratt's account is about leader- and researcher-watching, recognising the influence on our understandings of leadership (through literature at least) of the ways in which the evidence has been collected and interpreted.

Four years later, Gronn's article provides the map of an increasingly complex terrain, in which signposts often point in different directions and there appear to be no connections between the natural features. The final article in the selection by Ron Glatter brings us back to earth with its reminder that watching leaders must be informed by an understanding of the context within which they are working. His final comment, that 'we are moving into uncharted territory', may seem to belie the value of the map that I have identified as emerging during the twenty-five years. Yet the characteristics of the work of these four map-makers ensure that the journey is always challenging, rarely comfortable (because it is about problem-finding, not problem-solving) and always honest. As well as reflecting changes in our conceptions of educational leadership, they also reflect the ever-evolving relationship between researchers as commentators and the leaders and managers with whom they work. The following selection is about researcher- as well as leader-watching.

Inevitably uncharted or only partially revealed areas remain. Whatever challenges there have been to the concept and practice of educational leadership over the last twenty-five years, it is still centre stage particularly in relation to leading secondary schools. The journal's pages reveal occasional excursions into leadership in other phases and other countries. There are some but not many discussions too of other management roles but rarely with the same challenging lens as that used to scrutinise leadership. Headteachers or school principals remain the main players in the educational leadership game, in spite of successive governments' attempts to temper their individual powers through mandated partnerships. Noticeable too is the absence of any women writers in this selection. Elsewhere I have described how gender has remained mainly segregated from other issues in this journal rather than integrated into our understanding of the behaviour of men and women in education management (Hall, 1997). There I propose a number of ways in which a gender perspective can contribute to alternative conceptions of educational leadership. In the meantime it remains a ghost at the leader-watching feast, sometimes (as in Gronn's piece) more visible than others. Similarly none of the four articles represents the critical perspectives on educational leadership which, together with gender perspectives, highlight the emancipatory potential of leadership and what some see as its contamination by managerialism. Finally the discourse about leading and managing that is represented in these four articles must be understood against the radically changing context of education over the past twenty-five years and the changing ways of interpreting educational management itself. Together they show how our understanding of educational leadership comes from watching researchers watching heads, watching heads watching themselves, watching leaders in settings other than education, and watching policy-makers frame the context for the practice of leadership. As Gronn points out, the literature on leadership is immense. The purpose of this introduction to my selection is to concentrate on how these four influential writers have encapsulated key ideas arising from their own leader-watching activities.

KEEPING THE LEADER IN SIGHT

Meredydd Hughes' report of his research on secondary headship set the direction for the debate, in England and Wales at least, for years to come. It also represents the limitations of the discourse about school leadership at the time. His main contribution was in his attempt to construct a model for understanding school leadership, based on systematic analysis of information gained from leaders themselves. At this stage, although he acknowledges the desirability of including others' views in constructing the picture, they remain largely absent and the word 'followers' does not appear. In his approach, the headteacher is firmly centre stage and Hughes' purpose is to demystify a school leadership role that had remained unquestioned for the preceding seventy years or more. His interest is prompted by the changing dimensions of the role (one which, as a former secondary head, he knew well) and the challenges and dilemmas these changes were creating for its incumbents. In throwing out his own challenge to traditional stereotypes of headship, by identifying its contrasting 'professional' and 'administrator' components, he leaves unchallenged its association with men as leaders (only headmasters are referred to). Nor in this early discussion is the common equation of leadership with the headteacher's role questioned. As Gronn points out some twenty years and many headship studies later, it can no longer be assumed that leadership and headship are connected.

The importance of Hughes' contribution was in showing how the executive and professional aspects of the headteacher's role are analytically distinct but closely interrelated. In arguing for a new, unified model of secondary headship he captured the beginnings of a dilemma that continues to haunt educators as they search to preserve the integrity of their professional identities in the market place of contemporary schooling. Working within a positivistic paradigm (interpretative approaches like that of Ribbins and Sherratt only came later), Hughes dissects the headteacher's role to show the possibility of combining the chief executive and the innovative dimension of the leading professional components in ways that lead to positive outcomes both for heads and for their schools. The transformations that have occurred since he proposed his fourfold typology are in our conceptions of the chief executive aspects of the job which, for most secondary heads now, are part of their professional persona, reinforced by the heavy investment in their training for the tasks and skills required. The 'personal' dimension of the leading professional concept has also changed, particularly where secondary heads are concerned. In secondary headship, personal teaching and pastoral emphasis are no longer definers of being a leading professional. Instead the 'innovator' role is writ large, as headteachers play their central part in managing multiple change, together with their battle to define and protect educational values. The transformation is perhaps less marked in primary headship where there is continuity (in the primary headteacher's 'ego identification' with their schools and self-recognition as powerful individuals) and change (more management and school maintenance tasks, more politics and a more public role) (Hall and Southworth, 1997, p. 157). The centrality of the headteacher's role, at the time when Hughes was writing, was accompanied by very limited use of delegation to offset its demands on one individual. Then heads were faced with a choice between personal involvement and executive functions. He rightly recognised that 'survivor' heads were those who recognised the need to delegate the 'personal'. Now, the reconceptualised 'personal' cannot be delegated since it is, in its transformation, once more the core of the leader's identity.

WATCHING BY WALKING ALONGSIDE

Ribbins and Sherratt locate their journey towards an understanding of educational experience in their perception of the value of a partnership between the researcher and headteacher, which creates the possibility of an account that combines the biographical and autobiographical. They do not share Hughes' inhibitions about including the views of 'followers' (though they also do not use that word) and systematically build these into their evolving understanding. The headteacher, however, is still centre stage in their analysis in spite of the radically altered context in which, as Ribbins himself points out elsewhere, the head's autonomy is substantially tempered by increased governor powers. The fact that the outcomes of these conversations are only just about to be published (six years on) testifies to the long-term nature of the enterprise and the demands it makes on time and the continuity of personal relationships. Like Hughes, Ribbins and Sherratt are proposing a way of understanding headship that challenges what has gone before and involves dilemmas which cannot be ignored. Whereas for Hughes the challenges and the dilemmas were in the character of school leadership itself, for these authors in this article at least they reside in the methods for collecting the data to arrive at an understanding. Their concern is not with correlations and measurement but with meanings and interpretations and how these are mediated through the researcher's and headteacher's perspectives. Their claim to a 'new approach for the study of headship' rests on a belief that current questions about the role of the contemporary headteacher call for not just more research but new methods of research.

If the headteacher is, in this account, still centre stage, there is a new dimension in his willingness and ability to reflect on his role and performance. Sherratt emerges as the reflective practitioner *par excellence*, using the opportunities and tools provided by Ribbins as researcher-cum-consultant to understand and provide an account of what he does and why. He provides a positive answer to those who question what is in it for heads to engage in this kind of reflection. He also foreshadows the current emphasis of the Teacher Training Agency (TTA 1996a) on the need for practitioners to be their own researchers, if research is to have an impact on practice. Unlike the Hughes account, this paper captures the immediacy of the research process, allowing both headteacher and researcher to emerge in their own right, unmediated by others' interpretations. As Sherratt rightly points out, the method enables them to overcome the problem of challenging the gap between what headteachers say and what they actually do. In this respect, this study leads the way for others (e.g. Southworth, 1995; Hall, 1996) which show the need for research accounts of school leadership to include observation and context as well as interview data.

As Gronn points out in his article, more and better leader watching must include longitudinal, naturalistic and biographical investigations.

Unfortunately the paper came too soon to provide the 'uniquely rich account of headship' it was aiming for, particularly in terms of how schools were responding to the demands made on them after the 1988 Education Reform Act. The effects on the head's role of working to secure grant-maintained status for the school are touched on and echo Hughes' earlier identification of the 'innovator' side of the role. Particularly notable, in view of Gronn's analysis in which 'influence' and 'identification' are the key components of leadership, is Sherratt's recognition of the need for him to be 'more directly and significantly influential' both inside and outside the school.

MAPPING THE TERRITORY

If Ribbins and Sherratt's article raises issues of whose account counts within the interpretative model they use, Gronn has no inhibitions about drawing eclectically on a wide range of different sources to argue for the limitations of current definitions of educational leadership. His paper was the hardest to edit, the original being almost three times the length presented here. It offers, however, a map of contemporary thinking on the theory and practice of leadership that could not be omitted. An avid leader-watcher himself, he uses the occasion of this article to review the results of others' leader-watching and the influence of their commentaries on our understanding of the phenomenon. He includes research and writing about leadership both in and outside of education, seemingly sharing Ron Glatter's view that the boundaries between the two should be permeable and not exclusive.

If Hughes' article was about challenging old conceptions of school leadership, Gronn's is about challenging the new, particularly those ideas and authors he sees as leading us up blind alleyways or following false trails. For him, leader-watching must include follower-watching; one cannot be understood without the other. The journey must, too, pay constant attention to the morality of leadership and travellers must not be seduced by pragmatists hawking their wares at the crossroads. He is less concerned in this article with building his own model of leadership as with challenging those developed by others, often inadequately or inappropriately. His dissection of the validity of 'transactional' and 'transformational' models of leadership highlights the complexity of the concepts and the dangers of their simplistic use by those concerned with developing educational leaders. While Hughes signposted the territory, Gronn, like Ribbins and Sherratt, is more concerned with the journey itself and how it sets the relations between leaders and followers. He expresses concern at the dearth of detailed ethnographic case studies of the dynamics of leadership and followership in action; and it is regrettable that the two case study examples he describes to support his argument had to be omitted in this abridged version. Readers are strongly recommended to read the original article.

Gronn is like a dog herding (some might say worrying) sheep in his determination not to let a single fashionable idea escape without being first thoroughly scrutinised. He challenges the over-easy association of leadership and headship and of leadership and management; the failure to understand the relationship between preparedness to lead and willingness to be led; the leader's role in transforming school culture (in whose interests?); the reduction of leadership, by those who see heads as primarily expert problem-solvers, to something that goes on in the head of the leader. He draws on critical theory perspectives to question the appropriateness of the transformation of school leaders into super-managers skilled in micropolitics. Finally he raises a crucial question: does headship make a difference? Together with the other authors in this selection he clearly thinks it does, but not in what he cites as its 'romantic' version; nor as something which is 'done' to followers. He ends with a clarion call to leaders and leader-watchers to heed the morality of leadership and followership, its embeddedness in the biographies (in the broadest sense) of those who lead and follow and the continuous need for vigilance against its corruption by the context in which it occurs.

LOOKING FOR A NEW MAP?

Ron Glatter's career as a leader-watcher easily spans the twenty-five years since Meredydd Hughes published the research with which this section began. As the title of Glatter's paper implies, his interest is as much in the context for leadership (the prevalent social agenda and values) as the process or people themselves. In his argument, leader-watching only makes sense if leaders can be shown to make a difference to schools; and that question is only important if schools can be shown to make a difference to all their pupils, not just some. Implicit in his discussion is his belief that schools and their leaders can make a difference but only in so far as the context within which they operate makes that possible. There are echoes, in his identification of the tensions and dilemmas of the uneasy relationship between centralisation and marketisation, of Hughes' critique of the negative effects of constrained autonomy on school leaders' effectiveness. The move in many education systems now towards self-governance and financial autonomy for schools would appear to create the conditions for innovativeness and proactivity as a chief executive and leading professional that Hughes' research revealed as desirable.

However, as Glatter points out, the current rhetoric of the 'self-governing school' is constrained by the 'serious limitations of close bureaucratic supervision'. Like Hughes twenty-five years ago, he sees many heads experiencing themselves as 'the powerless minions of a centralised and powerful bureaucracy'. Glatter also criticises the potential of self-governance to become self-centred and ignore the social agenda. His critique resembles Gronn's, when he points to perceptions of leadership which are divorced from concerns for moral values and culture. Crucially, Glatter reminds us that any further leader-watching must include both followers and context. As he says, the claim that 'leaders make things happen' should be replaced by 'things make leaders happen'. He calls for a new orientation in the leader-watching journey, from a narrow concentration on the individual leader with a defined leadership role to a more broadly conceived and focused view of leaders, followers and context. For researchers and other watchers, the challenges and dilemmas of leader-watching become the challenges and dilemmas of leadership-watching. The biggest challenge of all is to those responsible for professional development for leadership in education. Support for learning to lead, as these four authors have shown, requires understanding of self, of followers (who may also be the official leaders), of the political, policy and social context and the moral values and culture which give schools as organisations their distinctive characters and styles.

Research Report:
The Professional-as-Administrator:
The Case of the Secondary School Head

MEREDYDD G. HUGHES

In summing up his extensive studies of scientists in research establishments, Abrahamson (1967) observed that 'to most administrators, professionals are a major source of frustration'. Professionals prize their autonomy and are not readily amenable to hierarchical control, preferring a 'group of equals' pattern (Wardwell, 1955). The organisational loyalty of professionals is also suspect, their prior commitment being to their specialised work activity and to their links, both formal and informal, with fellow workers outside their particular organisation (Reissman, 1949; Kornhauser, 1963; Blau and Scott, 1963; Cotgrove and Box, 1970).

A technique commonly used in seeking to resolve, or at least to diminish, the almost inevitable conflict which results when professional and organisational perspectives differ is to appoint professionals or ex-professionals as administrators of professionally staffed organisations (Etzioni, 1964). The professional-as-administrator, it is argued, is uniquely capable of achieving accommodation between the organisation's emphasis on superordinate control and the professionals' desire for colleague control (Barber, 1963, pp. 669–88). Inevitably, as in all 'boundary' roles, there is some degree of role strain for the professional-as-administrator: 'professional norms stressing autonomous integrity for practitioners still make a claim upon him, which he considers legitimate, but so does the organisation's need for control' (Abrahamson, 1967, p. 83). Such positions often have a considerable prestige, however, and it has been noted that, though there is some tendency among professionals to disparage administrative roles, the expression of such sentiments does not normally inhibit the acceptance of administrative responsibilities when the opportunity is presented (Goss, 1962; Barber, 1963).

It may be claimed that the professional-as-administrator construct has relevance to many positions in the administration of education (Taylor, 1964;

Browning, 1972; David, 1973). The present article reports selected aspects of recent research (Hughes, 1972a), in which the construct was applied to the role of the secondary school head. The secondary school head is the *chief executive* of a professionally staffed organisation, and may also be regarded as the *leading professional* of that organisation.

In the study, 72 heads from a stratified random sample of maintained secondary schools ranging in size from under 400 pupils (6 modern schools) to over 1600 pupils (5 comprehensive schools), and 123 members of staff, similarly selected, responded to items relevant to two role models of headship: the head as Chief Executive (the CE role model) and the head as Leading Professional (the LP role model). The heads were asked to indicate, on a five-point scale, their self-expectations, i.e. the behaviour they regarded as desirable in the context of their school, and also their perception of their actual behaviour. Because of unease expressed during a pilot study, staff were asked only for their expectations for the head's role.

Avoiding technicalities as far as possible, it is proposed in the following, *firstly* to indicate some of the interrelationships which were found within the CE role model, demonstrating in particular the articulation of what may be called the internal and external sectors; *secondly*, to identify two independent parameters within the LP role model; and, *finally*, to explore the interpenetration of the two structures, with a view to facilitating the emergence of a more unified role model of secondary school headship.

THE CE ROLE MODEL

Nearly all executives, according to Chester Barnard (1938, p. 215), do a considerable amount of non-executive work, which is sometimes more valuable than the executive work which they do. Nevertheless, 'executive work is not that *of* the organisation but the specialised work of *maintaining* the organisation in operation' (author's italics). Accepting Barnard's dictum that the executive functions relate to the work, within and outside the organisation, which is essential to its vitality and endurance, we differentiate between an internal and an external sector of the role model: the chief executive is concerned both with what happens within the organisation and with the relation of the organisation to the wider system of which it is a part. An elementary application of systems analysis then suggests the hypothesis that the two aspects are interrelated: ...

The internal aspect is broadly dealt with in the provision of the Ministry of Education's Model Articles of Government (AM 25, 26.1.45) that '... the Headmaster shall control the internal organisation, management and discipline of the school, shall exercise supervision...', etc. Within this general framework, statements were included in the internal sector of the role model relating to two types of executive function which may be regarded as complementary: (a) the division and allocation of work (including the clarification of staff responsi-bilities and delegation of responsibilities by the head); (b) the co-ordination and control of organisational activity (including staff supervision, an insistence on deadlines and a general emphasis on efficient procedures). A correlational analysis of responses to individual items, taken in pairs, was performed at each of the three levels of response (i.e. heads' expectations, heads' reported behaviour and staff expectations), using the English Electric 4-50 Computer at Cardiff University College, and significant positive correlations were obtained involving each of the items. From this it may be concluded that the internal sector of the CE role model, as constructed, can be regarded as a configurative whole, in which the parts are consistent, and mutually interrelated.

Items in the external sector were chosen to explore the head's relationship as Chief Executive to institutional authority in the guise of the school's governing body and the local education authority. Topics considered were the head's freedom to invite visitors to the school without reference to outside authority, his access as normal practice to his chairman of governors, and the effectiveness of his involvement, if any, in the appointment of members of staff. Again an underlying common factor emerged in the statistical analysis, which at each of the three levels of response, may be interpreted as being related to the status and autonomy granted to the head by external authority.

We are now in a position to state and consider a problem of some interest concerning the interrelation of environmental influences and the functioning of a school. Is there a relationship, in terms of expectations and in terms of behaviour, between the standing and autonomy of the head in relation to external authority and the internal governance of the school? Such a relationship is frequently claimed or implied in the professional literature. Lewis, for instance, in a Head Masters Association publication (1967), states that 'the privilege of making his own appointments contributes significantly to the head's status, on which the standing and effectiveness of the school so much depends'. Baron (1956, p. 13) has noted that essentially the same point was made in the Board of Education Prefatory Memorandum to the 1905–6 *Regulations for Secondary Schools*, which states that

> experience proves that in a school of the secondary type full efficiency can be secured and the best teaching and organisational power attracted, only where the Head Master or Head Mistress is entrusted with a large amount of responsibility.... In particular the appointment and dismissal of Assistant Staff is a matter in which a voice ought to be secured to the Head Master.

The issue also exercised the Public School Commission (1970) when considering the possible absorption of the direct grant schools into the state system. Arising from such statements, the hypothesis is advanced that there will be at least *some* significant correlations between responses relating to the internal and external sectors of the CE role model. Refraining from predicting the direction of the relationships, we use the more stringent two-tail tests of statistical significance.

The correlational analysis amply confirmed the hypothesis. Both in terms of expectations and behaviour, the head whose position is less recognised by external authority takes less initiative in defining staff responsibilities and delegates less readily. He is less likely to supervise staff closely, insist on deadlines or emphasise efficiency. A person who feels that his authority is limited or uncertain, i.e. that he is 'under-powered', to use Musgrove's phrase (1971), in relation to his responsibilities is naturally on the defensive. He is understandably reluctant to risk taking positive measures in the deployment or supervision of staff or to share with others the little authority which he has. On the other hand, the head whose position in relation to external authority is assured is more likely both to take initiatives himself in executive matters and to delegate effectively to members of staff.

The findings reported above provide grounds for formulating a general proposition in the following terms: *the occupant of an executive position who is granted little authority and recognition by his superiors, tends to behave in relation to his subordinates in a cautious and defensive manner, which exposes him to as little risk as possible.* Conversely the executive who is granted an appreciable measure of autonomy and recognition by his superiors is more likely, in his relations with subordinates, both to adopt a positive approach himself and to encourage others to become involved in executive functions.

It is relevant to note that the above proposition receives support from studies in the very different cultural milieu of the United States. Thus Seeman (1960) found that school executives in Ohio whose status was precarious or ambiguous adopted a conservative type of leadership behaviour, which he interpreted in terms of 'inauthenticity'. On the other hand, leaders who rated themselves as high in status 'described their leadership not only as high in authority and responsibility, but also in delegation'. Seeman concluded that 'leadership behaviour and ideology are, in significant part, functions of status considerations which stem from the community and culture surrounding the given organisation'. Carlson (1965) found a similar relationship between the status of school superintendents and their encouragement of curriculum innovation in the schools under their control. Also noteworthy is the finding of Gross and Herriott (1965) that the executive professional leadership provided by elementary school principals is positively and significantly related to the perception by the principals of the professional behaviour of their administrative superiors, including the extent to which the higher administrators involve the principal in the appointment of his teachers.

Returning to implications from the present study, conducted within the educational system of England and Wales, the evidence suggests that it is unrealistic for governing bodies and local education authorities to expect the heads of their educational institutions to adopt a positive and dynamic approach to managerial responsibilities and staff involvement unless they are prepared, at the same time, to grant a generous measure of institutional autonomy. In a wider setting our findings, and the American studies which have been cited, have relevance to the centralisation-versus-devolution issue which invariably looms large in international seminars on educational administration and is a major concern of UNESCO and OECD in their studies of educational planning and the management of innovation (Lyons, 1970; Dalin, 1973). It may well be that professional initiative and the exercise of discretion cannot properly be expected from school executives who are regarded, and who regard themselves, as the powerless minions of a centralised and powerful bureaucracy.

THE LP ROLE MODEL

Considerations of space make it necessary to report on this section more briefly in the present paper. The formulation of items was based on a review of the professional literature and on the writer's personal experience as a secondary school head, with some revision as a result of a pilot study.

A correlational analysis of the responses, taken in pairs, to the items finally chosen, revealed two distinct factors in the concept of the head as leading professional. Firstly, there is what may be called a *traditional* (or local) dimension, which is significantly related to high scores on the head's regular teaching and his pastoral relationship to, and personal involvement with, both staff and pupils.

Secondly there is an *innovating* (or cosmopolitan) dimension, which is indicative of an openness to external professional influences. Significant positive correlations at each of the three levels of response were found among the responses under the following headings:

- the head's readiness to take the initiative in getting staff to try out new ideas and media

- the head's involvement in educational activities outside his own school, e.g. the meetings of professional bodies;

- the importance attached to the head finding time for personal study.

The data showed clearly that the heads who expected (and were expected by staff) to be professionally active outside their school, expected (and were expected by staff) to give positive encouragement to innovation within their schools, a result confirmed in terms of the heads' reported behaviour responses. The conclusion which may be drawn, i.e. that there is an 'innovative' dimension which provides a link between the in-school and out-of-school aspects of the head as leading professional provides a new element in the discussion of the head as educational innovator (Hoyles, 1968; Hoyle, 1969; Tucker, 1970).

An interesting finding in the study was that the traditional and innovating aspects are largely independent of each other, rather than antithetical aspects of the head's role; i.e. the two dimensions may be regarded as orthogonal. A typology of heads may thus be based on the following diagram:

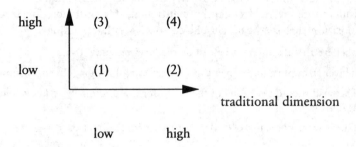

The four categories may be labelled as follows:

(1) *The abdicator* – below average in personal teaching and pastoral emphasis and in openness to external professional influences.

(2) *The traditionalist* – above average in personal teaching and pastoral emphasis but below average in openness to external professional influences.

(3) *The innovator* – below average in personal teaching and pastoral emphasis but above average in openness to external professional influences.

(4) *The extended professional* – above average in personal teaching and pastoral emphasis and in openness to external professional influences.

The 'abdicator' type in its most extreme form is probably non-existent, but the other three types were easily recognisable in the research. A correlation of responses with the size of school showed some tendency for the small-school head to be a 'traditionalist' and for the large-school head to be an 'innovator', but there were numerous instances of heads, irrespective of the size of school, who placed a high emphasis on both aspects.

Large-school heads in the latter category might properly be called '*over extended professionals*' (Hughes, 1972b). Several of them admitted, during interview, that they sought to live up to expectations of personal involvement with pupils which they themselves recognised to be unrealistic, e.g. 'One should try to know all pupils, however large the school may be, though it is impossible in a large school'. Similarly Bernbaum (1970) found large-school heads reluctant to relinquish traditional human-relations aspects of their work, a result confirmed by Cohen (1970) and by Bates (1971). It is a matter for concern that there are still far too many heads who carry too great a responsibility for their school's success on their own shoulders (Benn and Simon, 1970; Conway, 1970).

THE INTERPENETRATION OF THE ROLE MODELS

The incidental comments of heads and staff, during interview, provided cumulative evidence that the executive and professional aspects of the head's role, though analytically distinct, are closely interrelated. Organisational considerations were frequently mentioned, for instance, in favour of the proposition that the head 'should do some regular teaching':

> I believe that discipline is helped by the head teaching. (head)

> It gives an opportunity of being around the school without obviously snooping. (head)

> The head should teach one of the tough forms occasionally to know what we are up against. (staff)

> This is what keeps the Old Man in touch with reality. (staff)

Similarly the reservations sometimes expressed by heads and staff of larger schools were often linked to organisational considerations:

> I have always felt it important to have a foot in the classroom, regarding myself as still a teacher, but now I am not so sure. I still *do* teach, but I have become very doubtful about it, feeling that there is an element of escapism in getting away to the classroom. Am I justified? Ought I not to be more accessible and be about the school more? (head)

> The previous head taught too much and was not available to staff as much as was desirable. (staff)

> After all, his main job is to run the school. (staff)

The above remarks serve to illustrate the fact that a crude formulation of the professional-organisational dilemma in terms of the polar extremities of a single continuum would be singularly naive. The relationship between responses within the two role models may properly be expected to be much more complex, and this proved in fact to be so. When an inter-model correlational analysis was performed, nearly a half of the item pairs yielded no significant relationship, while the rest provided one cluster of negative significant correlations and another cluster of positive significant correlations. We consider these in turn.

(a) The negative correlations

These were confined almost entirely to one area, revealing a conflict between 'traditional' elements of the LP role model and aspects of the CE role model. In particular, there was a significant negative relationship between responses favourable to the head's personal involvement with individual pupils (pastoral care of pupils, knowing pupils by name, personally writing reports on pupils, etc.) and responses indicative of an emphasis on executive functions (the delegation of routine matters, stressing efficient procedures, etc.)...

The severe difficulties experienced by large-school heads seeking to conform to the traditional stereotype have already been noted. There is evidence, however, that a change of emphasis is occurring both in the schools and in the professional literature (Holden, 1969; Hughes, 1971). As a consequence, the counselling function is no longer regarded as an essential part of the head's role, but is able to develop an independent institutional existence with a distinctive professional expertise and ideology (Halmos, 1965). The head is no less 'concerned' than formerly, but his professional care is increasingly expressed in the planning and maintenance of a comprehensive system of counselling and guidance, involving house tutors or year tutors, counsellors and careers staff, rather than in attempting personally to give an all-round one-man service (Halmos, 1970).

(b) The positive correlations

LP role model responses indicative of an 'innovating' emphasis correlated significantly and positively with responses within the CE role model. Thus the head who reports taking the initiative in getting staff to try out new ideas tends to rate himself highly on sorting out staff responsibilities, supervising staff, insisting on deadlines and emphasising efficiency. Members of staff who expect the head to encourage innovation are more tolerant than other staff of his insistence on deadlines, and are more likely to approve of his being much in evidence about the school. The head's professional leadership is seen, by heads and staff, to have organisational implications.

The innovating head, it appears, relies partly on exerting influence on staff colleagues as a fellow professional. Equally, however, he accepts his position as chief executive, and uses the organisational controls which are available to him to get things moving. Professional and executive considerations reinforce each other as complementary aspects of a coherent and unified strategy.

The seeming paradox is also evident in the positive correlations, significant at each of the three levels of response, which link the personal guidance of inexperienced staff by the head (an aspect of his professional role) and the head's close supervision of staff (an aspect of his executive role). It seems that the fact that the chief executive of the organisation regards himself, and is regarded by the professional staff, as one of them, makes it unrealistic to seek to distinguish with any precision between his guidance of staff in the interest of their personal development and their supervision in the interest of the organisation.

TOWARDS A UNIFIED ROLE MODEL OF HEADSHIP

In the research which is only partially reported in the present article the relevance of the LP–CE construct was further explored in relation to three areas of potential difficulty for heads: namely, the head's social interaction with staff, the school's relationship with parents, and the issues of pupil and staff participation. Though it is not practicable to report these aspects here, it may be stated that the findings provide further confirmation of the importance of the distinction drawn between a 'traditional' and an 'innovating' aspect of the head's professionalism. It is already clear from the inter-model correlational analysis reported above that the 'traditional' emphasis is potentially in conflict with the basic features of the chief executive role, whereas an 'innovator' emphasis is more easily reconciled with the head's managerial responsibilities.

Though they are useful as analytical and heuristic devices, it has to be recognised that our role models are but abstractions, which only partially reflect the reality. In seeking to develop a more unified role model it is therefore salutary to recall that many heads to some extent, and some heads to a great extent, succeed in simultaneously activating and integrating the two contrasting and potentially conflicting aspects of their total role. For the head of a small school in a stable environment, this may not be too difficult, but it may be concluded from the research reported above that when these conditions do not apply a change of emphasis within the head's concept of his professionalism (and within staff concepts of the head's professionalism) may be necessary for some heads if the total role is to be successfully enacted without excessive strain.

In a specific context it has been shown that the professional-as-administrator fulfils his mediating role to a large extent by providing the kind of supervision of professional staff and the kind of organisational leadership in responding to external change, which is acceptable to professionals. Other aspects of his professionalism may be inappropriate and even counterproductive.

Much therefore depends on the interpretation given by the professional-as-administrator to his professional role. If his professionalism is restricted and modelled on traditional stereotypes, his best endeavours could well exacerbate the problems of a large and complex organisation, subject to pressures from within and without. If the emphasis is on his leadership and encouragement of colleagues in their joint efforts, his contribution could be invaluable in enabling the combined expertise of a professional staff to be mobilised for the achievement of agreed organisational objectives.

Managing the Secondary School in the 1990s: A New View of Headship

PETER RIBBINS AND BRIAN SHERRATT

1. PREFACE

Secondary schools face a plethora of change. Some have tackled this effectively and others have struggled. The way in which the role of headship is interpreted and enacted has been repeatedly identified by researchers, by professional educators and by parents as a crucial variable in determining the nature and quality of a school's response to demands for change. Given this, we know remarkably little about how particular heads see their role. There are, of course, many surveys of headship of one kind or another and a number of case studies of individual secondary schools which, amongst other things, examine aspects of the role of the head. Such studies normally seek to say something about the views of heads and draw upon direct quotations from interviews which the researcher has conducted with the head to do so. There are also a small number of case studies of secondary schools as a whole or of aspects of such schools which have been written by their headteachers. In producing these studies such heads often draw heavily on their own experience and their accounts frequently contain descriptions, explanations and justifications of how and why they acted in the ways they did. With this in mind why is yet another study worth undertaking and what can it hope to add to our understanding of headship?

It is possible to advance plausible reasons for engaging in further studies of headship. For example, relatively few studies of this kind exist and several which are currently available were undertaken many years ago. Few would deny that the context within which contemporary heads must operate has been significantly changed over the last few years. This alone would justify further studies of headship. But in undertaking such a study we have tried to develop a new approach. An approach in which the head is not regarded as just the subject of another's research but rather as a full partner within the research process. The authors, one of whom is currently head of a very large successful comprehensive school and the other an experienced researcher within secondary schools, are together attempting to pioneer an approach to the study of headship which they describe as a dialectic of biography and autobiography.

The context of our study is Great Barr Grant Maintained School in Birmingham and at the time of writing we have been engaged in it more or less actively for just over 20 months. The evidence which we have collected to date is extraordinarily rich and it should enable us when we finally come to write it up to throw some light upon the kinds of things which more conventional studies are unable to explore. It is not our intention in this paper to report upon substantive issues. This would be premature given the current state of the research. Rather we will try to say something about the project in general and about the approach in particular and will present this in the form of an edited and revised transcript of a discussion which we conducted specifically for this purpose.

2. TOWARDS A NEW APPROACH FOR THE STUDY OF HEADSHIP: A DISCUSSION

PR: I want to raise a number of issues about what we are doing in this research project, how we are doing it, why we are doing it in the kind of way we are, what the advantages and difficulties are in doing it as we are and to illustrate these things with an example or two as we go along...

I wanted to undertake the study within a large successful urban comprehensive school and Great Barr seemed to fit this description well. I envisaged an in-depth longitudinal case study of the kind I had undertaken in other secondary schools in the past. The research would, I thought, focus on issues which derive from the 1988 Act and other recent legislation including such things as the introduction of a national curriculum, more open enrolment, local management of schools, the redistribution of powers and duties between elected members, governors, the head and other teachers. At the time I had no reason to believe that the school would take the decision which it subsequently did to seek grant-maintained status. From a research point of view, this added a considerable additional opportunity to examine the consequences of the Act.

When the research began I had intended to use a methodology based on the kind of partially ethnographic approach which I had used in other similar studies (see Ribbins, 1986). This means observing what people do, talking to them, reading what they write and doing all this over an extended period of time. During the last 20 months I have been engaged in this and in doing so have interviewed about 25 staff in all, some more than once. In time, I hope to talk to all the staff and governors. I have also made a number of observations including meetings of staff and of the governing body. Finally, I have collected two large boxes of documents from the school. More of all this will need to be done in the future.

For me, an important but subsidiary interest was to explore the claim that a crucial variable in determining the quality of a school is the nature and quality of the leadership which it gets, especially from the head. So from the beginning I saw the need to study your attitudes and actions. Therefore we have engaged in a series of discussions. To date, we have met 17 times in meetings lasting up to two hours. As a result of our discussions my initial conception of the project gradually evolved into what we now see as its present form. This has meant your role as head has become a central focus of the research and not just one aspect amongst many others. In an important sense the study has become an examination of the ways in which you understand, interpret and enact your headship at a crucial period in the life of the school and during a period of radical transformation.

Many of the case studies of secondary schools reported over the last 20 years have given prominence to the role of the headteacher. Even so I find it helpful to think in terms of three main kinds of approaches to such research. The first two are studies by heads or former heads. In the first, practising heads give an account of what they have tried to do – studies by Poster, Dawson and others are of this kind. In these the reader is given an opportunity to learn from a head what it is he or she is trying to do and why. In the second, heads analyse headship in schools based upon systematic research into the attitudes and activities of other heads. Some distinguished researchers into headship, such as Meredydd Hughes (1975) and Anne Jones (1987) are cases in point.

In the third case a head or a group of heads are the subject of research by professional researchers. There are two main versions of this. The first are studies which focus on the views of heads in some general sense. They can be very illuminating as the recent book on secondary headship by Mortimer and Mortimer (1991) demonstrates. Whatever their merits, such reports do not seek to study particular heads in the context of the schools within which they are located. This latter is the approach which I have adopted in the studies of secondary schools I have been involved in at Rivendell, Revelstone, Mallory and elsewhere. It has been characteristic of the research undertaken by Ball, Burgess, Lacey and others. In most such studies the school is not identified. Elizabeth Richardson's (1973) report on Nailsea is an exception. She reports on what he said and did but it is clearly her account we are being given not his....

As our research progressed we began to look for other ways of studying headship. Ways which might enable us to produce accounts of headship much richer than are possible using the approaches described above. Could, for example, a researcher and a head work together closely over a significant period of time as co-researchers and in doing so develop the kind of novel approach to the study of headship which we sought. This, we knew, would be difficult for you. As head you would be both the principal subject of the research and a fully fledged researcher within a project in which you are the main subject of that research. To achieve this means that you will need to reflect carefully upon what you are doing and why you are doing it. A task for us has been to work out methods of enabling you to do this.

Over the last year or so we have begun to work out three ways of enabling you to do this. Firstly, the continuing series of conversations which you and I have been having. As these have taken place we have had the time to build up a high level of trust and respect for each other. Both these things seem essential if the approach we are trying to develop is to have any hope of producing worthwhile understandings. We are both, you more than I, taking a considerable risk in what we are doing.

Secondly, your production of a series of frank diaries describing your life as a head. Would that we could publish these as they stand. They offer a fantastically detailed and illuminating account of your thinking. But for obvious reasons this may not be possible and we will have to think carefully about how we are going to use them.

The third method is to try to set your own accounts against those of other key actors who play a significant part in determining the kind of school Great Barr is to be and the ways in which it will respond to external demands for change. In undertaking this we have focused in particular on the staff and governors. For a comprehensive examination we would have had to explore the views of parents, pupils and others but limitations of resource have made this impossible. My role in our conversations has been to try to describe, analyse, explain to you what it is I see that you are trying to do. This must involve an attempt to interpret what you have told me and to reflect this back to you. Since, at the same time, I am talking to other staff and governors I can reflect their views back to you and explore with you your response to this in the light of your own views. From all this we hope eventually to be able to offer an account of headship which will be richer than any currently available. We have come to think of our approach to the study of headship as involving a dialectic of biography and autobiography. We need to say something more about this.

The biographical aspect is based in part upon the account of the school and your place and role in it which I build up using traditional methods. It would draw on the collections of documents I have made, my interviews with you, my access to your diaries, my discussions with staff and governors, my observations of you in action and my observations of staff and governors in action. This is beginning to enable me to give an account of your headship in context. My discussions with you alone would probably have enabled me to give a remarkably full account of headship but without talking to others this would have been limited. By talking to staff and governors I can locate your account within the context of the views and actions of others in the school. So much for the biographical aspect of our research. What of its autobiographical dimension?

A dictionary might define 'autobiography' as 'an account of one's life written or told by oneself'. It is the form of literature which consists of stories that people write or tell about their own lives and experiences. In a sense your diaries and what you say to me in our discussions amount to a sketch for such an autobiography. What then of the notion of a dialectic between biography and autobiography? This comes from the juxtaposition of our accounts against each other.

In these comments I have tried to set out what we are trying to do and have sought to offer a description and explanation of our developing thinking about the research we are engaged in together. Is this how you see it?

BS: Yes I do. A veritable *tour de force*!

PR: How did you see the project in the beginning? . . .

BS: . . .In the beginning I saw it as a study of how the school was responding to the implementation of the Education Reform Act in general and the National Curriculum in particular. But over the last year much more has happened as we secured grant-maintained status in terms of what this means for relationships with the governors, the introduction of new budgetary arrangements and the revision of the management roles of senior staff. Even without the developments in our thinking which you describe, all this would have made our project even more interesting than it was when we set out. In part this is because my own role changed significantly as a result of LMS and even more so with our GM status. These changes have meant that as the head I feel I have become much more directly and significantly influential in the things which we set out to look at . . .

I think you have always thought of me as a central actor in the management of the changes entailed by the Act. But in becoming GM I took a leading role. I had little option but to stand centre stage. Partly because at that stage my chairman of governors, for reasons of diplomacy, was unable to do so. This meant I had to lead the campaign and so was far more aware of the broader implications, processes and politics of what I was trying to do than I might otherwise have been. Similarly, being involved in the research encouraged me to be more reflective and introspective . . . .

It also became more public.

PR: But even this could have been encompassed within a traditional qualitative research approach. But in the event we have been trying to develop another and relatively novel approach to studying and understanding such change and of the role of the head within it. We began to realise that we had become very interested in exploring together what you were doing and why you were doing it. Our conversations gave more and more prominence to this topic as we began to understand we could undertake such an exploration in a much more worthwhile way if we worked together not as researcher and researched but as co-researchers.

BS: That's right. We were trying to describe a period in which I as head was dealing with a series of complex and often sensitive technical and political issues, situations and even confrontations. The scope of headship was fundamentally changed in a situation in which the nature and level of parental involvement reached a pitch which had never existed before.

PR: This was a very demanding and stressful time for you. I suspect that if we had not already begun to work together as co-researchers we could never have achieved this during those tense and hectic months. I also doubt if I alone could hope to achieve the kind of account of headship which I expect we will be able to produce together. For you, this was and is a very risky time. Why should you expose yourself to the risks entailed in sharing your innermost thoughts about what you were doing and why with someone who regarded you as an interesting subject for his research? Even so it may be worth asking you why you should choose to do this now and as a full and equal participant in the research? For my own part I suspect that you are interested in exploring your own motives and actions as a head and feel you might achieve a clearer understanding if we work together than if you worked on your own. Could it also be that you would have had no reason to engage in the systematic, in-depth self-reflection in which you have engaged over the last year if we had not been involved in this project together?

BS: Yes; that is right. I had already become used to working in this way and engaging in the kind of introspection you mention. Because I had become used to saying what I was thinking or feeling at the time this made me more prepared to divulge things which perhaps I would not normally want to talk about to other people. Also I found that the diaries and our conversations helped me to clarify what I was doing.

PR: Another benefit in terms of our attempt to understand headship has been that you have made explicit in a systematic and continuing way and at the time your thoughts about what you were trying to do...

BS: It may be that our conversations have helped me not only to clarify my ideas and thinking about what I have done but also about what I might do.

PR: It is almost as if the study has become a piece of action research and my role has become that of consultant. Has it modified how you have thought and acted over time? Have you become more critical of what you do?

BS: It has encouraged me to a greater extent than I might have to try to look at things from the perspective of those who might be diametrically opposed to what I am trying to do, for example, in the pursuit of grant-maintained status. In this, I think that trying to take on board perspectives which are very different to my own has helped me to cope with the knowledge that there were people who either did not like or were unsure about what was happening. It helped me to see this objectively and dispassionately rather than taking it to heart.

PR: From the point of view of the research this means that to an extent you have been reflecting on these events as researcher as well as participant? This may help bridge the divide between researcher and practitioner which is too often found in such studies – you are both researcher and practitioner.

In undertaking this phase of our research we have had to grapple with a number of methodological and practical difficulties. Given that we are trying to develop a new kind of approach this is not surprising. But some of the practical problems we have encountered have had little to do with the novel character of our research approach and more to do with the demands you have faced in managing a major and difficult period of change. For example, we had planned to meet once every two weeks during term time to discuss developments and had hoped that each couple of weeks you would produce a taped diary account of about three-quarters of an hour in length. We have not managed to achieve either of these things. However, we have met some 17 times and you have taped 11 diary entries over the last year. On six or seven occasions we have managed to follow up the diary entries with discussions but would hope in the future to be able to do this on a rather more regular and systematic basis. At these meetings we would hope to feed into our discussions what I am hearing from other staff and the governors and to explore your reactions to this....

In a conventional research study of this kind you would not as head expect to have access to the transcripts of the interviews I undertake with other staff. Even in our research there are possible problems with this which we should discuss. One is that if staff know you will have access to what they say to me how will this affect what they are prepared to tell me? After all as the head you have an important role in determining the quality of their life within the school and of their future career prospects. How might this influence what they say to me? To try to minimise this we agreed that I would make it clear that unless they specifically asked for all or some of their interview to be kept confidential, you would have access to transcripts. To date, following interviews with a quarter of the staff none have asked for this with regard to the whole interview and only a few have asked that some aspect of what they have to say be kept confidential. We have been scrupulous in observing to the letter such requests...

BS: How have I undertaken the diary? Ideally, on a daily basis. This has the great advantage of noting ideas and experiences while they are fresh in my mind. It is less satisfactory to do it at one sitting once every two weeks. On the other hand this helps, or helps me, to weed out what appear in retrospect to be the less significant features of the past couple of weeks as I sit down to reflect upon them. There is a certain discipline involved in having to do all this which is sometimes very difficult to achieve...

PR: What ground rules have you established to help you with the diary?

BS: I have tried to describe events during the course of the week which I feel have been significant, primarily from the point of view of a head managing a large school. Very often these have hinged upon the need to make decisions on policies and tactics with respect to the achievement of certain stated or unstated goals during the course of the week.

PR: Reading through them they have seemed very open and frank. You have tried to think through the various tactics which you might use or have used and the tactics which others might use or have used to block or support what you are trying to do. You also speculate on why staff and others take the line they have – expedience, self-interest, principle or whatever.

BS: Also what people say may not be what they mean or believe. Nor is it always a perfect guide to what they do. In some cases they might appear to be enthusiastic when talking to you or in a public meeting but in private they may be opposed and work to encourage others to be hostile as well.

PR: What you have done is to record some quite frank descriptions of your own motives and methods and some quite frank speculations as to why other people act in the ways in which they do act.

BS: I think we all do this and I think it is essential for a head to be able to speculate in this way if he or she is to motivate people, to match tasks to individuals and this is true of effective leadership in all kinds of contexts and not something special to effective headship. I also think if our research is to be worthwhile I need to say what I really think.

PR: Was it difficult to be as frank as you have been in the tapes?

BS: I have not found it that difficult once the trust between us had developed. I have always realised that this is a serious piece of research and have come to be excited by it as I became aware of how novel and innovative it is. I saw little point in continuing unless I was prepared to be frank about what I was experiencing, feeling and thinking. And of course it will be very interesting in a couple of years to listen to or read back what I have said. It will give me the chance to reflect at some later stage on whether I had judged the situations I was talking about adequately. Few of us get the chance to do this at least in such a systematic way...
  It is important to say that they are not just an account of what I have tried to do but also touch upon the problems I have experienced along the way. It would be difficult to get at this subsequently without access to a record of one's thoughts and feelings which were made at the time.

PR: In describing how we have gone about this research there are three main things which we might talk about. Firstly, there are a number of technical things to do with the way in which we have undertaken the research. For example, how, when and where did we undertake our discussions? How were they recorded? How were they transcribed? Secondly, there are issues about the substance and method of the research. What should it focus on? To what ground rules should we work? Thirdly, given that the transcripts of our discussions and your diaries are highly confidential documents, we have had to think carefully about how they were to be produced and stored. The fact that you are both researcher and manager makes this especially important.

We have used the terms 'biography and autobiography' several times in this conversation. Perhaps we need to try to say what we mean by these terms at the level of the school and the head. Let us begin at the level of the school. In interviews with staff I have been inviting them to tell me what they think is happening. Since I am going to use this to tell the tale of the school we might think of this as biography. But since it is their account of their own school and their place within it, you could argue that this is the stuff of autobiography. I think what you are doing in your diaries is much more evidently a kind of autobiography – in undertaking this you are producing a detailed and frank account of your life and work as head. The account I am offering, derived as it is from observations of different aspects of the school in action, from school documents, from discussions with you and other staff and governors and from access to your diaries, is a kind of biography of both you and of the school.

BS: Yes, I think your part can aptly be described as biographical. But you might need to be careful since if you become too attached to the school and the people in it you might lose your detachment and objectivity. This is not something I can avoid. My accounts of the school and of my place within it are clearly autobiographical; there is a sense in which I experience the school as an extension of myself.

PR: I take your warning about the danger of becoming too involved. What I hope to achieve is the status of insider/outsider. As one spends time in a place insiders can to a degree forget you are an outsider or else they can accord you a kind of 'honorary insider' status.

BS: Some objectivity is essential to your role in our research. But as you become more and more involved it may be increasingly difficult to sustain this necessary level of detachment, however important it is for you to do so. You risk becoming an insider?

PR: It could be. I agree I need to bring a degree of detachment to my part in the research. Given my past experience I feel sure I will be able to do it at the level of the school as a whole. But in any case I think it helps to like the people you are studying. If you cannot do this you must try to respect them. I do not see myself as a professional organisational assassin nor do I accept contracts on individuals.

BS: Nevertheless you will need to bring a degree of detachment to our relationship as well.

PR: If I do not, my value to the research is diminished to the degree to which I lose this detachment. I risk becoming an echo rather than an alter ego. But what can happen in such research is not just that the external researcher risks becoming an insider but that those with whom (s)he works closely risk becoming quasi-researchers or outsiders. This happens if their commitment to the research/researcher becomes greater than their commitment to the school.

PR: . . . I think we might follow up the point you made that you see the school as a kind of extension of yourself. What did you mean by that?

BS: I know that may not be a very helpful way of putting it but there are times when I feel like that. When things go particularly well or badly then I do feel as if it is a kind of extension of myself. Whether other heads feel like this I don't know. . . .

BS: Perhaps we ought to see my responses to your questions as autobiographical. I don't necessarily have time to sit down and ask myself what you are going to ask when we meet. You come in, ask questions and I start talking in response. Since I do not know what you are going to ask me I cannot plan carefully in advance what I am going to say in response. As such I suppose my answers are autobiographical. Of course there will be certain things you ask which are essentially factual – for example, our plans for building development or our budgetary arrangements – when I give you the facts. It is when I tell you about how I feel or what I think that I am engaged in autobiographical activity. When I tell you the details of our building plans or budget my answer is in the biographical mode. You can also argue that autobiography entails a description of oneself and since in these cases I am being asked for a description of someone or something else then in answering I am engaged in biography.

PR: I wonder if you might have missed an important step in the argument. I am not asking you to tell me other people's views but what you think other people's views are. I can go directly to them and ask them for their perceptions of things if I wish to know this. Given the division of labour we have agreed on we might even say that it is my responsibility to seek these as necessary. When I ask them for their views what I get is their views, or at least what they are prepared to tell me. When I ask you about their views, I am not expecting you to go along to ask them but to tell me what you think they think. Taken as a whole when we work together to produce an account of the school and of your role within it your part is to offer an autobiography of your headship. What I can do is produce a biography of your headship. What we have a chance to do together is to produce something which is more than either and more than either of us can possibly achieve alone; something which is part biography and part autobiography. I do not know of anybody else who has tried to do this and I do not know of any other way of doing it . . .

BS: An advantage for those who might read our report is that, unlike other research into headship, you get much more than just the view of a researcher; you get the view of the head as well. Traditional research on headship can be irritating to practitioners because it sometimes does not sufficiently take into account the dilemmas of headship as these are experienced by heads themselves in situ. There are things which as a manager practitioner I can speak on from personal experience. On the other hand, the rigour and detachment which you as a professional researcher bring to bear offers an important corrective against any tendency I might have to give too much weight to my views about aspects of the school and how people see these which are highly questionable. I might get something off my chest in the diary about how something seems to me at the time and you might be able to present me with evidence which challenges my view. It is these kinds of things which are all too often missing in the general run of such research into headship within schools. They will be the stuff of our research.

PR: That was well put but I think we might explore one or two caveats which I have about some of the things you have said. Firstly, I am essentially a subjectivist. I would not claim that the kind of accounts I have given of the schools and people I have studied over the last 16 years are objective in some absolute sense. I am happy to acknowledge that these are my accounts and not the accounts of the people who were the subjects of my research. I try to base what I have to say on as full and as clear an account of the way in which the people involved within the institution I am studying see things too. Nevertheless I take a view of a world which is socially created and sustained, a world of multiple realities. We make our social world and every part of it, we don't just take it. For me what is different about our research is that I believe that the account we can give together must be richer than any account I could possibly give on my own of your exercise of headship at Great Barr.

BS: In this research you will not just be using my words as you have used the words of the heads you have studied in the past. In our study my words will not only be used but I will also be saying something in my own right.

PR: And furthermore you will have an important role in determining what we report you to have said and how that is to be interpreted. At best we might offer an account of headship which is personalised but not idiosyncratic.

BS: Monitoring any gap between what I say and what I do will not just be a matter of talking to me but also talking to others. Furthermore if there is a gap we can hope to explain why. This should go a long way to preventing the doubtful accounts which I have sometimes read from my fellow heads when they set out to describe what they do and why....

PR: ... We have talked about the advantages of the approach but there are also difficulties. It is one thing to collect the kind of data we have described, another to decide what and how we can report. Particularly since we have decided to identify the school.

BS: I don't think we have any option about this.

PR: In our conversations with others we have never said that this is going to be an anonymised study. We should be aware of the potential advantages of such anonymity....There are also practical concerns such as the fact that you are likely to continue to be head of the school after our book or any papers are published and the views and decisions we record and report may have consequences for the way in which individual staff and governors view their prospects at the school. In practical terms we will have hard decisions to make about what we can report when this can be directly or indirectly traced back to individuals. We would not have these difficulties to this extent if the study was anonymous but this does not seem to be a real option for us as we see things at this point. Even if we did decide to make the study anonymous it is not easy to see how we would do this since you would be a co-author.

BS: ...What it means at the very least is that we are going to gather material which is much richer than we will be able to use. In a sense the project may be at its most interesting now. It will not be easy but we should still be able to say something about headship using the methods which we are developing which is different in kind from anything else which exists currently. In doing so we should also be able to say a good deal about the way in which a large successful comprehensive school and its staff and governors are coping with a difficult present and planning for an uncertain future.

From Transactions to Transformations: A New World Order in the Study of Leadership?

PETER GRONN

When asked by a friar (the Duke of Vienna in disguise) towards the end of Shakespeare's *Measure for Measure* of what disposition was the duke, the noble lord Escalus replies (III, ii): 'One that, above all other strifes, contended especially to know himself'. Earlier, to the lord deputy during his forthcoming absence, Angelo, the duke had confessed (I, i):

> ... I love the people,
> But do not like to stage me to their eyes:
> Though it do well, I do not relish well
> Their loud applause, and *Aves* vehement:
> Nor do I think he man of safe discretion,
> That does affect it.

After 14 years of statutes 'let slip' and of decrees 'Dead to infliction', therefore, when:

> .... liberty plucks justice by the nose;
> The baby beats the nurse, and quite athwart
> Goes all decorum...

the duke had departed, ostensibly to a monastery, but fully intending to see 'If power change purpose, what our seemers be' (I, iv).

Needless to say, the duke's rather stealthily contrived device for inspecting the outcome of his own leadership or its lack, disguised as 'a looker-on here in Vienna' (V, i), is beyond the reach of most leaders, who are forced to rely instead on more indirect means of insight into what their own leadership does and what their followers think and do in response to it. Yet Shakespeare's ingenious example of the duke who, it will be recalled, had allowed his subjects to indulge themselves in permissiveness, but did not have the stomach to inflict tyrannous punishment on his realm – after all, he was, said Escalus, 'a gentleman of all temperance' (III, ii) – brings to light a number of dimensions of leaders and their leading, and of followers and their following. This paper discusses five aspects of leadership: its meaning, its significance, the most appropriate ways in which to frame an understanding of it, the current state of knowledge about it and its genesis, or where leadership comes from.

The final part of the paper brings together the implications of these points for leading and following in education. For reasons which are not entirely clear... the received wisdom amongst commentators is that the 1970s marked a sea-change in the study of leadership.... Among the more ardent proponents of a new paradigm in leadership the most popular way of typifying the transition has been to contrast a new version of leading which accomplishes leadership *outcomes* (or transformations) with an older variety focusing on the mechanics of leadership *processes* or transactions.

This paper, however, takes issue with this claim. First, it is shown that while there certainly has been a switch in focus, mainly from political leaders and small group leaders to organizations, to executive organizational levels and then to what leaders achieve, the continuity of recent developments with previous approaches to leadership far outweighs their discontinuity. Second, despite the new focus, age-old questions about leadership remain unanswered. In particular, it is shown that two important new developments – transformational leadership and managerial leadership – are deficient, owing to an impoverished understanding of context and process. The former approach attributes undue *agency* to individual leaders, while the latter over-emphasizes the constraints of *structure*....

DEFINING LEADERSHIP

Unlike Shakespeare's duke-in-disguise, no one has the luxury of being in a privileged or transcendent position from which to discourse on leadership. Any definition, therefore (and the one below is no exception), will reflect that particular commentator's presuppositions about the parameters of leader-followership. Nevertheless, whatever the cultural, ethnic, gender and social class components of the context concerned, the two core attributes which best define a 'leader' are influence and identification, while 'leading' is defined as the framing of meaning and the mobilization of support for a meaningful course of action.

There is now increasingly broad acceptance that leadership is a form of direct or indirect influence (Hunt, 1991, p. 57). Influence entails a significant effect on an individual or group's well-being, interests, policies or behaviour, and its exercise is usually thought of as legitimate by those subjected to it. The leader, then, is that person who, as Gouldner (1950, pp. 17–18) suggested, 'stimulates patterning of the behaviour in some group' and whose influence may be grounded in any perceived skill, attribute or endowment. Identification, something usually associated with psychoanalytic perspectives on leadership (see Shamir, 1991, pp. 83–6), expresses the emotional connection between leaders and followers. Thus, the leader is the person with whom followers (for a variety of motives) identify, the one whom they would prefer to imitate, who inspires them or who represents their deep-seated aspirations and hopes.

There is also an emerging consensus that leading is an inherently symbolic activity (Bolman and Deal, 1994, pp. 83; Schein, 1992, pp. 19–20). To frame meaning (the capacity to make sense of one's own and others' experiences of the world in palatable ways) is synonymous with the everyday sense-making intrinsic to what it means to be human. But the significance of a leader's act of sense-making is her or his capacity to invoke key symbols which reinforce the meaning of the events and circumstances they frame. And the willingness of followers to be influenced and to identify ensures their almost automatic preparedness for leaders to frame meanings on their behalf and to submit themselves to the former's version of events. Smircich and Morgan (1982, pp. 258, original emphasis) refer to this as 'an *obligation* or a perceived *right* on the part of certain individuals to define the reality of others'. Readily available stocks of definitions (i.e. words, images, discourse and ideologies) facilitate the leader's manipulation of symbols and the mobilization of support in the pursuit of particular group or organizational interests. Thus, if a leader's symbols have semantic force for followers, then she or he is, in effect, responsible for 'instilling meaning in organization action and events' and able to 'construct reality for the followers' (Griffin *et al.*, 1987, pp. 202).

Commentators also agree with Jacobs and Jaques's (1991) disavowal (see earlier) of any automatic connection between leadership and headship. Gibb's (1968, p. 213) reference to the 'unidirectional influence which few people would want to call leadership' traditionally evident in relations between, for example, master and slave, teacher and pupil, and officer and men, suggests headship entails reflex compliance by subordinates. But the exercise of the authority of office over others, by virtue of headship, is not the same thing as leadership (Biggart and Hamilton, 1987, p. 432). At the same time, however, terms designating headship roles, like 'principal', 'headmaster' and 'head-mistress', may carry with them expectations of leadership on the part of senior or chief executive incumbents and its exercise by heads still has to be allowed for as a possibility. Thus, 'a head *may* be a leader but is not one inevitably' (Lantis, 1987, p. 191, original emphasis).

Commentators remain divided over two important points of definition. The first is that if headship is qualitatively distinct from leadership, then so, presumably, are management and administration. After all, 'it is obvious that a person can be a leader without being a manager, and a person can be a manager without leading' (Yukl, 1989, p. 253). Leaving aside any differences in preferred cultural and public/corporate sector usage of terms, administrators and managers are, essentially, officials in executive status systems who are authorized to get others to get work done, and for whose work, as well as their own, they are held accountable (Jaques, 1970, p. 133). This distinction between leadership, on the one hand, and management and administration, on the other, does find ready acceptance (e.g. Kotter, 1990; Zaleznik, 1977), but for different reasons from those being suggested here, whereas Hodgkinson

(1983, p. 195, original emphasis), by contrast, remains adamant that 'administration is leadership' and 'leadership is administration'.

Faced with having to classify actual instances of persons engaged in leading and managing, we may find hard-and-fast distinctions like those above difficult to sustain (see Bryman, 1992, pp. 174–5), but the acknowledgement of them as conceptual possibilities leads to one further point of disagreement amongst researchers. This takes two forms. The first is the acceptance of a division of labour between leaders and followers, with the former seen as superior in kind to the latter... The second form is the related argument (e.g. Zaleznik, 1977, 1990) that leaders are qualitatively different from, and leadership a more important function than, managers and management respectively. And the criticism (Krantz and Gilmore, 1990, p. 189) that any endorsement of such a dualism amounts to a potentially 'debilitating split' for the health of organizations has prompted some commentators (e.g. Jaques, 1989, pp. 121–2) to view leadership as an essential part of a manager's role – a notion reminiscent of Selznick's (1957) older idea of institutional leadership.

These points of contention bear directly on schooling and education because the expectation that educational administrators can and will be leaders remains pervasive. Thus, W. D. Greenfield (1995, p. 66) has recently exhorted school personnel to 'rely on influence associated with leadership rather than on authority associated with their office or position' in enacting their roles. It may be that this is wishful thinking, however (at least in the case of heads), because Evetts (1994, p. 46) has discovered a dramatic diminution in leadership in the UK as school principals have become corporate managers under local management of schools (LMS). Is the ubiquitous significance attached to leadership, therefore, justified? Does leadership make a difference (or, as the duke said: 'power change purpose')? And if so, what is the difference that it makes?

THE SIGNIFICANCE OF LEADERSHIP

Increasingly, connections are being sought between leadership and the restructuring of organizations and their cultures, and between leadership and standards of enhanced organizational performance. Broadly, leader-watchers agree that qualitative differences can be made to organization members' behaviour, some seeing these as for the best and others as for the worst, but they disagree on whether such changes are to be attributed causally to the actions of individuals presumed to be leaders or to some other factors altogether.

...Any argument about the impact of leadership has to contend with one other problem: that attributional influence, rather than causality, is being assessed by researchers. The 'Romance of Leadership' is what Meindl, Ehrlich and Dukerich (1985, p. 79) have called the deep-seated 'faith in the potential if not in the actual efficacy of those individuals who occupy the élite positions of formal organizational authority' held by most organization members. That is, of all the possible causal explanations for event outcomes, significance is mostly attributed in the popular mind to the idea of a 'leader' or 'leadership' as *the* causal entity rendering ill-structured, complex problems meaningful and explicable. Be it in the treatment of leadership in press reports, dissertation topics, small business periodicals or in undergraduates' responses to organizational vignettes during experiments, leaders, typically, are accorded potency and given credit for securing positive outcomes and blamed for circumstances that go wrong (Meindl et al., 1985, p. 96). Thus, if informants are asked whether leaders, their subordinates, other people or environmental factors influence hypothetical organizational outcomes, as Shamir (1992, pp. 393–4) did, they are more likely to nominate a leader than any other alternative.

This deeply ingrained romanticized significance accorded leadership is the outcome of generations of cultural conditioning fuelled, historically, by élites' sanctioning of leader archetypes like heroism and greatness (two statuses well and truly on the rise again: see Gronn, 1993a, 1995). The question of causality currently bites deepest in education in respect of any connection between educational leadership and enhanced school effectiveness. Here the signs are not good. Thus, a leading proponent of structural reform (Caldwell, 1994, p. 52) finds 'little evidence of a direct cause-and-effect relationship between a shift to school-based management and improved outcomes for students'. One reason for this might be the inadequate maps of causality and the barren models of followership contexts informing the search for effective leaders.

When, therefore, does leadership work and under what kinds of circumstances?

CONCEPTIONS OF LEADER-FOLLOWERSHIP

Overwhelmingly, the conventional cause-effect relationship between leaders and followers runs as follows. Leadership is seen as something performed by superior, better individuals (invariably, ageing white males), rather than by groups, located in *top* positions, and as something done *to* or *for* other inferior, lesser people. Causal significance is achieved when relevant counter-factual conditions are satisfied (e.g. the outcomes for followers otherwise would not have transpired but for the leader's leadership; all rival candidate explanations for the outcomes have been eliminated). Finally, the prevailing assumption is that leaders can be known (either by repute or by virtue of role incumbency) and can be designated as such in advance of or *before* an investigation rather than the reverse: individuals presumed to be leaders act and the effects which they achieve subsequently confirm their leadership capacity (Bryman, 1992, pp. 7–8; Dachler, 1988, pp. 267–75). All these features remain as true of the so-called 'new' leadership (see later) as of the old body of theory it purports to supplant.

But when this a priori attribution of agency to leaders and one-way-street leadership is jettisoned in favour of an approach which accords primacy to followership, as called for recently by Meindl (1990, p. 185) and Bryman (1992, p. 177), a qualitatively different level of understanding emerges. And follower-centredness makes a lot of sense; for, in the current rush to embrace the transformational, charismatic and visionary leadership models comprising the 'new' leadership, it is often forgotten that Max Weber, the originator of the concept of charisma, emphasized the crucial role played by followers. 'It is the recognition on the part of *those subject to authority* which is decisive for the validity of charisma', Weber (1922/1978, p. 242, emphasis added) wrote. Likewise the famous scholar-practitioner, Chester Barnard (1938/1982, p. 165, original emphasis), was equally adamant that 'the necessity of the assent of the individual to establish authority *for him [or her]* is inescapable'. Two things which the analysis of followership does bring to light are followers' implicit theories of leadership and the psychological tugs-of-war in which leaders and followers engage....

Apart from Meindl's (1990, pp. 189–97) recent hypothesis that potential followers are made receptive to collective followership status through informal processes of social contagion, independent of particular leaders' attributes, understanding of follower motivation has largely been the preserve of psychoanalytic theory. It has been pointed out elsewhere (Gronn, 1995, p. 22) how the proponents of the 'new' leadership (e.g. Bass, 1985) acknowledge the psychodynamic complexity of followership contexts but then, curiously, gloss over them in their subsequent research. Yet understanding the connection between the preparedness to lead and the willingness to be led is vital. And, given that conferral of leader status is always contingent upon followers' perceptions of its legitimacy, it is their psychological readiness to be led which renders followers acutely vulnerable to leader manipulation. The main processes of psychological investment in the leader (identification, idealization, transference and projection) underwrite two sorts of collective follower responses: primitive, emotionally regressive forms of resistance, splitting, persecution and scapegoating, or more positive, pro-social expressions of hope, idealism and utopia (Kets de Vries, 1988). Faced with either of these possibilities one useful antidote for any leader is the Duke of Vienna's introspective desire, above all else, 'to know himself', but recent research in the field has moved in the opposite direction in the quest for a better understanding of leader behaviour....

FOUR 'NEW' TYPES OF LEADERSHIP

The leadership under the microscope in the last two decades – described as 'new' by Bryman (1992, p. 144), because of its central concern with vision – displays, for Meindl (1990, p. 181), merely a 'new look'. Four strands of it connect directly with Weber's idea of charisma. Transformational leadership, first articulated by Bass (1985) who, with the aid of Burns's (1978) 'transforming' leader, extended House's (1977) original suggestions, and charismatic leadership itself, comprise the two most prominent models. When not seen as distinct, stand-alone types, these two categories are used interchangeably or charisma is treated as a component part of transformational behaviour (but rarely the other way round). Charisma is also one defining attribute of a third related category, visionary leadership, although the prime concern of proponents of this type (e.g. Sashkin, 1988; Schein, 1992; Westley and Mintzberg, 1988) is with the cognitive skills essential to the realization of executive-level visions. The link via charisma between all three types has led recently to calls (by House and Shamir, 1993) for their synthesis.

Sensitive to the dominance of followers to which charismatic inspiration lends itself, some commentators have striven for more follower-centred types. Thus, Howell (1988) has differentiated 'personalized', submission-inducing charismatic leadership from a 'socialized' version which allows for follower empowerment and autonomous followership. Further, it is argued, some followers are more receptive to the charismatic leadership emerging in extraordinary circumstances, or crises, while others are affected by the visionary charisma of extraordinary individuals, whatever the circumstances (Boal and Bryson, 1988). Finally, alarmed at the desiccation of any ethical uplift and moral development of followers when Burns's (1978) original idealist 'transforming' leader suddenly became a 'transformational' one, Graham (1988, 1991) emphasizes similar prosocial outcomes to Howell and has distinguished the fourth strand in the 'new' bundle: servant leadership. Rather than followers being mesmerized through blind faith to a charismatic figure, Graham's type combines leader inspiration with the morality of humility and service; it is a direct reversion back to Burns's original category, but is renamed servant leadership to avoid any confusion between the words 'transforming' and 'transformational' (Graham, 1991, p. 116).

For the unwary student of leadership, however, these enticing new distinctions often overlap or are blurred when used and the individual definitional components of the categories defy precise specification. Moreover, the meaning of transformational leadership has evolved over a ten-year period. Oddly (although this probably reflects its connection with organizational contexts), the factors which comprise it continue to be couched in a superior–subordinate relationship. One potentially fatal criticism (Hunt, 1991, p. 189) of it has been that the survey items used by its proponents to obtain subordinate ratings of leader effects muddle up descriptions of leader behaviour and follower attributions (i.e. imputed effects) – a confusion readily conceded (Bass and Avolio, 1993, pp. 57–8) as requiring rectification. The four 'i's of transformational leadership, as they are called, are: *inspirational leadership* (the heightening of subordinate motivation through charisma), *individualized consideration* (treatment of subordinates according to their personal needs), *intellectual stimulation* (influence on subordinates' thinking and imagination) and *idealized influence* (subordinates' identification with and emulation of the leader's vision). Leaders embodying these characteristics are transformational primarily because they motivate people to perform at peak levels way beyond their normal expectations (Avolio and Bass, 1988, p. 33).

Burns (1978) contrasted his original transforming leader with a transactional type – a category retained by Bass (1985, pp. 121–49). Transactional leadership, essentially, comprises a technology of control that facilitates an exchange relationship with followers (such as increased output in return for material incentives) entailing reliance on the management by exception and contingent reward or inducement typical of supervisory management levels. Advocates of transformations, however, retain a curious love–hate relationship towards transactions – the situational mechanics of getting other people to do things. Sometimes the transactional–transformational contrast is one of differences in kind, at others of degree, and at others still of differences in evolutionary stages. Transformational leader–follower relationships, on the one hand, are seen as more significant than transactional ones – as well as superior to all preceding leadership types (which are dismissed as merely transactional) – whenever transformational leadership is touted as 'a new paradigm' (Avolio and Bass, 1988, p. 29) as Meindl (1990, p. 181) quite rightly observes. And, to the extent that transactional exchanges typify management relationships generally, the distinction between transactional and transformational types really implies the more global one already canvassed (see earlier and see Gronn, 1995, pp. 17–20): that between managers and leaders. To add to the confusion, transformational leadership, on the other hand, is also seen as an extension of transactional leadership, or as a special case of it, and transformational leaders, apparently, cannot be successful without being transactional as well (Avolio and Bass, 1988, pp. 30–4; Sashkin, 1992, p. 156).

....Managerial leadership theory begins with the fact of an uncertain and ambiguous, but rapidly complex and changing, strategic decision-making environment. The continuity here is with the emphasis both the object-relations and the Kleinan perspectives (evident in Jaques's early Tavistock phase) place on the anxiety with which the human organism must cope to ensure its balanced maturation and development. Structures, comprising bounded well-defined roles, therefore, represent a defence against anxiety (Jaques, 1957)....

In this structural view, then, the aforementioned distinction between leaders and followers is meaningless: there are no leader–follower role relationships; indeed, there are no leaders – 'we have found that the notion of "a leader" or "the leader" simply gets in the way' (Jaques and Clement, 1991, p. 6). Likewise, there is no split between leaders and managers. The hierarchy of roles comprises core managerial work (planning, communicating, appraising, setting output targets, finding resources, coaching, selecting and inducting, etc.), to which leadership at every level is the 'value-added' component. All managers carry leadership accountability, and to that extent are managerial leaders:

> everyone is capable of exercising effective leadership in roles that carry leadership accountability, so long as they value the role and are competent to carry the basic requirements of that role, and so long as that role is properly structured and the organization has properly instituted practices. (Jaques and Clement, 1991, p. 7)

...Both transformational and managerial leadership have significant shortcomings. On the one hand, driven by the desire to engineer organizational transformations, theorists reduce charisma to a technology of context-free behavioural effects on followers. Yet this clouds understanding by imputing unwarranted causal agency to leaders and by trivializing the processes of leader–followership in particular contexts. On the other hand, in the desire to ensure requisite systemic adaptation to the demands of the environment, managerial leadership risks diminishing leaders', let alone followers', agency altogether....

FORMING LEADERS AND FORMING FOLLOWERS

The need to reproduce a leadership stratum was always a concern of classical management theorists (e.g. Barnard, 1956, pp. 82–3, 88; Selznick, 1957, p. 15). Yet, apart from a few recent suggestions (Gronn, 1993b, pp. 346-9; 1994, pp. 227–9), current knowledge of the processes of leader formation is insufficient to answer Kets de Vries's (1993, p. 3) important question: 'What determines who will become a leader and who will not?'

Despite their different emphases both approaches to leadership agree on the importance of leader cognition, although their understanding of cognition and the importance they attach to it differs. (Any differences, of course, are significant for the assessment and selection of potential leaders.) Broadly, transformational theorists have advocated short-term cognitive skill training and structural theorists have stressed career-long cognitive development. For each approach specific proposals are speculative. Bass and Avolio (1993, pp. 73–4) remain optimistic regarding workshops for training managers in transformational behaviours and skills, but most of the research to date (Kuhnert, 1994; Kuhnert and Lewis, 1987; Wofford and Goodwin, 1994) has been confined to modelling cognitive capacity and is devoid of data on actual leaders' cognition (although see Leithwood, 1995, pp. 123–31; Leithwood et al., 1994, Chapters 10–12). Interestingly, Avolio and Gibbons (1988, p. 291) consider transformational leadership from a life-history perspective and caution against relying solely on short-term learning or training strategies.

... One useful, but neglected, source of data on the origins of leadership is biography. Indeed, Avolio and Bass (1988, p. 46) note the relative absence of psychohistorical studies of leaders despite 'the wealth of information in biographies of world-class leaders' available. Highlighting such personal dimensions as a particular leader's conception of her or his role, their motivation and ambition, etc. – in addition to the formative cultural influences on that leader, and the ways in which various pathways facilitated or impeded the assumption of leadership roles – ensures that agency and structure are brought together in a Weberian approach to biographical data....

LEADERSHIP IN THE NEW EDUCATIONAL DISPENSATION

Proponents of educational restructuring emphasize school leaders' roles in transforming school cultures. Thus, 'as effective leaders they give abundant feedback and positive reinforcement to teachers and students and at the same time build the culture for these behaviours to permeate all levels and members of the school community' (Dimmock, 1995, p. 294; and see Leithwood *et al.*, 1994, pp. 128–46). This observation prompts three questions: first, why does school leadership comprise cultural transformation? Second, given Dimmock's rather normative use of 'effective' (i.e. that leaders *should do* as he recommends), is there any empirical evidence of cultural transformation actually taking place in schools? Third, what does it really mean to transform a school's culture?

TRANSFORMING SCHOOL CULTURES

The emphasis on cultural transformation in schooling is a direct consequence of the emergence of a wider enterprise culture in education (and other public policy sectors) as part of the 'new managerialism', the main contours of which are well-documented. Its diffusion and adoption, owing to policy-copying (Whitty, 1994, pp. 1–2), is strongest in Scandinavian and Anglo-American member countries of the OECD (Hood, 1995, p. 102). Its two main doctrines include removing differences between the public and private sectors in the control of services, and shifting the emphasis in accountability for the delivery of services away from adherence to set procedures towards outcomes and results....

For individual schools, accountability-driven school-based management entails evaluation of their performance in attaining outcomes measured against predetermined indicators of quality. School managers, as a result, are judged on the extent to which they secure and sustain quality in the so-called 'core technology' of teaching and learning. Inexorably, therefore, the logic of school restructuring entails 'backward-mapping': a kind of reverse rationalism in which traditional top-down, ends-means organizational arrangements are stood on their head. Briefly summarized, the result is meant to be an effective school in which quality outcomes determine the particular 'configuration' or choice of learning styles and processes, which, in turn, determines the selection of appropriate teaching strategies as well as the flexible organizational structures which facilitate these processes. Lastly, all of these mechanisms are dependent for their coherence and success on 'specific forms of leadership, management, resourcing and culture-building' and it is the senior leadership which 'sets the school culture and the prevailing values' (Dimmock, 1995, pp. 289, 291). Such restructured, responsive and effective schools are often characterized, figuratively, as being structurally loose, but culturally tight.

TRANSFORMED SCHOOLS: NORMATIVE FANTASY OR EMPIRICAL FACT?

The fine detail of the cultural-transformation-of-schooling idea has been given extensive attention by Leithwood (1994, 1995). Like Sashkin, Leithwood has endeavoured to reconcile leader cognition and leader behaviour (but without any reliance on Jaques's particular structural version of complexity) in order to match them to school contexts. Curiously, he seems ambivalent about transformational leadership: sometimes he and his colleagues (Leithwood *et al.*, 1994, pp. 10, 97, 113, 128) appear to embrace it yet, at others, they either bypass, ignore or recast its attributes (Leithwood *et al.*, 1994, pp. 144, 254) in preference for a description of school leaders as expert problem-solvers – the authors' aim being to facilitate school leaders' problem-solving in restructured schools.

Leithwood's (1995, pp. 117–18) constructivist model locates leaders' cognitive or 'internal processes' in a causal chain. These processes are said to 'determine' leaders' behaviours (e.g. transformational leadership) which, in turn, are meant to 'potentially contribute' to the learning outcomes desired by schools, those leaders' behaviours being mediated by the internal processes of other school personnel and by 'collective internal processes' such as school culture. Leithwood's (1995, p. 131) ambitious hope is that the leader's internal cognitive mechanisms will redefine the meaning of effective leadership 'by focusing attention on those expert, internal, cognitive processes which give rise to situationally sensitive and necessarily contingent sets of overt leadership practices, rather than on those practices themselves'. One consequence of defining leaders as expert problem-solvers is to evoke, yet again, the aforesaid presumption of leader superiority. Thus, compared with their less expert peers, expert problem-solving school leaders 'more adequately anticipate many of the constraints' of problem-solving. They are 'better able to control intense moods and remain calm during problem-solving' and are 'more self-confident about their ability to solve ill-structured problems' and so on (Leithwood, 1995, pp. 121–2). The three core tasks of expert school leaders are the standard fare of apologists for cultural realignment: articulating a vision, devising strategies to attain that vision and empowering followers.

This cognitive view reduces leadership to something that goes on in the head of the leader: it is devoid of any recognition of the existence of follower attributions and implicit theories (despite its stress on empowerment), nor is it aware that leadership is a socially constructed process. Not only that but leadership here also seems to be something that is *done to* someone else, whether they like it or not....

The second effect has been to heighten their need for micro-political skills in the battle to procure scarce resources and to produce a greater likelihood of conflict in schools. Evetts (1993, p. 63) also found that heads bargain less with their local authorities under LMS but more and more with industry and business, their own staff and their governors. The constant need of these secondary heads to negotiate over staffing levels and the distribution of performance allowances, as part of formula-funding, is confirmed by Huckman and Hill's (1994) study of five English primary schools. For good reasons (entirely rational given the particular texture of micro-politics in their schools, but anything but rational from the perspective of backward-mapping), heads have played safe on staffing. Thus, it is less disruptive to distribute performance allowances evenly than to single out individuals for special rewards, and budgets are simply too tight to permit any increases in salaries (Huckman and Hill, 1994, p. 195).

The significance of these findings is that the need for a continued ethnographic focus on the processes of leading and managing is underscored once again. Yet the insistence that leadership become an instrument for attaining outcomes, and that this switch in focus somehow represents a fundamental break with previous practice, merely diverts attention from the realities of organizational life...

The much maligned process focus on leadership, therefore, in the sense of the day-to-day, and even moment-by-moment, situational exigencies of context continues to be important in at least two ways. First, it confirms what has always been the case in the managing and leading of schools: that there is a constant interplay of personalities, interests and ideologies in the battle for resources (Gronn, 1986), the intensity and precise make-up of which will vary according to the nature of the external political imperatives. On that score little or nothing has changed. Second, it highlights the need to always ask one disarmingly simple and sceptical question of all normative models of leadership: what do they look like in practice?

VISIONARY LEADERSHIP AND TRANSFORMING SCHOOLS

The other problem with normative models which cast leaders as engineers of school culture lies with the conception of culture itself. Once education is reduced to a commodity, and consumption norms replace citizenship norms, culture becomes seen as a second-order concept; as in the corporate sector, something to be adjusted at will according to whether or not it facilitates growth, profit or an increased market share. But in education, as Bottery (1994) suggests, culture has always been a first-order consideration to do with the development of individual potential and a just society. Rendering culture in education isomorphic with corporate culture, however, means schools and colleges risk abandoning any sense of a wider ethical commitment or mission:...

In this and similar ways terms like mission and vision, which appear frequently in the lexicon of outcome-based, instrumental rationality, but which are not new, are made to serve new purposes. Yet, in the older, classical idealist conception of leadership (e.g. Selznick, 1957, pp. 62–3) defining an organization's mission and values meant shaping its enduring institutional character. Indeed, so crucial is the aesthetic and moral activity of leadership in this process of institutional character-building, according to Barnard (1938/1982, p. 282), that organizations only endure 'in proportion to the breadth of the morality by which they are governed'. In the classical view, the image of the organizational leader is of a kind of great moral helmsman or woman (as the case may be). Schools have always helped shape the character structure, and therefore the leadership character, of entire societies....

CONCLUSION...

The purpose of the paper was to review some of the more recent developments in the wider fields of leadership and in educational leadership. It has been argued that the current concentration on organizational performance and outcomes by commentators creates the impression of newness and difference when in fact what has really happened is that scholars of leadership have simply readjusted their previous focus. There have been no big breakthroughs which justify the idea of a new paradigm, watershed or quantum leap. No matter what the field of interest in question, however, this kind of switch in attention is best seen as a natural and inevitable consequence of endeavouring to remain relevant – in this case to those for whom a knowledge of leadership is deemed important. It has been pointed out that the continuities with the work of previous scholars on leadership, particularly Weber, remain strong, and the issues which have been in contention for so long (e.g. what leadership means; whether it is the same thing as management or something different; whether or not it really does make a difference, and so on) remain matters which continue to divide scholars.

As regards the methodological approaches taken to trying to understand leadership better, so much of the field has been shown to be dominated by what Avolio and Bass (1988, p. 47) refer to as 'static cross-sectional' research. Here a plea has been made for more and better contextualized leader-watching or on-looking: longitudinal, naturalistic and biographical investigations, particularly the latter, to better enrich knowledge of where leadership comes from and to ascertain what leading and following look like when scrutinized in any depth. Finally, scepticism has been expressed about the nature and role of leadership envisaged for the current wave of school reform. The underlying logic of the proposed new school leadership, the validity of the causal role being attributed to school leaders, the intense drive to (behaviourally and cognitively) psychologize leadership even further, the disregard of followership and the superficiality of the conceptions of schooling thought to require leadership, have all been called into serious question.

As Hunt (1991, p. 267) says, 'last things last'. What about the Duke of Vienna's brief spell of leader-watching? Power, he discovered, had not of itself changed purpose in Angelo's Vienna. Instead, disguised, the duke had witnessed (V, i):

> ... corruption boil and bubble,
> Till it o'er run the stew: laws, for all faults
> But faults so countenanced that the strong statutes
> Stand like the forfeits in a barber's shop,
> As much in mock as mark.

He returned from his on-looking, 'not changing heart with habit' after his sojourn in the field as a friar, to be 'still attorney'd' at Vienna's service, having learnt, through Angelo's fall from grace, an invaluable lesson about himself and the strength of character required of a leader (111, ii):

He, who the sword of heaven will bear,
Should be as holy as severe;
Pattern in himself to know,
Grace to stand, and virtue go;
More nor less to others paying,
Than by self-offences weighing.
Shame to him, whose cruel striking
Kills for faults of his own liking!

Context and Capability in Educational Management

RON GLATTER

INTRODUCTION

I took the invitation to address BEMAS's 25th Annual Conference as an opportunity to reflect and to offer a personal perspective on aspects of the current scene.

...Before I explain what this article will cover, I will make three general points. First, my comments are heavily informed by the work that I and my colleagues at The Open University, notably Philip Woods and Carl Bagley (the latter is now at Staffordshire University), have been doing over a number of years on the ESRC-funded Parental and School Choice Interaction (PASCI) study (ESRC reference R000234079).

...Second, there is I think a general 'position' underlying most of what I have to say. This is that we in 'mainstream' educational management have become too preoccupied with what might be called the institutional side of leadership and management, to the extent of disregarding or at least under-emphasizing policy and contextual factors. In doing so we may be playing into the hands of those who accuse educational management of being too technocratic and mechanistic and of paying insufficient regard to values...

Third, to the extent that I have a specific position on educational policy matters it is a fairly conventional but nevertheless neglected one, and it informs much of the discussion to follow. It was set for me by a document that was published 33 years ago and which had a defining influence on my outlook and subsequent work. This was the Newsom Report of 1963, *Half Our Future* (Ministry of Education, 1963), which chronicled the national neglect of pupils of average and below-average ability and made what seems an unanswerable case, on both social and economic grounds, for placing this group at the top of our list of national priorities. Since then many others have taken up this theme, not least the National Commission on Education (1993), yet most of the public debate and policy developments seem still to be focused on the needs of pupils of higher ability and, less frequently, on the relatively small group with clearly identifiable special educational needs. As the introduction to Newsom so rightly said, the problem is as much one of attitude as of organization, and it remains so to this day.

I have four aims in this article: to develop a discussion around some contextual factors impacting on schools; to make some comments on what 'best practice outside education' might mean in relation to educational management; to reflect on issues concerning leadership in the light of my previous arguments; and, last, to draw some implications for continuing professional development in a situation of increased central control of this activity, at least in England and Wales.

REINVENTING CONTEXT

I wish to take up three issues under this heading: inter-institutional differences; the significance of structure; and the role of the media.

Inter-institutional differences

When the work of the school effectiveness researchers first came to general attention, it gave a significant boost to studies and training in educational management. The message that 'schools make a difference' lent academic credence to common observation. I remember myself feeling the liberation that the statistical substantiation of that insight provided. Even more, in attempting to account for the differences between schools, researchers such as Rutter and his colleagues (Rutter *et al.*, 1979) concluded that leadership and management *must* play a significant part, though their methodology did not allow them to investigate this. The school improvement movement reinforced the emphasis on school individuality through its detailed studies of improvement processes. More recently, the two streams of research – school effectiveness and school improvement – have begun to try to coordinate their methods and outcomes. Eventually, politicians caught on, perhaps recognizing yet another opportunity for scapegoating schools and teachers, or at least for passing the buck to them, and in the past two or three years the air of political rhetoric has been thick with the 'schools make a difference' refrain.

Perhaps we should now ask whether we have overstepped the mark in relegating contextual factors virtually to the status of a sideshow. The mainly statistical studies in the school effectiveness tradition appear to demonstrate rather limited variances between schools. . . .

Even where the assessments of effectiveness are done on a broader and more judgemental basis, contextual factors are generally highly significant. While accepting that quite a wide range of mixes of resources can be associated with success, John Gray makes these three striking observations on the link between resources and effectiveness:

1. In 20 years of reading research on the characteristics of effective schools, we have only once come across a case of an 'excellent' school where the physical environment left something to be desired....

2. In many years of reading HMI's published reports on secondary schools we can only remember two or three occasions where their overall rating was highly favourable and the roof (or something similar) was in need of repair....

3. We have never read an account of a 'good' school which had serious staffing difficulties. (Gray, 1995, p. 21)

Gray does not conclude that the 'schools make a difference' thesis is wrong – of course they make a difference, he insists, but the crucial questions are how much, and why? The dangers, it seems to me, lie in implying that the process of improvement is easy, quick or commonly successful and that hostile contextual factors can readily be overcome.

The significance of structure

A fascinating aspect of the political context in the pre-election period in which this article was written was the debate about whether structure is or is not important in relation to educational outcomes....

If we want to improve the system as a whole, especially for the 'Newsom children', structures are crucial. One example is school admissions systems. Donald Hirsch, whose comparative studies of choice and competition for the Organization for Economic Cooperation and Development (OECD) have formed a very useful background to our own work, has put this neatly:

> One important element of *across-the-board improvement* is that schools [should] achieve a greater equality of esteem, and that the more that schools are allowed to become privileged enclaves the more perceptions of schools, and ultimately the reality of their performance, will become polarized. (Hirsch, 1995, pp. 16–17, my italics)

...I want to say something about this centralization that has been such a pervasive feature of our system over the past eight years. We all feel the effects of the decisions of central government and of its agencies much more directly than we could have imagined possible only a few years ago. In the areas of the curriculum, teacher training and Continuing Professional Development (CPD), further education funding, research, inspection and many others, the central state now has a pivotal role and this seems to be constantly expanding....

I do not have space to go into the ramifications of the debate about markets and competition. Let me just say that the term 'self-governing school' sounds impressive in its rhetoric but the reality is rather different. First, the school is self-governing only in relation to the 'middle tier', i.e. what has come to be called the local democratic framework. It is actually less self-governing in relation to the central state. Second, the pressures of the market and the fragmented system of governance can easily turn 'the self-governing school' into 'the self-centred school'. Indeed the structure is arguably designed to achieve just this, and we need to consider as a society, as a nation, whether this is what we want from our schools. The key, related, questions 'Where should power lie?' and 'To whom should the schools belong?' are rarely addressed explicitly, except by central government itself (DfEE, 1996). It is time that they were.

Nor is there clarity about how competitive the system should be. Even before the 1988 Act, there was intense competition in many areas of the country, mainly because of falling rolls. It is not realistic to suppose that competition could be legislated away – the idea of 'choice' is much too popular for that – though its parameters could be modified, for example through formula changes, and incentives could be provided for collaboration...

We have suggested in one of our papers (Glatter et al., 1997) what policy changes would be needed to create a much more diverse and competitive system, if it were decided to go in that direction, because we have been struck by another paradox. Although the policy rhetoric is all about choice, diversity and avoiding dull uniformity, what is actually emerging on the whole is less variety, more homogeneity, and much less incentive to innovate....

Role of the media

The last issue I want to take up under the general heading of 'Reinventing Context' (and I could of course have identified many more) is the role of the media in defining the agenda of educational discourse, or what I call the 'ideas context'. Given the extent of coverage of educational matters by the media, I have been surprised by how little research has been done on this topic in recent years. I am only aware of one study, by Mike Wallace (1995): this provides very valuable starting-points....

My argument would be that educational managers face a rather monolithic ideas context set by the bulk of the media, which is focused around what might be called an authoritarian/conservative consensus. This monolithic ideas context stimulates and reinforces the main policy drives, influencing the opposition as much as the government. A fertile area for investigation!

BEST PRACTICE OUTSIDE EDUCATION

I now want to change focus quite substantially, by moving away from issues of context, without forgetting them entirely, to look at questions of leadership and professional development. I consider first what is known as 'practice outside education'. Some 'mainstream' educational management people agonize about the whole issue of borrowing from non-educational contexts, but I myself have never found it particularly troublesome, probably because I tend to oversimplify it. I had to tackle it as part of the brief for the project sponsored by the Calouste Gulbenkian Foundation on educational management training which I under-took at the London Institute of Education with my great mentor Professor George Baron some years ago. In the book which resulted from the project I concluded that training for educational management should mainly be provided on a 'specialist' basis because this would give a more effective use of time and money, and emphatically not for narrow parochial reasons. I went on: 'It is scarcely possible to conceive of administrative training without substantial borrowing from studies of management in other contexts. . . .This work must be reinterpreted for its relevance to education and, where appropriate, studies to test such relevance should be mounted' (Glatter, 1972, p. 9). It reads somewhat glibly now, but seems reasonable enough. Recently the term 'best management practice outside education' has come into use, for example by the Teacher Training Agency (TTA) in their list of key principles for the new National Professional Qualification for Headship (Teacher Training Agency, 1996b). This term merits further comments.

First, it is not always very clear what constitutes best practice in management outside education. As in education itself, there are different approaches and contending schools of thought. The picture is complicated by the speed with which many fads and fashions – trumpeted for a while as the acme of good practice – come and go. When I was writing up the Gulbenkian report we were in the process of bidding farewell to two of the most hyped systems of that era, one developed in the private sector, management by objectives (MBO), and the other in the public sector, planning-programming-budgeting systems (PPBS). I tried to give a rounded assessment of each of these in the report, but, struck by the lack of evidence of much successful implementation, I concluded: 'The dangers of "selling" a particular technique or set of techniques, and sending course members back to their work with inaccurate expectations, are very great' (Glatter, 1972, p. 47). In the present day, ideas which only recently were strongly promoted, like downsizing and business re-engineering, appear to be under a dark cloud and even Total Quality Management (TQM) is said to be losing its lustre (Caulkin, 1996).

Second, as is by now well-known in particular through the work of Charles Handy (1994) and Will Hutton (1995), and also the 'Tomorrow's Company' Inquiry by the Royal Society of Arts (Cleaver, 1995), there is an increasingly influential radical critique of British business culture and methods, attacking their alleged short-termism, hierarchical approach and lack of attention to building consensual trust relationships both within the company and with other organizations. This practice is contrasted with that in many European and Pacific Rim countries, and is said to account to a large extent for those countries' greater economic success. The irony here is that many educational institutions are probably much closer to the model of the stakeholder organization advocated by these critics than is the typical British business. Arguably, the system as a whole was closer to that model before the process of nationalization which Jenkins describes started to take hold.

Third, and perhaps most interesting, some apparent examples of trends in good practice outside education seem to conflict with the dominant rationalistic paradigm within education. One example is the approach to detailed strategic planning. In fact, as John Kay, an influential writer and leading consultant on this subject, points out, there has been growing disenchantment with this type of approach in the business world: 'Elaborately quantified corporate plans lay gathering dust on the shelves of managers who went on making the decisions they would have made had the plan never existed' (Kay, 1993, p. 341). Because of this dissatisfaction, says Kay, the familiar idea that 'successful strategies are often opportunistic and adaptive, rather than calculated and planned' (p. 356) has recovered ground and 'rationalism is in retreat, but by no means routed' (p. 354). Kay is far from alone in this analysis (see also e.g. Bailey and Johnson, 1992; Mintzberg, 1994).

...My brief overall conclusions are that, first, identifying best management practice outside education will require the judgement of a Solomon, and, second, deciding what elements of this would really be of value in education will involve some notions of cultural compatibility.

LEADERSHIP AND AMBIGUITY

I have space only to refer briefly to a few themes. In the light of my earlier comments, my insistence on the contingent nature of success in leadership will not be surprising. I am reminded here of the assessment by the late US journalist I. F. Stone, in an interview he gave in which he looked back on a long and distinguished career observing powerful people and great events:

> You cannot understand events without understanding that power is a prison... T]here are very severe limits: if you have no power, you're free. But in every prison there is some leeway – someone with courage and ingenuity can do more than one who's lazy or a coward. Find out what can be done and judge on that: you must always have a sense of the possible. (Quoted by Lloyd, 1986, p. 19)

Closer to home, our Centre at the Open University has recently put together a series of case studies on managing change in FE. One of these is a study of strategic management and competitive advantage in 14 colleges in London, Birmingham and South Wales (Bassett-Jones and Brewer, 1997). The authors comment on the role of chance and local history and circumstance in shaping market success, saying what I suspect we all know, that indifferent management can be good enough to secure survival in some contexts, while even talented leadership can fail to prevent closure or amalgamation in others.

In their splendid book *Reframing Organizations: Artistry, Choice and Leadership*, Bolman and Deal (1991) put forward three propositions towards a more realistic view of leadership. They regard leadership as a subtle and intricate process. Their first heading is *leadership and context*: 'Traditional notions of the solitary, heroic leader have led us to focus too much on the actors and too little on the stage on which they play their parts.' For the adage 'Leaders make things happen' we should substitute 'Things make leaders happen'. Their second heading is *leadership as relationship*. Leadership is not a one-way process: it is 'not simply a matter of what a leader does but of what occurs in the relationship between a leader and others'. It is an interactive relationship. 'Leaders both shape and are shaped by their constituents.' Finally there is *leadership and position*. Leadership is not provided *only* by people in high positions. 'Such a view leads us to ask too much of too few. It encourages senior managers to take more responsibility than they can discharge' (Bolman and Deal, 1991, pp. 408–11). Their whole analysis is, in my view, highly perceptive and rewarding.

Then of course there is the question of dilemmas, to which Grace has drawn attention. In his recent book he quotes Chester Barnard's dictum that 'leadership is the conjunction of technical competence and moral complexity' (Grace, 1995, p. 63). We have thankfully come a long way since Barrow argued in a piece presciently called 'Competence and the Head' that virtually the only quality necessary for headship was 'philosophic competence', because only this would ensure that the head had the conceptual clarity and logical coherence to be able to issue sound policy directives (Barrow, 1976). Still, in its search for certainty, the 'can-do' culture of the present day tends to dismiss the dilemmas and ambiguities that are the stuff of leadership activity and are pervasive in organizational life.

The competitive market and the new strategic functions of educational leaders have reinforced the importance of the art of managing dilemmas (often referred to in conversation as 'juggling'!). I wrote about this topic in a paper (Glatter, 1996) for the 1994 International Inter-visitation Programme which had 'dilemmas' as its main theme. I gave several examples from our work of the kinds of dilemma of strategic choice which the current competitive climate creates for those guiding the affairs of institutions. One of the most sensitive and difficult is what balance to strike between acting separately and acting collaboratively with other institutions. This requires leaders to exercise fine judgement based on their own and their colleagues' values and a shrewd reading of the local situation. There are no easy answers to it. As Larry Cuban has said, the best we can do with such dilemmas is to try to reframe them through explicit analysis and thus seek to 'create better compromises and more elegant tightrope walks' (Cuban, 1992, p. 8).

PROFESSIONAL DEVELOPMENT AND CAPABILITY

What is the relevance of all this for professional development? Some time ago I drew attention to the then embryonic 'Education for Capability' movement of the Royal Society of Arts and its possible implications for our work in educational management. I claimed that hardly anyone involved in the field saw running an educational institution as simply a technical process – I believe that is still true. But at the same time we were not concerned only with purveying knowledge for its own sake or developing understanding – our purposes had to go beyond purely academic ones: we had to become involved in the areas of method and skill development and to have a central focus on leadership and management action (Glatter, 1980).

Two of the early contributions on capability are relevant here. One came from Correlli Barnett, who defined capability as 'an ability successfully to tackle the practical situations of life. This also means possessing the specialized skills and knowledge necessary to tackle the operational problems of a particular professional sphere' (1979, p. 118). The other was from Tyrrell Burgess: 'What is important is not a particular fact or even a particular ordered collection of facts but *method*. It is method rather than information which gives mastery...' (1979, p. 152). I argued that methods, or implementation skills as they might now be more commonly called, were as important as knowledge, understanding and value orientations. It is probably this concern with methods, with the messiness of the real world, its ambiguities, dilemmas, constraints – power as a prison – which makes our critics so uncomfortable, and provokes them to urge us to breathe the purer air of leadership, *beyond* education management (Grace, 1995). But erecting this kind of dichotomy between something pure called 'leadership' and something dirty called 'management', or between values and purposes on the one hand and methods and skills on the other, would be disastrous. It would create exactly that divorce between values and methods which the critics claim to abhor....

Then there is the question of an individual's wider, social, analytical and professional understanding. As Kay has observed: 'Practical knowledge which is not based on some more fundamental analysis is usually knowledge of only the most superficial kind' (1993, p. 355)....

Now, 25 years after the foundation of BEMAS, leadership and management development has moved centre stage in education. Politicians with their urgent time-scales have fastened on to it as a key plank in their educational platforms. BEMAS can take much credit for this.

The TTA, with their new headship qualification and their initiatives in middle management, have set out on a hugely ambitious programme – nothing of its scale or complexity has been attempted elsewhere to my knowledge. The risks and dangers are obvious, particularly of establishing a heavy bureaucratic apparatus which all our experience, both within education and outside it, shows would be counterproductive.

But there are hopeful signs that we can avoid this. For example, Anthea Millett, the TTA's Chief Executive, has said the headship qualification will seek to develop heads 'who are well-prepared to lead effective and flourishing schools, where debate, challenge and improvement are the norm and where pupils get a taste for learning that will stay with them throughout their lives' (Millett, 1996)....

We are moving into uncharted territory. It is vital that BEMAS monitor the developments closely and seek to influence their direction. The second 25 years promise to be at least as interesting as were the first, and probably far more challenging.

References

Abrahamson, M. (1967) *The Professional in the Organisation*. Chicago: Rand McNally.

Aguayo, R. (1992) Deming the American who Taught the Japanese about Quality. *World Executive's Digest* (June).

Aitken, R. (1983) *Comprehensive Education for Life*. Coventry: Coventry City Council.

Allison, G. T. (1971) *Essence of Decision: Explaining the Cuban Missile Crisis*. Boston: Little Brown.

Anderson, B. (1991) *Imagined Communities: Reflections on the Origins and Spread of Nationalism*. London: Verso.

Argyris, C. and Schön, D. A. (1976) *Theory in Practice: Increasing Professional Effectiveness*. San Francisco: Jossey Bass.

Avolio, B. J. and Bass, B. M. (1988) Transformational Leadership, Charisma and Beyond, in J. G. Hunt, B. R. Baliga, H. P. Dachler and C. A. Schreisheim (eds.) *Emerging Leadership Vistas*. Lexington, MA: D. C. Heath.

Avolio, B. J. and Gibbons, T. C. (1988) Developing Transformational Leaders: A Life Span Approach, in J. A. Conger and R. K. Kanungo (eds.) *Charismatic Leadership: The Elusive Factor in Organizational Effectiveness*. San Francisco, CA: Jossey-Bass.

Bailey, A. and Johnson, G. (1992) How Strategies Develop in Organizations, in D. Faulkner and G. Johnson, *The Challenge of Strategic Management*. London: Kogan Page.

Bailey, T. (1982). The Question of Legitimation: A Response to Hoyle. *Educational Management and Administration*, Vol. 10, No. 2, pp. 99–105.

Ball, S. (1993a) Education policy, power relations and teachers work. *British Journal of Educational Studies*, Vol. 41, No. 2, pp. 106–21.

Ball, S. (1993b) Education markets, choice and social class: the market as a class strategy in the UK and USA. *British Journal of the Sociology of Education*, Vol. 14, No. 1, pp. 3–19.

Ball, S. (1993c) The Education Reform Act: market forces and parental choice, in A. Cashden and J. Harris (eds.) *Education in the 1990s*. Sheffield: Sheffield Hallam Pavic Publications.

Barber, B. (1963) Some problems in the sociology of the professions. *Daedalus*, No. 92.

Barnard, C. I. (1938/1982). *The Functions of the Executive*. Cambridge, MA: Harvard University Press.

Barnard, C. I. (1956) The Nature of Leadership, in C. I. Barnard, *Organization and Management: Selected Papers*. Cambridge, MA: Harvard University Press.

Barnes, J. (1984) *Flaubert's Parrot*. London: Pan Books.

Barnes, A. Humble S., Davies J. L. and Lyons G. (1978) Governing Schools: Has the Taylor Report got the Balance Right? *Educational Administration*, Vol. 6, No. 1, pp. 1–19.

Barnett, C. (1979) Technology, Education and Industrial and Economic Strength. *Royal Society of Arts Journal*, Vol. 127, No. 5271, pp. 117–27.

Baron, G. (1956) Some aspects of the 'Headmaster tradition'. *Researches and Studies*, No. 14, pp. 7–16.

Baron G. (1979a) Research in Educational Administration in Britain. *Educational Administration*, Vol. 8, No. 1, pp. 1–33.

Baron, G. (1979b) The British Educational Administration Society: The next seven years. *Educational Administration: Approaches to Professional Development*. Proceedings of the Seventh Annual Conference of BEMAS, Westfield College, University of London, September, pp. 1–11.

Baron, G. and Taylor, W. (1969) (eds.) *Educational Administration and the Social Sciences*. London: Athlone Press.

Barrow, R. (1976) Competence and the Head, in R. S. Peters (ed.) *The Role of the Head*. London: Routledge & Kegan Paul.

Bass, B. M. (1985) *Leadership and Performance Beyond Expectations*. New York: Free Press.

Bass, B. M. and Avolio, B. J. (1993) Transformational Leadership: A Response to Critics, in M. M. Chemers and R. Ayman (eds.) *Leadership Theory and Research: Perspectives and Directions*. San Diego, CA: Academic Press.

Bassett-Jones, N. and Brewer, R. (1997). Strategic Management and Competitive Advantage, in R. Levačić and R. Glatter (eds.) *The Strategic Management of Change in Further Education*. London: Further Education Development Agency.

Bates, A. W. (1971) The Administration of Comprehensive Schools. PhD Thesis, University of London.

Bates, R. (1989) Is there a new paradigm in educational administration? Unpublished paper. Deakin University, Victoria, Australia.

Bates, R. (1993) On Knowing: Cultural and Critical Approaches to Educational Administration. *Educational Management and Administration*, Vol. 21 No. 3, pp. 171–76.

Bauman, Z. (1978) *Hermeneutics and Social Science: Approaches to Understanding*. London: Hutchinson.

Bauman, Z. (1993) *Postmodern Ethics*. Oxford: Blackwell.

Beck, U., Giddens, A. and Lash, S. (1994) *Reflexive Modernization: Politics, Tradition and Aesthetics in the Modern Social Order*. Cambridge: Polity Press.

Benn, C. and Simon, B. (1970) *Half Way There: Report on the British Comprehensive School Reform*. London: McGraw Hill.

Bernbaum, G. (1970) The role of the headmaster: final report. A mimeographed report to the Social Science Research Council.

Best, R. (1977) Sketch for a sociology of art. *British Journal of Aesthetics*, Vol. 17, No 1, pp. 68–81.

Best, R. E., Jarvis, C. B. and Ribbins, P. M. (1979). Researching Pastoral Care. *Educational Management and Administration*, Vol. 8, No. 1, pp. 48–74.

Best, R., Ribbins, P. and Jarvis, C. with Oddy, D. (1983). *Education and Care*. Oxford: Blackwell.

Bhindi, N. (1992) The Asian Manager. Paper presented to the ASEAN Perspectives on Excellence in Leadership (APEL) Research Workshop, University Brunei, Dar es Salaam, 24 November.

Bhindi, N. (1995a) An Asia-Pacific Perspective on Management and Leadership. Paper presented to Malaysian Educators, Australian Catholic University, Sydney, 31 October.

Bhindi, N. (1995b) Educational Administration in a Multicultural Context: Some Leadership Challenges. Paper presented to the Canberra Chapter of the Australian Council for Educational Administration, 29 August.

Bhindi, N. (1996) Cutting Edge or Holding Pattern: School Leadership for the 21st Century. Keynote Paper, South Coast Principals Conference, Queensland, Australia, 7 June.

Biggart, N. W. and Hamilton, G. G. (1987) An Institutional Theory of Leadership. *Journal of Applied Behavioral Science*, Vol. 23, No. 4, pp. 429–41.

Blau, Peter M. and Scott, W. R. (1963) *Formal Organizations: A Comparative Approach*. London: Routledge & Kegan Paul.

Block, P. (1993) *Stewardship: Choosing Service Over Self Interest*. San Francisco, CA: Beffett-Koehler.

Boal, K. B. and Bryson, J. M. (1988) Charismatic Leadership: A Phenomenological and Structural Approach, in J. G. Hunt, B. R. Baliga, H. P. Dachler and C. A. Schriesheim (eds.) *Emerging Leadership Vistas*. Lexington, MA: D. C. Heath.

Bogue, E. G. (1994). *Leadership by Design*. San Francisco, CA: Jossey-Bass.

Bolam, R., Smith, G. and Canter, H. (1979) *Local Education Authority Advisers and Educational Innovation*. Windsor: NFER.

Bolman, L. G. and Deal, T. E. (1991) *Reframing Organizations: Artistry, Choice and Leadership*. San Francisco, CA: Jossey-Bass.

Bolman, L. G. and Deal, T. E. (1994) Looking for Leadership: Another Search Party's Report. *Educational Administration Quarterly*, Vol. 30, No.1, pp. 77–96.

Boomer, G. (1985) A celebration of teaching. *The Australian Teacher*. Vol. 11, pp. 13–20.

Bondi, L. (1988) Falling Rolls and School Costs. *Educational Management and Administration*, Vol. 16, No. 3, pp. 199–211.

Bonjour, L. (1985) *The Structure of Empirical Knowledge*. Cambridge, Mass: Harvard University Press.

Bottery, M. (1994) Education and the Convergence of Management Codes. *Educational Studies*, Vol. 20, No. 3, pp. 329–43.

Boulton, A. R. (1986) A Developed Formula for the Distribution of Capitation Allowances. *Educational Management and Administration*, Vol. 14, No. 1, pp. 31–8.

Brams, S. (1975) *Game Theory and Politics*. New York: Free Press.

Browning, P. (1972) Some changes in LEA administration. *London Educational Review*, Vol. 1 No. 3, pp. 4–12.

Brubaker, R. (1984) *The Limits of Rationality: An Essay on the Social and Moral Thought of Max Weber*. London: George Allen & Unwin.

Bryman, A. (1992) *Charisma and Leadership in Organizations*. London: Sage.

Bullock, A. and Thomas, H. (1993) Comparing school formula allocations: an exploration of some problems, in G. Wallace (ed.) *Local Management, Central Control: Schools in the Market Place*. Bournemouth: Hyde Publications.

Bullock, A. and Thomas, H. (1997) *Schools at the Centre? A Study of Decentralization*. London: Routledge.

Burgess, T. (1979) New Ways to Learn. *Royal Society of Arts Journal*, Vol. 127, No. 5271, pp. 143–53.

Burns, J. M. (1978) *Leadership*. New York: Harper & Row.

Burns, T. (1955) The reference of conduct in small groups. *Human Relations*, Vol. 8, pp. 467–86.

Bush, T., Coleman, M. and Glover, D. (1993) *Managing Autonomous Schools: The Grant-Maintained Experience*. Buckingham: Open University Press.

Busher, H. and Saran, R. (1994) Towards a Model of School Leadership. *Educational Management and Administration*, Vol. 22, No. 1, pp. 5–13.

Bush, T. and Goulding, S. (1984) The National Advisory Body and College Management. *Educational Management and Administration*, Vol. 12, No. 1, pp. 49–58.

Caldwell, B. J. (1994) Australian Perspectives on Leadership: The Principal's Role in Radical Decentralisation in Victoria's Schools of the Future. *Australian Educational Researcher* Vol. 21, No. 2, pp. 45–62.

Caldwell, B. J. and Spinks, J. M. (1992) *Leading the Self-Managing School*. Lewes: Falmer Press.

Carlisle, M. (1982) Address to the Association of Representatives of Old Pupils at Ellesmere College, Shropshire, reported in the *Daily Telegraph*, October.

Carlson, R. O. (1965) *Adoption of Educational Innovations*. Eugene, Oregon: Centre for the Advanced Study of Educational Administration, University of Oregon.

Carr, E. H. (1964) *What is History?* Harmondsworth: Penguin.

Carr, W. and Kemmis, S. (1986) *Becoming Critical: Education, Knowledge and Action Research*. London: Falmer.

Caulkin, S. (1996) Hey, What's the Big Idea? *The Observer*, 21 July.

Chaitin, G. J. (1975) Randomness and mathematical proof. *Scientific American*, Vol. 232, No. 5, pp. 47–51.

Chaleff, I. (1995). All Hail the Brave Follower! *Qantas Club Magazine* (November).

Champy, J. (1995) *Re-engineering Management: The Mandate for New Leadership*. New York: Harper-Collins.

Champy, J. and Hammer, M. (1993) *Re-engineering the Corporation*. New York: Harper-Collins.

Chu, C. N. (1992) *Thick Face, Black Heart*. London: Allen & Unwin.

Churchland, P. M. (1979) *Scientific Realism and the Plasticity of Mind*. Cambridge University Press.

Churchland, P. M. (1985) The ontological status of observables: in praise of the superempirical virtues, in P. M. Churchland and C. A. Hooker (eds.) *Images of Science*. University of Chicago Press.

Churchland, P. M. (1988) *Matter and Consciousness*. Cambridge, Mass: M.I.T. Press.

Churchland, P. S. (1986) *Neurophilosophy*. Cambridge, Mass: M.I.T. Press.

Cleaver, A. (1995) Tomorrow's Company. *Royal Society of Arts Journal*, Vol. 143, No. 5465, pp. 21–32.

Cohen, L. (1970) School size and headteachers' bureaucratic role conceptions. *Educational Review*, Vol. 23, pp. 50–8.

Conger, J. A. (1992) *Learning to Lead: The Art of Transforming Managers into Leaders*. San Francisco, CA: Jossey-Bass.

Conger, J. A. (1994) *Spirit at Work: Discovering the Spirituality in Leadership*. San Francisco, CA: Jossey-Bass.

Conway, E. S. (1970) *Going Comprehensive: A Study of the Administration of Comprehensive Schools*. London: Harrap.

Cotgrove, S. and Box, S. (1970) *Science, Industry and Society*. London: Allen and Unwin.

Cox, D. and Hoover, J. (1992) *Leadership When the Heat's On*. New York: McGraw Hill.

Covey, S. (1992) *Principle Centered Leadership*. New York: Simon & Schuster.

CPRS (Central Policy Review Staff) (1971) *A Framework for Government Research and Development*, Cmnd 4814. London: HMSO.

Crispin, A. and Marslen-Wilson, F. (1984) Extent of Central Control: LEA Responses to the 1981 Block Grant. *Educational Management and Administration*, Vol. 12, No. 1, pp. 37–48.

Crowe, K. (1993) Re-defining the profession: the approach of a government policy document to teachers in Australia. *Teaching and Teachers' Work*, Vol. 1, p. 2.

Crozier, M. (1964) *The Bureaucratic Phenomenon*. London: Tavistock.

Cuban, L. (1992) Managing Dilemmas while Building Professional Communities. *Educational Researcher*, January, pp. 4–11.

Cumming, C. E. (1971) *Studies in Educational Costs*. London: Chatto and Windus, Scottish Academic Press.

Cumming, C. E. (1973) The Power of Educational Research. *Educational Administration Bulletin*, Vol. 1, No. 2. pp. 36–8.

Dachler, H. P. (1988) Constraints on the Emergence of New Vistas in Leadership and Management Research: An Epistemological View, in J. G. Hunt, B. R. Baliga, H. P. Dachler and C. A. Schriesheim (eds.) *Emerging Leadership Vistas*. Lexington, MA: D. C. Heath.

Dalin, P. (ed.) (1973) *Strategies for Innovation in Education*. Paris: CERI, OECD.

David, M. (1973) Approaches to organisational change in LEAS. *Educational Administration Bulletin*, Vol. 2, pp. 24–33.

Day, C. (1982) *Classroom-Based In-Service Teacher Education: The Development and Evaluation of a Client-Centred Model*. Occasional Paper No. 9, ICAPE: University of Sussex.

Deem, R. (1996) The Future of Educational Research in the Context of the Social Sciences: A Special Case? *British Journal of Educational Studies*, Vol. 44, No. 2, pp. 143–58.

Deem, R., Brehoney, K. and New, S. (1993) Education for all? Three schools go to market, in G. Wallace (ed.) *Local Management, Central Control; Schools in the Market Place*. Bournemouth: Hyde Publications.

Dennett, D. (1991) Real Patterns. *Journal of Philosophy*, Vol. 88, No. 1, pp. 27–51.

Dennison, W. F. (1988) Education 2000 – Trends, Influences and Constraints to the Turn of the Century. *Educational Management and Administration*, Vol. 16, No. 1, pp. 33–42.

DES/Welsh Office (1977) *A New Partnership for Our Schools* (The Taylor Report). London: HMSO.

DES (1988) *Education (Special Educational Needs) Regulations 1994*. London: HMSO.

DES (1990) *Standards in Education 1988–89: The Annual Report of HM Senior Chief Inspector of Schools*. London: HMSO.

DES (1991a) *Education and Training for the Twenty-First Century*. London: HMSO.

DES (1991b) Circular 10/91: *Schoolteachers' pay and conditions of employment*. 26 June.

DfE (1992) *Choice and Diversity: A New Framework for Schools*, Cm 2021. London: HMSO.

DfEE (1995) *Superhighways for Education*. London: HMSO.

DfEE (1996) *Self Government for Schools*, Cm 3315. London: HMSO.

DfEE (1997a) *The Learning Age: a renaissance for a new Britain*. London: HMSO.

DfEE (1997b) *Learning for the Twenty-First Century*. First Report of the National Advisory Group for Continuing Education and Lifelong Learning (The Fryer Report). London: HMSO.

Dimmock, C. (1995) School Leadership: Securing Quality Teaching and Learnng, in C. W. Evers and J. D. Chapman (eds.) *Educational Administration: An Australian Perspective.* Sydney: Allen and Unwin.

DoE (Department of the Environment) (1972) *The New Local Authorities: Management and Structure, report by a study group* (The Bains Report). London: HMSO.

Drake, K. (1981) The Financing of Vocational Training: Some Methodological Issues, in P. Ribbins and H. Thomas (eds.) *Research in Educational Management and Administration*, Proceedings of the second BEMAS/SSRC Research Seminar, pp. 15–26.

Duignan, P. and Bhindi, N. (1995) A Quest for Authentic Leadership. BEMAS Annual Conference, Oxford, September.

Duignan, P. and Macpherson, R. J. S. (1992) *Educative Leadership: A Practical Theory for New Administrators and Managers.* London: Falmer Press.

Earley, P. (1993) Developing Competence in Schools: A Critique of Standards-based Approaches to Management Development. *Educational Management and Administration*, Vol. 21, No. 4, pp. 233–44.

Elliott, J. (1991) *Action Research for Education Change.* Buckingham: Open University Press.

Elstein, A. S., Shulman, L. S. and Sprafka, S. A. (1978). *Medical Problem Solving: An Analysis of Clinical Reasoning.* Cambridge, MA: Harvard University Press.

Eraut, M. (1982) What is learned in in-service education and how: a knowledge use perspective. *British Journal of In-Service Education*, Vol. 9, No. 1, pp. 6–14.

Eraut, M. (1985) Knowledge creation and knowledge use in professional contexts. *Studies in Higher Education*, Vol. 10, No. 2, pp. 117–33.

Eraut, M. (1988) Learning about management: the role of the management course, in C. Day and C. Poster (eds.) *Educational Management Purposes and Practices.* London: Routledge.

Eraut, M. (1992) Developing the professional knowledge base: conceptions of theory and practice, competence and effectiveness, in R. A. Barnett (ed.) *Learning to Effect* (Proceedings 1992 SRHE Conference). Buckingham: Open University Press.

Eraut, M. (1993a) The acquisition and use of educational theory by beginning teachers, in G. Harvard and P. Hodkinson (eds.) *Action and Reaction in Teacher Education.* Ablex, Norwood: New Jersey.

Eraut, M. (1993b) The Characterisation and Development of Professional Expertise in School Management and Teaching. *Educational Management and Administration*, Vol. 21, No. 4, pp. 223–32.

Eraut, M. (1994) Developing professional knowledge within a client-centred orientation, in T. Guskey and M. Huberman (eds.) *Teacher Professional Development in Education: a Multiple Perspective Approach.* Lisse, Netherlands: Swets and Zeitlinger.

ESRC (Economic and Social Research Council) (1997) Thematic Priorities Updated. *Social Sciences*, Swindon: ESRC, Issue 36, October, pp. 1–2.

Etzioni, A. (1964) *Modern Organisations.* Englewood Cliffs, New Jersey: Prentice Hall.

Evers, C. W. and Lakomski, G. (1991) *Knowing Educational Administration: Contemporary Methodological Controversies in Educational Administration.* London: Pergamon Press.

Evers, C. and Lakomski, G. (1993) Justifying Educational Administration. *Educational Management and Administration*, Vol. 21, No. 3, pp. 140–52.

Evetts, J. (1993) LMS and Headship: Changing Contexts for Micro-politics. *Educational Review*, Vol. 45, No. 1, pp. 53–65.

Evetts, J. (1994) The New Headteacher: The Changing Work Culture of Secondary Headship. *School Organisation*, Vol. 14, No. 1, pp. 37–47.

Feyerabend, P. K. (1975) *Against Method*. London: Verso.

Field, J. (1997) Contracting Knowledge: Policy Developments in Educational Research and the Role of the European Union. *Scottish Journal of Adult and Continuing Education*, Vol. 4, No. 2, pp. 7–16.

Fox, M. (1991) *Creation Spirituality: Liberating Gifts for the Peoples of the Earth*. San Francisco, CA: Harper.

Fullan, M. and Hargreaves, A. (1991) *What's Worth Fighting For? Working Together for Your School*. Toronto: Ontario Teachers Federation.

Fullan, M. (1993) *Change Forces: Probing the Depths of Educational Reform*, London: Falmer Press.

Gass, J. R. (1971) *An Overview of Past Trends and Future Issues, Educational Policies for the 1970s*. Paris: OECD.

Gathorne-Hardy, J. (1979) *The Public School Phenomenon*. Harmondsworth: Penguin.

Geertz, C. (1980) Blurred genres. *The American Scholar*, Vol. 99, No. 2, p. 178.

Getzels, J. W., Lipham, J. M. and Campbell, R. F. (1968) *Educational Administration as a Social Process: Theory, Research, Practice*. New York: Harper & Row.

Gibb, C. A. (1968) Leadership, in G. Lindzey and E. Aronson (eds.) *The Handbook of Social Psychology*, Vol. 4, (2nd edition.). Reading, MA: Addison-Wesley.

Giddens, A. (1991) *Modernity and Self-Identity: Self and Society in the Late Modern Age*. Cambridge: Polity Press.

Giddens, A. (1992) *The Transformation of Intimacy: Sexuality, Love and Eroticism in Modern Societies*. Cambridge: Polity Press.

Giddens, A. (1995) *A Contemporary Critique of Historical Materialism* (2nd edn.). London: Macmillan. pp. 15–18.

Glaser, B. G. and Strauss, A. L. (1968) *The Discovery of Grounded Theory: Strategies for Qualitative Research*. London: Weidenfeld and Nicolson.

Glatter, R. (1972) *Management Development for the Education Profession*. London: Harrap.

Glatter, R. (1979) Future Developments in the Training of Educational Administrators. *Educational Administration: Approaches to Professional Development*. Proceedings of the Seventh Annual Conference of BEMAS, Westfield College, University of London, September, pp. 19–42.

Glatter, R. (1980) Educational 'Policy' and 'Management': One Field or Two?, in T. Bush, R. Glatter, J. Goodey and C. Riches (eds.). *Approaches to School Management*. London: Harper and Row.

Glatter, R. (1981) Research into Policy-making in Education: Introduction, *Research in Educational Management and Administration*. Proceedings of the Second BEMAS/SSRC Seminar, University of Birmingham, Occasional Publication of the British Educational Management and Administration Society, pp. 4–7.

Glatter, R. (1982) The Micropolitics of Education: Issues for Training. *Educational Management and Administration*, Vol. 10, No. 2, pp. 160–5.

Glatter, R. (1987) Towards an Agenda for Educational Management. *Educational Management and Administration*, Vol. 15, No. 1, pp. 5–12.

Glatter, R. (1996) Managing Dilemmas in Education: The Tightrope Walk of Strategic Choice in More Autonomous Institutions, in S. L. Jacobson, E. Hickox and R. Stevenson (eds.) *School Administration: Persistent Dilemmas in Preparation and Practice*. Westport, CT: Praeger.

Glatter, R., Woods, P. A. and Bagley, C. (1997). Diversity, Differentiation and Hierarchy: School Choice and Parental Preferences, in R. Glatter, P. A. Woods and C. Bagley (eds.) *Choice and Diversity in Schooling: Perspectives and Prospects*. London: Routledge.

Goss, M. E. W. (1962) Administration and the physician. *American Journal of Public Health*, Vol. 52, pp. 183–91.

Gouldner, A. W. (1950) Introduction, in A. W. Gouldner (ed.) *Studies in Leadership*. New York: Russell & Russell.

Grace, G. (1995) *School Leadership – Beyond Education Management: An Essay in Policy Scholarship*. London: Falmer Press.

Graham, J. W. (1988) Transformational Leadership: Fostering Follower Autonomy, not Automatic Followership, in J. G. Hunt, B. R. Baliga, H. P. Dachler and C. A. Schriesheim (eds.) *Emerging Leadership Vistas*. Lexington, MA: D. C. Heath.

Graham, J. W. (1991) Servant-leadership in Organizations: Inspirational and Moral. *Leadership Quarterly*, Vol. 2, No. 2, pp. 105–19.

Gray, H. L. (1972) Training in the Management of Education. *The Educational Administration Bulletin*, Vol. 1, No. 1, pp. 1–9.

Gray, J. (1995) The Quality of Schooling: Frameworks for Judgement, in J. Gray and B. Wilcox (eds.) *Good School, Bad School: Evaluating Performance and Encouraging Improvement*. Buckingham: Open University Press.

Greene, J. C., Caracelli, V. J. and Graham, W. F. (1989) Toward a conceptual framework for mixed-method evaluation designs. *Educational Evaluation and Policy Analysis*, Vol. 11, No. 3, pp. 255–74.

Greenfield, T. B. (1975) Theory about Organisations: A New Perspective and its Implications for Schools, in M. Hughes (ed.) *Administering Education: International Challenge*. London: Athlone Press.

Greenfield, T. B. (1976) Barr Greenfield and Organisational Theory: A Symposium. *Educational Administration*, Vol. 5, No. 1, pp. 1–12.

Greenfield, T. B. (1978a) Where Does Self Belong in The Study of Organisation? *Educational Administration*, Vol. 6, No. 1, pp. 81–101.

Greenfield, T. B. (1979a) Research in Educational Administration in the United States and Canada: An Overview and Critique. *Educational Administration*, Vol. 8, No. 1, pp. 207–45.

Greenfield, T. B. (1979b) Ideas versus data: how can the data speak for themselves?, in G. L. Immegart and W. L. Boyd (eds.) *Problem Finding in Educational Administration*. Lexington: Lexington Books.

Greenfield, T. B. (1980) The man who comes back through the door in the wall: discovering truth, discovering self, discovering organizations. *Educational Administration Quarterly*, Vol. 16, No. 3, pp. 26–59.

Greenfield, T. B. (1983) Against group mind: an anarchistic theory of organization, in L. R. Rattray Wood (ed.) *Reflective Readings in Educational Administration*, Victoria, Australia: Deakin University Press, pp. 293–301.

Greenfield, T. B. (1984) Leaders and schools: Wilfulness and nonnatural order in organizations, in T. J. Sergiovanni and J. E. Corbally (eds.) *Leadership and Organizational Culture. New Perspectives on Administrative Theory and Practice*. Urbana, Chicago: University of Illinois Press, 142–69.

Greenfield, T. B. (1986) The decline and fall of science in educational administration. *Interchange*, Vol. 17, No. 2, pp. 57–80.

Greenfield, T. B. (1991) Science and service: the making of the profession of educational administration, in Greenfield and Ribbins (1993b), pp. 199–228.

Greenfield, T. B. and Ribbins, P. (1993a) Educational administration as a humane science: conversations between Thomas Greenfield and Peter Ribbins, in Greenfield and Ribbins (1993b), pp. 229–271.

Greenfield, T. B. and Ribbins, P. (eds.) (1993b) *Greenfield on Educational Administration: Towards a Humane Science.* London: Routledge.

Greenfield, W. D. (1995) Towards a Theory of School Administration: The Centrality of Leadership. *Educational Administration Quarterly,* Vol. 31, No. 1, pp. 61–85.

Griffin, R. W., Skivington, K. D. and Moorhead, G. (1987) Symbolic and Interactional Perspectives on Leadership: An Integrative Framework. *Human Relations,* Vol. 40, No. 4, pp. 199–218.

Griffiths, D. E. (1959) *Administrative Theory.* New York: Appleton-Century-Crofts.

Griffiths, D. E. (1977) The Individual in Organisation: A Theoretical Perspective. *Educational Administration Quarterly,* Vol. 13, No. 2, p. 10.

Griffiths, D. E. (1979) Intellectual turmoil in educational administration. *Educational Administration Quarterly,* Vol. 15, No. 3, pp. 43–65.

Griffiths, D. E. (1988) Administrative theory, in N. J. Boyan (ed.) *Handbook of Research on Educational Administration.* Longman: New York, pp. 27–51.

Griffiths, D. E. (1991) Nontraditional Theory as Research. *Educational Administration Quarterly,* Vol. 27, No. 3, pp. 262–451.

Gronn, P. C. (1986) Politics, Power and the Management of Schools, in E. Hoyle and A. McMahon (eds.) *The Management of Schools.* London: Kogan Page.

Gronn, P. C. (1993a) Bewitching the Led: Hodgkinson on Leadership. *Journal of Educational Administration and Foundations,*Vol. 8, No. l, pp. 29–44.

Gronn, P. C. (1993b) Psychobiography on the Couch: Character, Biography and the Comparative Study of Leaders. *Journal of Applied Behavioural Science,* Vol. 29, No. 3, pp. 343–58.

Gronn, P. C. (1994) Educational Administration's Weber. *Educational Management and Administration,* Vol. 22, No. 4, pp. 224–31.

Gronn, P. C. (1995) Greatness Revisited: The Current Obsession with Transformational Leadership. *Leading & Managing,* Vol. 1, No.1, pp. 14–27.

Gronn, P. C. (1996) From Transactions to Transformations: A New World Order in the Study of Leadership. *Educational Management and Administration,* Vol. 24, No. 1, pp. 7–30.

Gross, N. and Herriott, R. E. (1965) *Staff Leadership in Public Schools.* New York: Wiley.

Guba, E. G. and Bidwell, C. E. (1957). *Administrative Relationships: Teacher Effectiveness, Teachers' Satisfaction, and Administrative Behavior.* Chicago: University of Chicago.

Gunn, B. (1995) The Paradigm Shift in University Management. *International Journal of Educational Management,* Vol. 9, No. 1. pp. 28–40.

Habermas, J. (1972) *Knowledge and Human Interests.* London: Heinemann Educational Books.

Hall, V. (1996) *Dancing on the Ceiling: A Study of Women Managers in Education.* London: Paul Chapman Publishing.

Hall, V. (1997) Dusting off the Phoenix: Gender and Educational Leadership Revisited. *Educational Management and Administration,* Vol. 25, No. 3, pp. 309–24.

Hall, V. and Southworth, G. (1997) Headship. *School Leadership and Management*, Vol. 17, No. 2, pp. 151–70.

Halmos, P. (1965) *The Faith of the Counsellor*. London: Constable.

Halmos, P. (1970) *The Personal Service Society*. London: Constable.

Halpin, A. W. (1957) *Administrative Theory in Education*. Chicago: Midwest Administration Center, University of Chicago. London: Macmillan.

Halpin, D. (1998) Editorial: Getting By Through Failing to Deliver Simple Truths. *British Journal of Educational Studies*, Vol. 46, No. 1, pp. 1–7.

Handy, C. (1994) *The Empty Raincoat: Making Sense of the Future*. London: Hutchinson.

Hanson, N. R. (1968) *Patterns of Discovery*. New York: Cambridge University Press.

Hargreaves, D. (1978) Whatever happened to symbolic interactionism?, in I. Barton and R. Meighan (eds.) *Sociological Interpretations of Schooling and Classrooms: A Reappraisal*. Nafferton: Nafferton Books, pp. 7–22.

Hargreaves, A. (1994) *Changing Teachers, Changing Times: teachers' work and culture in the postmodern age*. Cassell. Reviewed by Strain, M. (1994). Review Symposium. *Education Management and Administration*. Vol. 22, No. 4, pp. 270–2.

Hargreaves, D. (1996) *Teaching as a Research Based Profession: Possibilities and Prospects*. The Teacher Training Agency Annual Lecture, London.

Hartley, D. (1993) The evaluative state and self management in education: cause for reflection, in J. Smyth (ed.) *A Socially Critical View of the Self Managing School*. London and New York: Falmer Press.

Henson, J. (1987) An Evaluation of Aspects of Teacher Professionalism, as Evidenced by Salary and Structure Proposals. *Educational Management and Administration*, Vol. 15, No. 3, pp. 165–70.

Hinds, T. (1984) Local Financial Management: a Pilot Scheme. *Educational Management and Administration*, Vol. 12, No. 1, pp. 21–6.

Hirsch, D. (1995) The Other School Choice – How Should Over-Subscribed Schools Select their Pupils?, Open Lecture, 31 May, Institute of Education, University of London (mimeo).

Hirschhorn, L. (1990) *The Workplace Within: the Psychodynamics of Organisational Life*. London: MIT Press.

Hodgkinson, C. (1978a) The failure of organisational and administrative theory, *McGill Journal of Education*, Vol. 13, No. 3, pp. 271–8.

Hodgkinson, C. (1978b) *Towards a Philosophy of Administration*, Oxford: Basil Blackwell.

Hodgkinson, C. (1983) *The Philosophy of Leadership*. Oxford: Basil Blackwell.

Hodgkinson, C. (1988) The value bases and foundations of administrative action. *Journal of Educational Administration*, Vol. 3, No. 1, pp. 20–30.

Hodgkinson, C. (1990) Madness and malady in educational administration. Paper presented to the Canadian Association for the Study of Educational Administration. Victoria, Learned Societies of Canada Conference.

Hodgkinson, C. (1991) *Educational Leadership: The Moral Art*. Albany, NY: SUNY.

Hodgkinson, C. (1993) The Epistemological Axiology of Evers and Lakomski: Some un-Quinian Quibblings, *Educational Management and Administration*, Vol. 21, No. 3, pp. 177–84.

Holden, A. (1969) *Teachers as Counsellors*. London: Constable.

Hood, C. (1995) The 'New Public Management' in the 1980s: Variations on a Theme. *Accounting, Organizations and Society*, Vol. 20, No. 2/3, pp. 93–109.

Honey, J. R. de S. (1977) *Tom Brown's Universe*, London: Millington Books.

Hough, J. (1991) An Economist Looks at Education. *Educational Management and Administration*, Vol. 19, No. 4, pp. 218–32.

Hough, J. R. and Warburton, S. J. (1984) Studies of School Costs and Resources. *Educational Management and Administration*, Vol. 12, No. 1, pp. 27–31.

House, R. J. (1977) A 1976 Theory of Leadership, in J. G. Hunt and L. L. Larson (eds.) *Leadership: The Cutting Edge*. Carbondale, IL: Southern Illinois University Press.

House, R. J. and Shamir, B. (1993) Toward the Integration of Transformational, Charismatic and Visionary Theories, in M. M. Chemers and R. Ayman (eds.) *Leadership Theory and Research: Perspectives and Directions*. San Diego, CA: Academic Press.

Howell, J. M. (1988) Two Faces of Charisma: Socialized and Personalized Leadership in Organizations, in J. A. Conger and R. K. Kanungo (eds.) *Charismatic Leadership: The Elusive Factor in Organizational Effectiveness*. San Francisco, CA: Jossey-Bass.

Hoy, W. and Miskel, C. (1987) *Educational Administration: Theory, Research, and Practice* (3rd edition). New York: Random House.

Hoyle, E. (1969) How does the curriculum change? Systems and strategies. *Journal of Curriculum Studies*, Vol. 1 (Nov.), pp. 230–239.

Hoyle, E. (1981) The process of management. *Managerial Processes in Schools, Management and the School*. O.U. Course E 323 Block 3, pp. 6–51. Milton Keynes: Open University Press.

Hoyle, E. (1982) Micropolitics of Educational Organisations, *Educational Management and Administration*, Vol. 10, No. 2, pp. 87–92.

Hoyles, E. (1968) The Head as innovator, in B. Allen (ed.) *Headship in the 1970s*, Oxford: Blackwell.

Huckman, L. and Hill, T. (1994) Local Management of Schools: Rationality and Decision-making in the Employment of Teachers. *Oxford Review of Education*, Vol. 20, No. 2, pp. 185–97.

Hughes, M. (1972a) The Role of the Secondary School Head. Cardiff: University College Cardiff, University of Wales Ph.D. Thesis.

Hughes, M. (1972b) School headship in transition. *London Educational Review*, Vol. 1, No. 3, pp. 34–42.

Hughes, M. (1972c) Editorial. *Educational Administration Bulletin*, Vol. 1, No. 1, pp. I–II.

Hughes, M. (1975) The professional-as-administrator: the case of the secondary school head, in R. Peters. (ed.) *The Role of the Head*. London: Routledge & Kegan Paul.

Hughes, M. (1978) Critical Issues in the Preparation of Educational Administrators in Britain. Paper presented at the Fourth International Intervisitation Program on Educational Administration, Vancouver, Canada.

Hughes, M. (1982) Professional Development Provision for Senior Staff in Schools and Colleges. *Educational Management and Administration*, Vol. 10, No. 1, pp. 1–15.

Hughes, M. (1988) Comparative educational administration, in N. J. Boyan (ed.) *Handbook of Research on Educational Administration*, Longman: New York, pp. 655–75.

Hughes, M. (1997) From Bulletin to Journal: Metamorphosis and New Vistas. *Educational Management and Administration*, Vol. 25, No. 3, pp. 243–63.

Hughes, M. and Ribbins, P. (1979) Looking to the Future: Emerging Issues and Suggestions, *Educational Administration*, Vol. 8, No. 1, pp. 274–9.

Hughes, P. M. (1971) *Guidance and Counselling in Schools: A Response to Change*. Oxford: Pergamon.

Humphrey, C. and Thomas, H. (1986) Delegation to Schools. *Education*, Vol. 168, No. 24, pp. 513–14.

Hunt, J. G. (1991) *Leadership: A New Synthesis*. Newbury Park, CA: Sage.

Hutton, W. (1995) *The State We're In*. London: Jonathan Cape.

ILEA (1976) *The William Tyndale Junior and Infant Schools*. Report by Robin Auld QC (The Auld Report).

Imich, A. J. (1994) Exclusions from school: current trends and issues. *Educational Research*, Vol. 36, No. 1, pp. 3–11.

Inglis, F. (1986) Why managerialism is dire. *Education*, 3rd January.

Jacobs, T. O. and Jaques, E. (1991) Executive Leadership, in R. Gal and A. D. Mangelsdorff (eds.) *Handbook of Military Psychology*. Chichester: Wiley.

Jackson, N. (1993) Competence: a game of smoke and mirrors? in C. Collins (ed.) *Competencies: the Competencies Debate in Australian Education and Training*. Canberra: Australian College of Education.

Jaques, E. (1957) Social Systems as a Defence against Persecutory and Depressive Anxiety, in M. Klein (ed.) *New Directions in Psycho-Analysis*. New York: Basic Books.

Jaques, E. (1970) On Being a Manager, in E. Jaques, *Work, Creativity and Social Justice*. London: Heinemann.

Jaques, E. (1989) *Requisite Organization: the CEO's Guide to Creative Structure and Leadership*. Arlington, VA: Cason Hall.

Jaques, E. and Clement, S. D. (1991) *Executive Leadership: A Practical Guide to Managing Complexity*. Arlington, VA: Cason Hall.

Jesson, D. and Levačić, R. (1993) Patterns of resource allocation in schools: a research basis for developing a funding formula, in G. Wallace (ed.) *Local Management: Central Schools: Schools in the Market Place*. Bournemouth: Hyde Publications.

Jonathan, R. (1989) Choice and control in education: parental rights, individual liberties and social justice. *British Journal of Educational Studies*, Vol. 37, No. 4, pp. 321–8.

Jonathan, R. (1990) State education service or prisoner's dilemma: the 'hidden hand' as a source of education policy. *British Journal of Educational Studies*, Vol. 38, No. 2, pp. 116–32.

Jones, A. (1987) *Leadership for Tomorrow's Schools*. Oxford: Blackwell.

Kay, B. W. (1978) The DES and Educational Research. *Research Intelligence*, Vol. 4, No. 1.

Kay, J. (1993) *Foundations of Corporate Success: How Business Strategies Add Value*. Oxford: Oxford University Press.

Kelly, A. (1992) Turning the budget on its head. *Managing Schools Today*, Vol. 1, No. 7, pp. 24–7.

Keeves, J. P. (ed.) (1988) *Educational Research, Methodology, and Measurement – An International Handbook*. Oxford: Pergamon Press.

Kendell, R. and Byrne, D. R. (1978) *Educational Administration*, Vol. 6, No. 2, pp. 107–19.

Kets de Vries, M. F. R. (1988) Prisoners of Leadership. *Human Relations*, Vol. 41, No. 3, pp. 261–80.

Kets de Vries, M. F. R. (1993) *Leaders, Fools and Imposters: Essays on the Psychology of Leadership*. San Francisco, CA: Jossey-Bass.

Klein, P. and Saunders, B. (1993) *Ten Steps to a Learning Organization*. Arlington, VA: Great Ocean.

Knight, B. (1984) Attitudes to Educational Finance. *Educational Management and Administration*, Vol. 12, No. 1, pp. 15–19.

Kogan, M. (1975) *Educational Policy Making: a Study of Interest Groups and Parliament*. London: George Allen and Unwin.

Kornhauser, W. (1963) *Scientists in Industry: Conflict and Accommodation*. Berkeley, CA: University of California Press.

Kotter, J. P. (1990) What Leaders Really Do. *Harvard Business Review*, Vol. 90, No. 3, pp. 103–11.

Kouzes, J. M. and Posner, B. Z. (1987) *The Leadership Challenge: How to Get Extraordinary Things Done in Organizations*. San Francisco, CA: Jossey-Bass.

Kouzes, J. M. and Posner, B. Z. (1991) *Credibility: How Leaders Gain and Lose it: Why People Demand it*. San Francisco, CA: Jossey-Bass.

Krantz, J. and Gilmore, T. N. (1990) The Splitting of Leadership and Management as a Social Defense. *Human Relations*, Vol. 43, No. 2, pp. 183–204.

Kuhn, T. S. (1974) *The Structure of Scientific Revolutions*. Chicago, Illinois: University of Chicago Press.

Kuhnert, K. W. (1994) Transforming Leadership: Developing People Through Delegation, in B. M. Bass and B. J. Avolio (eds.) *Improving Organizational Effectiveness Through Transformational Leadership*. Thousand Oaks, CA: Sage.

Kuhnert, K. W. and Lewis, P. (1987) Transactional and Transformational Leadership: A Constructive/Developmental Analysis. *Academy of Management Review*, Vol. 12, No. 4, pp. 648–57.

Lakomski, G. (1987) Values and decision-making in educational administration. *Educational Administration Quarterly*, Vol. 23, No. 3, pp. 70–82.

Lakomski, G. (1989) The Journal of Educational Administration, What They Do and How Well They Do It, in Harman G. (ed.) *Review of Australian Research in Education*, No. 1. Armidale: New England, Australian Association for Research in Education.

Lakomski, G. (ed.) (1991) Beyond paradigms: coherentism and holism in educational research. *International Journal of Educational Research*, Vol. 15, No. 6, pp. 499–597.

Lantis, M. (1987) Two Important Roles in Organizations and Communities. *Human Organization*, Vol. 46, No. 3, pp. 189–99.

Lauder, H. (1987) The New Right and educational policy in New Zealand. *New Zealand Journal of Educational Studies*, Vol. 22, No. 1, pp. 3–23.

Laver, M. (1981) *The Politics of Private Desires*. Harmondsworth: Penguin Books.

Lee, T. (1992) Finding simple answers to complex questions: funding special needs under LMS, in G. Wallace (ed.) *Local Management of Schools: Research and Experience*. Clevedon, Avon: Multi-lingual Matters.

Le Grand, J. (1991) *Equity and Choice: An Essay in Applied Social Policy*. Cambridge, MA: Ballinger; London: Harper Collins.

Leithwood, K. A. (1994) Leadership for School Restructuring. *Educational Administration Quarterly*, Vol. 30, No. 4, pp. 498–518.

Leithwood, K. (1995) Cognitive Perspectives on School Leadership. *Journal of School Leadership*, Vol. 5, No. 2, pp. 115–35.

Leithwood, K., Begley, P. T. and Cousins, J. B. (1994) *Developing Expert Leadership for Future Schools.* London: Falmer.

Levačić, R. (1989) Rules and Formulae for Allocating and Spending Delegated Budgets: A Consideration of General Principles. *Educational Management and Administration,* Vol. 17, No. 2, pp. 79–90.

Levačić, R. (1992) Local management of schools: aim, scope and impact. *Educational Management and Administration,* Vol. 20, No. 1, pp. 16–29.

Levačić, R (1995) *Local Management of Schools: analysis and practice.* Milton Keynes: Open University Press.

Lewis, C. H. (1967) *The Head of a School.* London: Head Masters Association.

Lipham, J. M. (1988) Getzels's models in educational administration, in N. J. Boyan (ed.) *Handbook of Research on Educational Administration,* New York: Longman, pp. 171–84.

Lloyd, J. (1986) Busy Izzy in Search of Truth. *New Statesman,* 15 August, pp. 18–20.

Lycan, W. G. (1988). *Judgement and Justification.* Cambridge: Cambridge University Press.

Lyons R. F. (ed.) (1970) *Administrative Aspects of Educational Planning.* Paris: IEP, UNESCO.

MacIntyre, A. (1981) *After Virtue: A Study in Moral Theory.* London: Duckworth.

Maddock, T. (1991) The role of authority and reason in education and educational administration. *Educational Administration Quarterly,* Vol. 27, No. 1, pp. 90–102.

Magsaysay, J. (1996) The Diversity Debates (editorial). *World Executive's Digest,* February, p. 6.

Mangham, I. (1979) *The Politics of Organizational Change.* London: Associated Business Press.

March, J. G. and Simon, A. A. (1958) *Organisations.* New York: Wiley.

March, J. G. and Olsen, J. (1976) *Ambiguity and Choice in Organisations.* Bergen: Universitetsforlaget.

Marginson, S. (1989) Human-capital theory and education policy. Unpublished paper, University of New South Wales.

Maw, J. (1984) *Education plc? Headteachers and the New Training Initiative.* Bedford Way Papers 20, Institute of Education, University of London.

McKenzie, M. L. (1973) Teaching and Study: Current Developments. *Educational Administration Bulletin,* Vol. 1, No. 2, pp. 34–6

Mead, R. (1990) *Cross-Cultural Management Communication.* New York: John Wiley and Sons.

Meindl, J. R. (1990) On Leadership: An Alternative to the Conventional Wisdom, in B. M. Staw and L. L. Cummings (eds.) *Research in Organizational Behavior,* Vol. 12, Greenwich, CT: JAI Press.

Meindl, J. R., Ehrlich, S. B. and Dukerich, J. M. (1985) The Romance of Leadership. *Administrative Science Quarterly,* Vol. 30, No. 1, pp. 78–102.

Messick, D. M. and Bazerman, M. H. (1996) Ethical Leadership and the Psychology of Decision-Making. *Sloan Management Review* (Winter), pp. 9–22.

Milakovich, M. (1991) TQM in the Public Sector. *National Productivity Review* (Spring), pp. 195–213.

Millett, A. (1996) A Head is More than a Manager. *The Times Educational Supplement,* 15 July.

Ministry of Education (1963) *Half Our Future: A Report of the Central Advisory Council for Education (England)*. London: HMSO.

Mintzberg, H. (1994) *The Rise and Fall of Strategic Planning*. London: Prentice Hall.

Monk, D. (1990) *Educational Finance: An Economic Approach*. New York: McGraw-Hill.

Morgan, G. (1996) *Images of Organisation* (2nd edition). Thousand Oaks, California: Sage Publications.

Morrison, J. (1973) Comment. *Educational Administration Bulletin*, Vol. 1, No. 2, pp. 39–40.

Mortimer, P. and Mortimer, J. (1991) *The Secondary Head: Roles, Responsibilities and Reflections*. London: Paul Chapman.

Mountford, B. (1984) The Management of Change in Small Schools. *Educational Management and Administration*, Vol. 12, No. 1, pp. 63–6.

Murphy, J. (1990) Delegation, quality and the local management of schools. Unpublished manuscript, Department of Commerce, University of Adelaide, Working Paper 90/1.

Murphy, J. (1995) Creative Leadership. Paper presented to the Annual Conference of the Australian Council for Educational Administration, Sydney, 4 July.

Musgrove, F. (1971) *Patterns of Power and Authority in English Education*. London: Methuen.

Nair, K. (1994) *A Higher Standard of Leadership: Lessons From the Life of Gandhi*. San Francisco, CA: Beffett-Koehler.

Nash, R. (1989) Tomorrow's schools: state power and parent participation. *New Zealand Journal of Educational Studies*, Vol. 24, No. 2, pp. 113–28.

National Commission on Education (1993) *Learning to Succeed: A Radical Look at Education Today and a Strategy for the Future*. London: Heinemann.

Noble, T. and Pym, B. (1970) Collegial authority and the receding locus of power. *British Journal of Sociology*, Vol. 21, No. 4, pp. 431–45.

North, R. (1991) Managing the Integration of Information Technology Across the Curriculum of the Secondary School. *Computers in Education*, Vol. 16, No. 1, pp. 13–16.

Osborne, D. and Gaebler, T. (1992) *Reinventing Government: How the Entrepreneurial Spirit is Transforming the Public Sector*. Reading, MA: Addison-Wesley.

OST (Office of Science and Technology) (1993) *Realising Our Potential: A Strategy for Science, Engineering and Technology*. London: HMSO.

Ouchi, W. G. (1981) A framework for understanding organizational failure. *Administrative Science Quarterly*, 28.

Ouston, J. (1993) Management Competences, School Effectiveness and Education Management. *Educational Management and Administration*, Vol. 21, No. 4, pp. 212–21.

Ouston, J. (1998) Managing in Turbulent Times, in A. Gold and J. Evans (1998) *Reflecting on School Management*. Lewes: Falmer Press (in press).

Owen, P. R., Davies, M. and Wayment, A. (1983) The Role of the Deputy Head in Secondary Schools. *Educational Management and Administration*, Vol. 11, No. 1, pp. 51–6.

Pascal, C. (1987) Democratic Primary School Government: Conflicts and Dichotomies. *Educational Management and Administration*, Vol. 15, No. 3, pp. 193–202.

Peters, T. J. and Waterman, R. H. (1982) *In Search of Excellence: Lessons from America's Best Run Companies*. New York: Harper & Row.

Pettigrew, A. (1973) *The Politics of Organization Decision-Making*. London: Tavistock.

Pirsig, M. (1992) *Lila: An Inquiry into Morals*. London: Corgi Books.

Pitner, N. (1988) The study of administrator effects and effectiveness, in N. J. Boyan, (ed.) *Handbook of Research on Educational Administration*. New York: Longman, pp. 99–122.

Popkewitz, T. S. (1997) The production of reason and power: curriculum history and intellectual traditions. *Journal of Curriculum Studies*, Vol. 29, pp. 131–64.

Power, S., Fitz, J. and Halpin, D. (1994) Parents, pupils and grant-maintained schools. *British Journal of Educational Research*, Vol. 20, No. 2, pp. 209–25.

Pratt, S. (1982) Editorial: Enter Micropolitics. *Educational Management and Administration*, Vol. 10, No. 2, pp. 77–85.

Pratt, S. (1983) Microcomputers in Secondary Schools. *Educational Management and Administration*, Vol. 11, No. 1, pp. 57–61.

Preston, P. (1996) Class wars unique to Britain, *The Guardian*, 14 June, p. 17.

Pring, R. (1983) Privatisation in Education. Paper for RICE, republished in Plaskow (ed.) *Education and Social Class*. London.

Public School Commission (1970) *Second Report, Vol. 1: Report on Independent Day Schools and Direct Grant Grammar Schools*. London: HMSO.

Pucik, V., Tichy, N. M. and Barnett, K. C., (eds.) (1993) *Globalizing Management: Creating and Leading the Competitive Organization*. New York: John Wiley and Sons.

Quine, W. V. (1960) *Word and Object*. Cambridge, Mass: M.I.T. Press.

Quine, W. V. (1981) *Theories and Things*. Cambridge, Mass: Harvard University Press.

Quine, W. V. (1990) *Pursuit of Truth*. Cambridge, Mass: Harvard University Press.

Quine, W. V. and Ullian, J. S. (1978) *The Web of Belief*, (2nd ed.). Random House: New York.

Ranson, S. (1984) Towards a Tertiary Tripartitism, in P. Broadfoot (ed.) *Selection, Certification and Control*. Lewes: Falmer Press.

Ranson S. (1992) Towards the Learning Society. *Educational Management and Administration*, Vol. 20, No. 2, pp. 68–79.

Reid, K. (1983) Institutional Factors and Persistent School Absenteeism. *Educational Management and Administration*, Vol. 11, No. 1, pp. 17–27.

Reilly, W. (1982) *Microcomputers in Wiltshire Secondary Schools*. Unpublished MEd dissertation, University of Bristol.

Reissman, L. (1949) A study of role conceptions in bureaucracy. *Social Forces*, Vol. 27, pp. 305–10.

Ribbins, P. (1985) Organisation theory and the study of educational institutions, in M. Hughes, P. Ribbins and H. Thomas, *Managing Education: The System and the Institution*. London: Holt, Rinehart and Winston, pp. 223–61.

Ribbins, P. (1986) Qualitative perspectives in research in secondary education, in T. Simkins (ed.) *Research in the Management of Secondary Education*. Sheffield: Sheffield Papers in Education Management.

Ribbins, P. (1992). Editorial: Reflections. *Educational Management and Administration*, Vol. 20, No. 2, p. 67.

Ribbins, P. and Sherratt, B. (1992) Managing the Secondary School in the 1990s: A New View of Headship. *Educational Management and Administration*, Vol. 20, No. 3, pp. 151–60.

Richardson, E. (1973, 1977) *The Teacher, the School and the Task of Management*. London: Heinemann.

Romagna, J. (1995) The Best of All Worlds. *World Executive's Digest* (October).

Rorty, R. (1989) *Contingency, Irony, and Solidarity*. Cambridge.

Rosenbluth, H. F. and Peters, D. M. (1992) *Customer Comes Second and Other Secrets of Exceptional Service*. New York: William Morrow.

Ruddock, J. (1995) Enlarging the Democratic Promise of Education. *British Educational Research Journal*, Vol. 21, No. 1, pp. 3–4.

Rutter, M., Maughan, B., Mortimore, P. and Ouston, J. (1979) *Fifteen Thousand Hours: Secondary Schools and their Effects on Children*. London: Open Books. (Republished in 1994 by Paul Chapman Publishing, London.).

Ryle, G. (1949) *The Concept of Mind*. Hutchinson.

Sallis J. (1977) *School Managers and Governors: Taylor and After*. London: Ward Lock Educational.

Sashkin, M. (1988) The Visionary Leader, in J. A. Conger and R. N. Kanungo (eds.) *Charismatic Leadership: The Elusive Factor in Organizational Effectiveness*, pp. 122–60. San Francisco, CA: Jossey-Bass.

Sashkin, M. (1992) Strategic Leadership Competencies, in R. L. Phillips and J. G. Hunt (eds.) *Strategic Leadership: A Multiorganizational-level Perspective*. Westport, CT: Quorum.

Schein, E. H. (1992) *Organizational Culture and Leadership* (2nd edition). San Francisco, CA: Jossey-Bass.

Schmoker, M. and Wilson, R. B. (1993) Transforming Schools Through Total Quality Education. *Phi Delta Kappan* (January), pp. 389–95.

Schön, D. (1983) *The Reflective Practitioner: how professionals think in action*. New York: Basic Books.

Schumacher, E. F. (1977). *A Guide for the Perplexed*. New York: Harper Colophon.

Scott, P. (1995) *The Meanings of Mass Higher Education*. Buckingham: Open University Press.

Schultz T. (1963) *The Economic Value of Education*. New York: Columbia University Press.

Seeman M. (1960) *Social Status and Leadership: The Case of the School Executive*. Columbus, Ohio: Bureau of Educational Research and Service, Ohio State University.

Selvarajah, C. T., Duignan, P., Suppiah, C., Lane, T. and Nuttman, C. (1995) In Search of the Asian Leader: An Exploratory Study. *Management International Review*, Vol. 35, No. 1, pp. 29–44.

Selznick, P. (1957) *Leadership in Administration: A Sociological Interpretation*. Evanston, IL: Row, Peterson.

Sernler, R. (1993) *Maverick! The Success Story behind the World's Most Unusual Workplace*. London: Arrow.

Senge, P. (1990) *The Fifth Discipline: The Art and Practice of the Learning Organization*. Sydney: Random House.

Senge, P. and Kofman, F. (1993) Communities of Commitment: The Heart of Learning Organizations. *Organizational Dynamics* (Autumn).

Sergiovanni, T. (1992) *Moral Leadership: Getting to the Heart of School Improvement*. San Francisco, CA: Jossey-Bass.

Shamir, B. (1991) The Charismatic Relationship: Alternative Explanations and Predictions. *Leadership Quarterly*, Vol. 2, No. 2, pp. 81–104.

Shamir, B. (1992) Attribution of Influence and Charisma to the Leader: The Romance of Leadership Revisited. *Journal of Applied Social Psychology*, Vol. 22, No. 5, pp. 386–407.

Sharp, R. and Green, A. (1975) *Education and Social Control: A Study in Progressive Primary Education*. London: Routledge & Kegan Paul.

Sheffield City Council (1992) *Resourcing Sheffield Schools*. Sheffield: Education Department, Sheffield City Council.

Shipman, M. (1976) Research and Local Government. *Research Intelligence*, Vol. 2, No. 2, p. 14.

Simkins, T. (1986) Patronage, Markets and Collegiality. *Educational Management and Administration*, Vol. 14, No. 1, pp. 17–30.

Simkins, T. (1994) Efficiency, effectiveness and the local management of schools. *Journal of Education Policy*, Vol. 9, No. 1, pp. 15–33.

Simkins, T. (1995) The Equity Consequences of Educational Reform. *Educational Management and Administration*, Vol. 23, No. 4, pp. 221–32.

Simon, B. (1978) Educational Research: Which Way? *Research Intelligence*, Vol. 4, No. 1.

Simon, H. (1945, 1964) *Administrative Behaviour: a Study of Decision Making Processes in Administrative Organization* (2nd Edition). New York: Collier Macmillan.

Smircich, L. and Morgan, G. (1982) Leadership: the Management of Meaning. *Journal of Applied Behavioral Science*, Vol. 18, No. 2, pp. 257–73.

Smith, J. and Blase, J. (1989) You can run but you cannot hide: Hermeneutics and its challenge to the field of educational leadership. *Organisational Theory Dialogue*, January, pp. 1–7.

Smyth, J. (1993) *A Socially Critical View of the Self-Managing School*. London and New York: Falmer Press.

Southworth, G. (1995) *Looking into Primary Headship: A Research Based Interpretation*. London: Falmer Press.

Stacey, R. (1992) *Managing Chaos*. London: Kogan Page. (Published in the USA as *Managing the Unknowable*, San Francisco: Jossey Bass.)

Stanton, M. (1978) School Evaluation: A Suggested Approach. *Educational Administration*, Vol. 6, No. 2, pp. 42–61.

Starratt, R. J. (1993) *The Drama of Leadership*. London: Falmer Press.

Starratt, R. J. (1994) *Building an Ethical School: A Practical Response to the Moral Crisis in Schools*. London: Falmer Press.

Stirling, M. (1992. How many pupils are being excluded? *British Journal of Special Education*, Vol. 19, No. 4, pp. 128–30.

Strain, M. (1993) Education Reform and Defamiliarization: the struggle for power and values in the control of schooling. *Education Management and Administration*, Vol. 21, No. 3, pp. 188–206.

Strain, M. (1996) Rationality, Autonomy and the Social Context of Education Management. *Educational Management and Administration*, Vol. 24, No. 1, pp. 49–63.

Suppes, P. (1974) The Place of Theory in Educational Research. *Educational Researcher*, Vol. 3, No. 6, p. 6.

Taylor, C. (1979) Interpretation and the sciences of man, in P. Rabinow and W. M. Sullivan (eds.) *Interpretive Social Science – A Reader*. Berkeley: University of California Press, pp. 25–71.

Taylor, C. (1985) *Philosophy and the Human Sciences*. Philosophical Papers 2, Cambridge.

Taylor, W. (1964) The training college principal. *Sociological Review*, Vol. 12, pp. 185–201.

Taylor, W. (ed.) (1973) *Research Perspectives in Education*. London: Routledge & Kegan Paul.

Taylor, W. (1981) Quality Control? Analysis and Comment. *Educational Administration*, Vol. 9, No. 2, pp. 1–20.

Teacher Training Agency (1996a) *Teaching as a Research Based Profession: Promoting Excellence in Teaching*. London: Teacher Training Agency.

Teacher Training Agency (1996b) The National Professional Qualification for Headship (NPQH): Key Principles and Draft National Standards for New Headteachers (mimeo).

Terry, R. W. (1993) *Authentic Leadership: Courage in Action*. San Francisco, CA: Jossey-Bass.

TES (1996) HMIs clash with Woodhead. *Times Educational Supplement*, 5 July, p. 1.

Thomas, H. (1984) Teachers in Decline? The Quality Consequences of the Management of Changing Rolls. *Educational Management and Administration*, Vol. 12, No. 1, pp. 1–14.

Thomas, H. (1987) Efficiency and opportunity in school finance autonomy. In H. Thomas and T. Simkins (eds.) *Economics and the Management of Education: Emerging Themes*. Lewes: Falmer Press.

Thomas, H. (1996). Efficiency, Equity and Exchange in Education. *Educational Management and Administration*, Vol. 24, No. 1, pp. 31–47.

Thomas, H. and Bullock, A. (1992) School Size and Local Management Funding Formulae. *Educational Management and Administration*, Vol. 20, No. 1, pp. 30–8.

Thomas, H. and Bullock, A. (1994) Money, Monitoring and Management, in P. Ribbins and E. Burridge (eds.) *Improving Education: Promoting Quality in Schools*. London: Cassell.

Thomas, R. (1978) *The British Philosophy of Administration: A Comparison of British and American Ideas, 1900–1939*. London: Longmans.

Thompson, J. D. (1967) *Organisations in Action*. New York: McGraw Hill.

Treston, K. (1994) Work and Spirituality, in F. Crowther and B. Caldwell (eds.) *The Workplace in Education: Australian Perspectives*. Sydney: Edward Arnold.

Trompennars, F. (1996) 'One Best Way' of Managing? *World Executive's Digest*, (February), pp. 14–16.

Tripp, D. (1992) *Critical Incidents in Teaching: the Development of Professional Judgement*. London: Routledge.

Tucker, M. (1970) Organisational change: the process of unstreaming, in M. G. Hughes (ed.) *Secondary School Administration: A Management Approach*. Oxford: Pergamon.

Tuijnman, A. and Wallin, E. (1995) *School Research at the Crossroads*. Stockholm: OECD/Stockholm Institute of Education Press.

Urban, G. (1981) The perils of foreign policy: a conversation with Dr Zbigniew Brzezinski. *Encounter*, May, pp. 13–30.

Wallace, M. (1995) An Unseen Hand: The Mass Media and Education Policy. Paper presented at the Annual Meeting of the American Educational Research Association, San Francisco, April.

Wardwell, W. I. (1955) Social integration, bureaucratization and the professions. *Social Forces*, Vol. 33, pp. 356–9.

Webb, R. and Vulliamy, E. (1996). Changing Role of the Primary-school Headteacher. *Educational Management and Administration*, Vol. 24, No. 3, pp. 301–15.

Weber, M. (1922/1978) *Economy and Society: An Outline of an Interpretive Sociology*, Vol. 1. (G. Roth and C. Wittich, eds.) Berkeley: University of California Press.

Weber, M. (1971) *Max Weber*, edited and introduced by J. E. T. Eldridge. London: Nelson.

Weber, M. (1978) *Economy and Society*. Berkeley: University of California Press.

Weick, K. E. (1979) *The Social Psychology of Organizing* (2nd edition) Reading, Mass: Addison Wesley.

Weick, C. W. and Leon, L. S. (1993) *The Learning Edge*. New York: McGraw-Hill.

Westley, F. R. and Mintzberg, H. (1988) Profiles of Strategic Vision: Levesque and Iacocca, in J. A. Conger and R. K. Kanungo (eds.) *Charismatic Leadership: The Elusive Factor in Organizational Effectiveness*. San Francisco, CA: Jossey-Bass.

Wheatley, M. J. (1992) *Leadership and the New Science: Learning about Organization from an Orderly Universe*. San Francisco, CA: Berrett-Koehler.

White, P. (1987) Self-esteem and the Management of Educational Institutions: A Question of Values. *Educational Management and Administration*, Vol. 15, No. 2, pp. 85–92.

Whitehead, J. D. and Whitehead, E. E. (1991) *The Promise of Partnership: Leadership and Ministry in an Adult Church*. San Francisco: Harper.

Whitty, G. (1994) Devolution in Education Systems: Implications for Teacher Professional Development and Pupil Performance. Paper presented to the National Industry Education Forum, Melbourne, August.

Whitty, G. Power, S. and Halpin, D. (1998) *Devolution and Choice in Education: the School, the State and the Market*. Buckingham: Open University Press.

Whyte, D. (1994) *The Heart Aroused: Poetry and the Preservation of the Soul in Corporate America*. New York: Doubleday.

Williams, M. (1977) *Groundless Belief*. Oxford: Blackwell.

Williams, M. (1980) Coherence, justification, and truth. *Review of Metaphysics*, Vol. 34, No. 2, pp. 243–272.

Willower, D. J. (1988) Synthesis and projection, in N. J. Boyan (ed.). *Handbook of Research on Educational Administration*. Longman: New York, pp. 729–45.

Willower, D. J. (1992) *Educational Administration: Philosophy, Praxis and Professing*. Madison: NCPEA.

Wise, A. E. (1967). *Rich Schools, Poor Schools*. Chicago: University of Chicago Press.

Wofford, J. C. and Goodwin, V. L. (1994). A Cognitive Interpretation of Transactional and Transformational Leadership Theories. *Leadership Quarterly*, Vol. 5, No. 2, pp. 161–86.

Young, P. (1980) Review of DES/HMI, *Aspects of Secondary Education in England* (London: HMSO). *Educational Management and Administration*, Vol. 9, No. 1, pp. 134–40.

Yukl, G. (1989) Managerial Leadership: A Review of Theory and Research. *Journal of Management*, Vol. 15, No. 2, pp. 251–89.

Zaleznik, A. (1977) Managers and Leaders: Are They Different? *Harvard Business Review*, Vol. 55, No. 3, pp. 67–78.

Zaleznik, A. (1990) *The Managerial Mystique: Restoring Leadership in Business*. New York: Harper & Row.

Index